Instant Pot® Cookbook

by Wendy Jo Peterson, MS, RDN and
Elizabeth Shaw, MS, RDN, CLT, CPT

Instant Pot® Cookbook For Dummies®

Published by: **John Wiley & Sons, Inc.**, 111 River Street, Hoboken, NJ 07030-5774, www.wiley.com

Copyright © 2020 by John Wiley & Sons, Inc., Hoboken, New Jersey

Published simultaneously in Canada

For general information on our other products and services, please contact our Customer Care Department within the U.S. at 877-762-2974, outside the U.S. at 317-572-3993, or fax 317-572-4002. For technical support, please visit https://hub.wiley.com/community/support/dummies.

Wiley publishes in a variety of print and electronic formats and by print-on-demand. Some material included with standard print versions of this book may not be included in e-books or in print-on-demand. If this book refers to media such as a CD or DVD that is not included in the version you purchased, you may download this material at http://booksupport.wiley.com. For more information about Wiley products, visit www.wiley.com.

Library of Congress Control Number: 2020901621

ISBN 978-1-119-64140-7 (pbk); ISBN 978-1-119-64141-4 (ebk); ISBN 978-1-119-64143-8 (ebk)

Manufactured in the United States of America

10 9 8 7 6 5 4 3 2 1

SKY10024139_011421

Recipes at a Glance

Main Courses

Side Dishes

Beverages

Desserts

Table of Contents

Introduction

Perhaps you received an Instant Pot for a gift, or snagged the latest Amazon Prime deal of a comparable brand when you saw it on sale. But here we are months later and where is that steal of a deal? Tucked nice and neatly in your hallway closet, yearning for its time to shine!

Consider this book a gentle nudge to encourage you to take your Instant Pot (or whatever brand of multiuse pressure cooker you have) out of the closet and let it do what it's meant to do: Provide delicious, nutritious meals in less time!

This book offers a plethora of new and exciting recipes you can create. You can do so much more than cooking meat and potatoes — though we highly recommend these traditional recipes, too! The Instant Pot can be a "set it and forget it" tool just like your slow cooker. It can transform your 30-minute dinner window into a magical Indian oasis with just a few simple ingredients.

All you need is the courage to unbox your pot, and you're in for a real treat! Get ready to take your taste buds to a whole new flavor experience. Buckle up and enjoy the Instant Pot ride that awaits!

About This Book

Think of this book as your own personal Instant Pot coach! But, fear not. For simplicity's sake, we refer to the multiuse pressure cooker as the Instant Pot, but you can apply many of the tips, tricks, and recipes to whatever multiuse pressure cooker you own.

In these pages, we get you ready to succeed using your pot. But we promise: With a little patience, practice, and determination — you'll be a pro in no time!

Each recipe in this book is designed to meet you where you are today, both in terms of your confidence with your pot and your nutritional needs. For instance, we give time-saving tips and notes throughout the book to ensure that you feel confident in making delicious dishes for you and your family.

As you get ready to make the recipes in this book, keep the following points in mind:

>> We highly recommend that you read the manual that comes with your pot.

>> We recommend that you read every recipe from beginning to end to ensure you have all the ingredients on hand before you start cooking.

>> We call for both fresh and dried herbs throughout the book. If you have one on hand but not the other, you can easily swap out fresh for dried, or vice versa: Just remember that 1 teaspoon of dried herbs is equivalent to 1 tablespoon of fresh.

>> Vegetarian recipes are marked with the tomato icon (🍅) in the Recipes in This Chapter lists, as well as in the Recipes at a Glance, which appears in front of the Table of Contents.

>> All temperatures listed are in Fahrenheit. For a temperature conversion to Celsius, see Appendix A.

>> We've created a special graphic to highlight not only the Instant Pot functions you'll be using for each recipe, but also the cook time and method of releasing the pressure from the pot. Here's a guide to what this graphic shows:

- **Upper-left quadrant:** The cooking function(s) that will be used to make the recipe.

- **Upper-right quadrant:** The pressure level to use for the cooking function(s).

- **Lower-left quadrant:** The time it takes to cook the recipe. Prep time and the time it takes for the Instant Pot to come to pressure are not included in this time.

- **Lower-right quadrant:** The type of release to use with the Sealing knob (natural or quick).

>> We list exactly which Instant Pot functions and methods you'll be using in each recipe right under the title. For recipes that use two functions (such as *Steam* and then *Pressure Cook*), we list them in the order used.

>> Though we've really tried to keep the recipes simple in nature, some do require some special kitchen tools (like a springform pan), and we identify them right at the top of the recipe as well.

>> Each recipe lists dietary types that the recipe fits. Here's a quick overview of the various diet categories we use:

- **Gluten-Free:** The recipe is void of gluten-containing ingredients. Be sure to check the labels of each ingredient you use to ensure it's free of gluten. Sometimes manufacturers include gluten in products that don't typically have them.

- **Keto:** The recipe is lower in carbohydrates than most recipes, with the bulk of macronutrients coming from protein and fat. If you're adhering to a strict keto diet, you may need to make some modifications to the recipe. See Chapter 24 for suggested meals to modify for keto compliance.

- **Mediterranean:** The recipe can be considered part of the Mediterranean Diet, which is rich in vegetables, fruits, whole grains, beans, nuts, seeds, and extra-virgin olive oil.

- **Vegan:** The recipe is free of all animal products, including dairy and eggs.

- **Vegetarian:** The recipe is free of animal meats, but it still uses dairy products and eggs.

>> We include information on the time it should take you to prepare and cook each recipe. Just be sure to factor in the pressurizing time of the Instant Pot. Each pot will vary with the time it will take to raise the internal pressure to begin the cooking function, which is *not* accounted for in the recipes. Typically, this ranges from 5 to 10 minutes, tops!

>> At the very bottom of the recipe, you'll see notes, tips, and variations you can try.

Finally, within this book, you may note that some web addresses break across two lines of text. If you're reading this book in print and want to visit one of these web pages, simply key in the web address exactly as it's noted in the text, pretending as though the line break doesn't exist. If you're reading this as an e-book, you've got it easy — just click the web address to be taken directly to the web page.

Foolish Assumptions

In writing this book, we made a few assumptions about you:

>> You have an Instant Pot or you're planning to get one soon. It doesn't matter which model of Instant Pot you have. Most recipes in this book work on every Instant Pot regardless of the model, with the exception of the recipes in Chapter 19, which use the newest *Bake* and *Sous Vide* functions.

>> You may be an Instant Pot whiz or your Instant Pot may still be sitting safe and sound in the box it came in. Whichever end of the spectrum you fall on (or somewhere in between), this book is for you!

>> You want to make healthy, delicious recipes for you and your family, and you don't have a ton of time on your hands.

If this sounds like you, you've come to the right place!

Icons Used in This Book

Throughout this book, you'll see the following icons in the margin. Here's a guide to what the icons mean:

TIP

The Tip icon marks information that can save you time and money as you're planning, shopping for, and preparing Instant Pot meals.

WARNING

We use the Warning icon when we're filling you in on important safety measures.

REMEMBER

This book is a reference, which means you don't have to commit it to memory and there won't be a test on Friday. But when we tell you something so important that you really should remember it, we use the Remember icon.

TECHNICAL
STUFF

When we get a little deep into the weeds on a subject, we use the Technical Stuff icon. If you're short on time, you can safely skip anything marked with this icon without missing the gist of the subject at hand.

Beyond the Book

In addition to the book you have in your hands, you can access some helpful extra content online. Check out the free Cheat Sheet by going to www.dummies.com and entering **Instant Pot Cookbook For Dummies** in the Search box.

Where to Go from Here

If you're brand-new to the Instant Pot, spend some time getting to know your pot in Part 1. We build up your confidence in Chapter 1, and then cover the basics in Chapter 2. Chapters 3 and 4 help you stock your kitchen for instant success. Chapter 5 is full of tips, tricks, and hacks to get the most out of your Instant Pot.

Part 2 is filled with meal-planning tips and guides to bring the Instant Pot into your weekly routine.

If you're already comfortable with the Instant Pot and you're itching to get going, Part 3 has tons of delicious recipes.

We hope you turn to this book again and again and that the Instant Pot becomes an indispensable part of your cooking routine!

1

Getting Started with the Instant Pot

Chapter **1**

Becoming the Boss of Your Instant Pot

We can't think of a better place to be your own boss than from the comfort of your own kitchen. And that's what this chapter is all about!

This chapter empowers and encourages you to be the boss of your Instant Pot. Sure, you may have been intimidated when you first unboxed it and heard its gentle roar, but rest assured, after you get to know the ins and outs of your Instant Pot, it'll start feeling like you own it (and not the other way around!).

REMEMBER

When we say "Instant Pot," we're referring to whatever multiuse pressure cooker you have. Some of the tips in this chapter (like those having to do with error messages) are Instant Pot-specific, but many of the troubleshooting tips can be used with whatever make and model of appliance you own.

Overcoming Your Instant Pot Fears

We've heard all kinds of stories about people who have purchased or been given an Instant Pot, but have kept it in their closets, waiting for the day when they had the courage to pull it out and dive in. If this sounds familiar, today is the day to unpack your pot and join us in the kitchen!

TIP

To help set you up for success (and give you a little encouragement to bite the bullet), here are a few tips we found helpful as we got comfortable with our own pots:

>> **Unbox your pot.** We mention this in Chapter 20, too, but seriously, just take it out of its box.

>> **Wash the metal pot, trivet, and lid.** You don't need anything special — just your standard dish soap.

>> **Give it a trial run.** Scared about ruining a recipe and creating food waste? Then just run a test trial using water for 1 minute under the *Pressure Cook* setting. Get comfortable with the valve and setting it to *Sealing*. Use both a *Natural Release* and a *Quick Release* to remove the steam so you can see what both functions are like.

>> **Keep your Instant Pot on the counter.** Don't move your Instant Pot after you've done your trial run! If you put it back in the box or in a hidden cabinet, you probably won't use it. Keep it visible and have your grocery list ready so you can whip up your first Instant Pot recipe this week!

>> **Start with a simple recipe.** There's no reason you have to make a lasagna right from the start. Start with something simple, like a soup or bowl recipe. Starting with something simple will help you see the versatility of the Instant Pot.

We hope one or all of these tips will inspire you to take charge of your pot! Trust us, when you jump on the Instant Pot train, you'll never turn back.

Staying Safe When Using Your Instant Pot

TIP

We get it: The Instant Pot can seem like a hazard if you're new to pressurized cooking. So, in this section, we share a few important safety tips you'll want to follow. When you know how to use your pot safely, you'll be eager to use it every day!

>> **Read your Instant Pot manual.** Yes, we know how tedious that sounds, but seriously, read it. The manual has specific notes right at the start that pertain to your specific pot model to ensure you're using it correctly.

>> **Avoid placing your Instant Pot near any external heat source (such as a stove or oven) and don't touch the hot surfaces of the pot.** Use your Instant Pot away from your cabinets and other kitchen appliances that are in use. We recommend using oven-safe mitts or the silicon mitts you can purchase with the pot.

>> **Only use your pot for its intended purpose.** Don't try to start a fire and make s'mores in the pot! And don't use the pot outside. The Instant Pot is intended for household use only.

>> **Make sure that your Instant Pot is securely closed before using it.** Don't move your Instant Pot when it's under pressure.

>> **Before you use it to cook something, check out your Instant Pot's functions.** Make sure the steam-release valve/handle, steam-release pipe, anti-block shield, and float valve are clear of clogging. (Don't know what those are? Read your manual!) If any of these things are clogged, refer to the Instant Pot manual for a quick fix.

>> **Don't touch the steam!** You can get a serious burn from the steam. Avoid placing your hands anywhere near or around the steam release valve/handle or float valve while the pot is depressurizing.

>> **Don't allow children or anyone who has reduced capability to perform common kitchen skills to use your Instant Pot.** We usually encourage getting kids involved in the kitchen, but kids have no business operating an Instant Pot. Allow kids to get involved in your Instant Pot meal by chopping, adding, or mixing the ingredients that go into the pot before pressure cooking. When it's time to release the pressure, have the kids step away and allow able-bodied adults to work with the pot.

>> **Do not submerge the cooker base in water.** Avoid getting the electrical cord wet and only use your pot with North American–compatible outlets. The Instant Pot is not designed for converters or adapters.

>> **To unplug your Instant Pot from the power outlet, press *Cancel* first; then remove it from the power source.** When cleaning your pot, also make sure it's unplugged.

Troubleshooting Your Instant Pot

As much as we wish we could be in the kitchen with you as you experiment with your pot, we know that's not possible. So, this section offers troubleshooting tips to refer back to when you encounter some of the most common problems that arise as you get to know your Instant Pot.

» **If you have trouble closing the lid:** Try repositioning the sealing ring to make sure it's nice and snug. Or, if the float valve is popped up, try pressing it down with fork prongs or another long utensil. Finally, if you're reheating something that perhaps didn't cook all the way, press *Quick Release* until the valve is in the *Vent* position; then slowly lower the lid back onto the cooker base to close.

» **If you have trouble opening the lid:** Be patient! This problem is likely because there is still pressure built up inside the pot. Do *not* try to force open the pot — you may experience severe burns if you try to do so. Make sure that the valve is set to *Venting,* and let the pot release the pressure free of obstruction.

» **If steam escapes from the lid while the pot is pressurizing:** We've seen this when the sealing ring isn't installed properly or needs to be cleaned or replaced. Make sure your vent is fully set to *Sealing.* Try these solutions, and if they don't work, contact Instant Pot customer support.

» **If steam escapes from the valve while it's in the locked position:** This can happen for a few reasons, but typically it's related to not having enough liquid in the inner pot or improperly setting the steam release valve. Try adding more of a thin liquid and make sure the valve is set to *Sealing.*

» **If strange cracking sounds are coming from the pot:** Some sounds are totally normal while the pot is coming to pressure, but other sounds are related to moisture on the outer surface of the inner pot. Wipe down the outer edges of the inner metal pot and always make sure it's fully dry before inserting it in the cooker base.

Here are some common error codes you may encounter and a guide to what they mean:

» **C1, C2, C6, C6H, or C6L:** There's a faulty sensor in the pot. Contact Instant Pot customer support.

» **C7, NoPr:** If the Instant Pot heating element is no longer functioning, you need to contact Instant Pot customer support. However, you may also encounter this error code if there's not enough liquid in the pot or the valve isn't in the correct position. Try adding more water and/or checking to make sure the valve is in the sealing position before contacting customer support.

» **C8:** The wrong inner metal pot has been inserted. Use the pot that is made for your Instant Pot.

» **Lid:** Open and close the lid. Also, note that no lid should be used for the *Sauté* function.

» **OvHt, Burn, Food burn:** When food particles (especially starchy foods like tomato sauce) build up on the bottom of your inner pot, you'll see this error code. Press *Cancel,* turn your Instant Pot off, release the pressure, and make sure the bottom of the metal pot is free of any food residue that is adhering to it.

» **PrSE:** Change the valve to the *Vent* position.

REMEMBER

If you encounter any other error code during your Instant Pot journey, don't fret! Just contact the customer support team for your pressure cooker — they can assist you in navigating any uncharted waters you encounter.

Getting Answers to Common Instant Pot Questions

Here are a few of the most common Instant Pot questions we've come across:

» **What's pot-in-pot (PIP) cooking?** PIP cooking is when you prepare your recipe in a pot that is specifically designed for the Instant Pot and then is placed inside the metal inner pot within the Instant Pot base to do its cooking.

Often, recipes like cheesecakes, lasagnas, dips, and baked goods are prepared with the PIP style of cooking. We talk about it a bit more in Chapter 4, but we highly recommend investing in a few basic Instant Pot accessories so you, too, can enjoy a delicious slice of the Cinnamon Walnut Monkey Bread (Chapter 18).

» **What adjustments are necessary for high altitudes?** Many Instant Pot models have built in technology that adjusts for altitude changes automatically. So, rest easy if you're cooking up in the Rockies or traveling through Yosemite — your Instant Pot will provide you with the same high-quality, dependable results you'd get at sea level.

» **Is it safe to leave the Instant Pot on when I'm not home?** Unless you have the models that allow a delayed start or Bluetooth capabilities to turn on and off your pot, we recommend that you plan your recipes around the times you'll be home. However, we highly encourage multitasking, and if you're waiting for a roast to cook, by all means, jump on a call, run on your treadmill, or head out into the garden. Just keep an eye on the clock so you know when to go back to perform the designated pressure release.

TIP

You can put frozen foods, even meat, into the Instant Pot to help shave time! Consider prepping meals ahead of time, so you can easily dump in the contents, set the pressure, and move on to other pressing tasks.

» **Can I wash the Instant Pot in the dishwasher?** Yes, you can! Or at least you can wash many of the pieces of the Instant Pot. Chapter 21 offers a deeper dive into this topic.

Chapter **2**

Instant Pot 101: Understanding the Pot

D r. Seuss once said, "It's not about what it is, it's about what it can become."

We couldn't love this statement more — and it applies as you begin your journey with the Instant Pot!

Whether you've been a loyal Instant Pot user from the beginning or you're just starting out, you'll quickly realize the versatility you have in creating timeless classics in minutes. Whether you're a baker, you're a slow cooker, or you're just looking for a multifunctional piece of equipment, there's an Instant Pot model (or similar multiuse pressure cooker) made just for you!

In this chapter, we cover what Instant Pot alternatives brands are on the market, as well as the basics of the Instant Pot. We take a look at its parts and various functions so you know exactly what your soon-to-be kitchen best friend can do for you. We also address the latest addition to the Instant Pot family and what you can do with this new model!

Exploring Other Multiuse Pressure Cookers on the Market

Instant Pot isn't the only brand making multiuse pressure cooker appliances. The following models are others on the market that have received high praise from online sources:

>> **Gourmia GPC 800:** With six smart programs for cooking various foods and 13 button settings, this model is an economical choice for many people. Whether you want to pressure cook, slow cook, or sauté, you can use the presets to create everything from soup to meat to rice and more! Sources say this model is comparable to the Instant Pot Lux (see "Considering the Various Instant Pot Models," later in this chapter).

>> **Mealthy Multipot:** This brand has not only two different sizes, but also nine different cooking functions, including pressure cook, slow cook, sauté, steam, cake, pasteurize, yogurt, rice, and hot pot! Sources say this model is similar to the Instant Pot Duo Plus (see "Considering the Various Instant Pot Models," later in this chapter), but it comes with many more accessories (more bang for your buck!).

>> **Mueller UltraPot 6Q Pressure Cooker:** If you're a fan of German-made products, you'll love this pot! This model has ten cooking functions, including functions to pressure cook, slow cook, sauté, and keep food warm, as well as settings to make the perfect rice, stew, yogurt, eggs, oatmeal, and soup. This model is similar to the Instant Pot Ultra (see "Considering the Various Instant Pot Models," later in this chapter), with the added bonus of having more cooking settings. Plus, it comes with many bonus tools to get you started.

>> **Ninja Foodi:** Word on the street is that this brand is vastly different from the Instant Pot because it can not only pressure cook and steam, but also bake, broil, and on some models even dehydrate the food. Plus, the Ninja Foodi also has two separate lids: one for pressure cooking and one for air frying! In other words, this appliance not only can roast your meats but also serve up some air-fried foods to go along with your favorite treats.

>> **TaoTronics TT-EE007:** This model has ten cooking functions, including functions to pressure cook, slow cook, sauté, and keep food warm, as well as settings to make the perfect rice, stew, yogurt, eggs, and soup. This model is similar to the Instant Pot Duo (see "Considering the Various Instant Pot Models," later in this chapter), with the added bonus of having more cooking settings.

REMEMBER

Whether your multiuse pressure cooker was made by one of these other brands or it's an Instant Pot brand itself, all can be used to create the recipes in this book! Use the manual that came with your appliance to adjust settings and modify the recipe for your brand specifically.

Exploring the Instant Pot

The first step to using your Instant Pot is getting to know all its parts. Subtle differences exist between each make and model of the pot, but the general structural components of the pot are the same (see Figure 2-1):

>> **Cooker base:** Meet the "meat and potatoes" of the Instant Pot! The cooker base is the home to the heating unit. It houses the inner pot. Be sure to keep the cooker base dry — don't submerge it in water.

>> **Power cord:** The newest version of the Instant Pot has an attached cord, whereas the previous models have a power cord that needs to be inserted into the pot and the wall.

>> **Control panel:** The control panel is where you'll choose the function(s) and set the timer.

>> **Inner pot:** When you open the lid, you see a shiny stainless-steel pot. This pot is removable and dishwasher safe. The inner pot has size markings on the inside and a max fill line. When using your Instant Pot, make sure to *never* exceed the max fill line.

>> **Lid (top and bottom):** The Instant Pot lid has many parts working to lock the pressure inside and keep your food cooking to perfection. The lid has robust functions — from an intricate steam-release valve that functions in both *Quick Release* and *Natural Release* modes, to the simple close and open lid position marker.

>> **Silicone sealing ring:** If your silicone ring is missing or not fitted correctly in the pot, your pot will be unable to come to pressure. These rings are essential!

TIP

You may want to keep a couple extra rings on hand. For example, we use red ones for savory foods and translucent ones with milder foods, like yogurt, cheesecake, and rice. The rings can carry a flavor or odor after cooking multiple items. Be sure to check out Chapter 21 for tips on how to keep your ring clean and odor-free.

>> **Anti-block shield:** The anti-block shield is on the inside of the lid next to where the float valve sits. The anti-block shield protects the exhaust valve. Both are important and need to be noted when cleaning and properly placed when the Instant Pot is in use.

>> **Float valve:** On the top of your lid, you'll see a metal piece near the venting mechanism — that's the float valve. When your pot is under pressure, the float valve rises up; as it depressurizes, it toggles down.

Float valve

Lid (top and bottom)

Silicone sealing ring

Anti-block shield

Inner pot

Control panel

FIGURE 2-1:
The parts of an
Instant Pot.

Cooker base

Power cord

© John Wiley & Sons, Inc.

Considering the Various Instant Pot Models

Did you know the very first Instant Pot made its debut back in 2010? It's amazing to see in just a decade how the pot has evolved and continues to evolve!

If you're wondering why your pot may have different functions than your friend's pot does, don't worry: This section is just for you. Nearly all Instant Pot models have the following basic functions: *Pressure Cook, Rice, Soup/Broth, Steam, Yogurt, Multigrain, Meat/Stew,* and *Poultry.* And, as you'll soon see in Part 3, almost all of the recipes in this book can be made using all of the Instant Pot models.

You likely have one of the following Instant Pot models in your home right now:

» **Max:** Includes up to 8 hours of pressure cooking at max pressure (15 pounds per square inch, or psi) to low pressure (6.5 psi), with *Sous Vide* and *Canning* functions and three *Keep Warm* settings up to 99 hours and 50 minutes. Optional custom temperature control for the *Sauté* function as well.

» **Ultra:** Includes up to 6 hours of high and low pressure and three *Keep Warm* settings up to 99 hours and 50 minutes. Optional custom temperature control for the *Sauté* function as well.

» **Duo Plus:** Includes up to 4 hours of high and low pressure and three *Keep Warm* settings up to 99 hours and 50 minutes.

» **Duo:** Includes up to 4 hours of high and low pressure and three *Keep Warm* settings up to 99 hours and 50 minutes.

» **Nova Plus:** Includes up to 4 hours of high and low pressure and three *Keep Warm* settings up to 99 hours and 50 minutes.

» **Viva:** Includes up to 4 hours of high and low pressure and three *Keep Warm* settings up to 99 hours and 50 minutes.

» **Lux:** Includes up to 4 hours of high pressure and two *Keep Warm* settings up to 10 hours. This model does not contain the *Yogurt* function.

» **DUO EVO Plus:** Includes up to 8 hours of high pressure and two *Keep Warm* settings up to 10 hours. *Sterilize* function included under *Pressure Cook* and *Steam.* Includes *Sous Vide* and *Bake* settings, where custom temperatures can be adjusted up to 347 degrees.

Finally, as if that wasn't enough information, there are also various *sizes* for each pot — 3 quart, 6 quart, and 8 quart.

TIP

The recipes in this book were tested in a 6-quart Instant Pot. Each pot size can feed a large number of people, depending on what specific recipe you're preparing, but rest easy knowing that you can also scale up (or down) a recipe to fit your family's needs. If you're looking to cook less or cook on the road, a 3-quart mini Instant Pot can work, too. You can cut recipes in half to accommodate. Just remember to keep the contents of the inner pot below the max fill line.

REMEMBER

Regardless of the Instant Pot model you own, you'll be able to successfully prepare (and enjoy) nearly every recipe in this book.

Looking at the Newest Instant Pot: The DUO EVO Plus

The star of the Instant Pot family recently made its debut. The DUO EVO Plus Instant Pot has a new function: *Bake!* The *Bake* function built in allows for a custom temperature range to be selected to proof and bake your favorite classics, like that Lemon Olive Oil Cake (Chapter 19).

TIP

Before you dive in, here are a few tips we've learned about the new baking feature we thought you'd like to know:

>> Pressure cook according to the baked item you're preparing first. There are five presets under the *Bake* setting: *Custom, Cake, Cheesecake, Pudding,* and *Proofing.*

>> Select the function, then set the time, pressure level, and temperature (if you're using the *Custom Bake* setting). Press the knob in to select and move to the next setting.

>> When pressure cooking first, don't forget to add water and use the metal trivet with the pot. The valve should also be set to sealing whenever pressure cooking is being used, even under the *Bake* function. Take note: The new *Bake* setting goes up to 347 degrees.

>> To create the crisp, browned, baked texture, finish cakes, cookies, and breads with the *Custom Bake* feature.

>> Don't use water when using the *Custom Bake* temperature setting.

>> Always add the trivet when using the *Custom Bake* function.

>> Keep the vent open when baking with a custom temperature.

The DUO EVO Plus is just the second pot in the line to have the *Sous Vide* function. Essentially, this function allows that tender, melt-in-your-mouth restaurant-quality end result for those traditionally tough cuts of meat. The *Sous Vide* function offers users the ability to select the protein source (such as eggs, poultry, beef, pork, or seafood) and customize the temperature as needed.

REMEMBER

Vegetables are pure perfection when cooked with *Sous Vide*. They come out crisp yet tender, just like fancy restaurants serve. One of our favorite recipes is the Sous Vide Shrimp Salad Sandwiches (Chapter 19). A perfect gourmet meal made from the comfort of your own home!

WARNING

When working with the *Sous Vide* function, be sure to keep the lid secured but venting open!

TIP

Check out a cool trick we learned using the water immersion method to help get all the air out of the bag before submerging in the water. See the nearby sidebar, "Water, water everywhere: The water immersion method," for more information.

CHECKING THE HEAT OF YOUR MEAT (AND OTHER FOOD ITEMS)

When you're cooking in your Instant Pot, use a meat thermometer to check the internal temperature to ensure that it's properly cooked. Here's a general food safety guide of what the internal temperature of various kinds of meat should be for safe eating:

- **Egg dishes (quiche, souffle, frittatas):** 145 degrees
- **Red meat (whole):** 145 degrees
- **Red meat (ground):** 160 degrees
- **Pork:** 145 degrees
- **Poultry:** 165 degrees
- **Seafood:** 145 degrees
- **Casseroles or leftovers:** 165 degrees

Looking at the Instant Pot's Features

The Instant Pot has a variety of features unique to its special design. Although the slow cooker of the past definitely had its time to shine, the Instant Pot has taken the elements we love about that appliance and done so much more.

To understand how the Instant Pot can function the way it does, you need to understand a bit more about the pot. Regardless of the model you have, every Instant Pot is a pressure-cooking unit that helps to cook food quickly under pressure, resulting in quality, time-efficient meals. Over the years, the Instant Pot has evolved to include more robust functions and settings (or Smart Programs, as you may see them referred to within the user manual). Figure 2-2 shows the Instant Pot Smart Programs panel.

REMEMBER

If you notice that your pot doesn't have some (or many) of these functions and settings, don't worry. This book is designed to allow you to enjoy a majority of the recipes regardless of the model of pot you have.

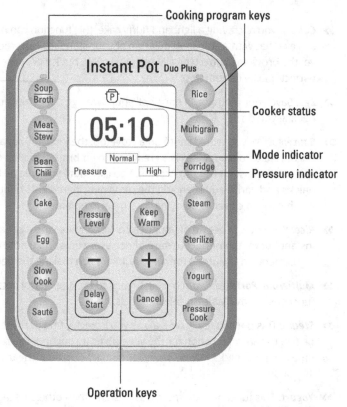

FIGURE 2-2:
The Instant Pot
Smart Programs
panel.

Here's a guide to the Instant Pot's functions:

>> **Manual/Pressure Cook:** Pressure builds up in the pot depending on whether you set it to low or high. The higher the pressure, the higher the temperature in the pot, so be mindful of this as you set the pressure for leaner cuts of meat.

>> **Soup/Broth:** This function allows pressure to build in the pot to cook soups and broths. The Instant Pot team has specifically programmed this function to take into account the nature of soups to prevent overcooking vegetables. However, be mindful of the time you set this for because it still reaches high temperatures.

>> **Meat/Stew:** Ready to have your mind blown as you take that tougher cut of meat and watch it transform into a moist, tender delight? This function can do that for you.

>> **Bean/Chili:** Beans are a staple we constantly make in the Instant Pot. Whether you're cooking dried beans from scratch or making a quick chili using canned beans, this function helps ensure that you don't end up with a mushy mess.

>> **Cake:** If you're craving a light and fluffy cake, this function can help you achieve that with a little manipulation of your standard cake recipe. You won't get the browning you'd typically see in an oven, but it'll produce a picture-perfect quality nonetheless.

>> **Egg:** Save your money and hard-boil your own eggs. This function can aid in helping you do so.

>> **Sauté:** Just as you would sauté on a stovetop, the Instant Pot has its own built-in *Sauté* function. This is a great way to embrace the all-in-one cooking method the Instant Pot can provide. You can sauté your recipe base (like onions and garlic) and then add the remaining ingredients right on top and get that much closer to enjoying your meal in no time.

>> **Rice:** Yes, you can get rid of your rice cooker and use the *Rice* setting on your Instant Pot for the perfect texture of rice every time. Take note of our adjustments in Chapter 8 for some quick tips on making the perfect rice.

>> **Multigrain/Porridge:** From baking breads to making hearty oats, these functions are available on select models.

>> **Steam:** This pot can really do it all, as you'll quickly find out when we enlist the help of the *Steam* function for the vegetables throughout the recipes. Tight on time and just need a few potatoes for dinner? This does the trick in under 10 minutes.

>> **Yogurt:** This function may seem less "instant" than others because it does take quite a bit of time, but we promise, the end result is well worth it. Save your hard-earned money and safely whip up a batch of your own homemade yogurt.

>> **Sterilize:** The high temperature of the Instant Pot allows you to perform a deep clean on glass jars to ensure a safe end result.

>> **Bake:** This function — brand-new on the latest Instant Pot — is sure to please the bakers in your house! It has a custom pressure control that allows it to be toggled on and off so you can let the heating unit of the cooker base work its magic to get the perfect baked texture.

>> **Sous Vide:** Low and slow is the motto of this function, which uses a bag and hot water to cook the food. It's typically used on proteins, but you can toss in vegetables to get a tender, melt-in-your-mouth end product within a few hours. **Remember:** You need to use resealable plastic bags or specific *sous vide* bags to insert the food in before placing it in the hot water bath. See the "Water, water everywhere: The water immersion method for sous vide" sidebar, earlier in this chapter, for more information.

After you press one of these functions, you then need to move on to adjusting some settings. Each function may have a few options, depending on the model of the pot you have, but here are the basic settings all pots have:

>> **High/Low:** Most functions allow you to adjust the temperature from High to Low (some models have a Normal temperature as well). This setting involves the pressure inside the pot and the temperature the pot will reach to cook your recipe.

>> **Keep Warm (On/Off):** This setting is used throughout this book to help keep the food warm. The default setting has it set to *On;* however, some of our recipes specify that this function needs to be set to *Off* for optimal results. Don't worry, we keep this clear in the recipes!

>> **+/–:** When you press this button, you get up to 4 hours of high and low pressure, and three *Keep Warm* settings up to 99 hours and 50 minutes.

Releasing Pressure Inside the Pot

What goes up, must come down, right? Well, that old adage applies to the Instant Pot as well! The temperature gradually rises inside the pot to build up pressure to cook the food, and you eventually have to release that pressure.

REMEMBER

The more liquid you have in the pot and the cooler the temperature, the longer the pot will take to come to pressure.

The lid that comes with your Instant Pot has a built-in mechanism that allows you to control the way in which the pressure is released inside the pot.

But before pressure can build up, you have to adjust the valve on the top part of the lid and make sure it's placed in the *Sealing* position. The *Sealing* position locks the lid in place and prevents steam from escaping, which would hinder your pot from heating up to the appropriate temperature to heat your food.

That same valve also has a *Venting* position, which allows the pressure to quickly release to avoid overcooking your food. To understand this a little bit better, you need to understand the pressure release options for the lid: Natural Release and Quick Release.

WARNING

If you release the pressure too quickly, steam and potentially some liquid may escape from the pot. Take note of our suggested pressure release method for each recipe.

Here are the two methods for releasing pressure from the Instant Pot:

>> **Natural Release:** *Natural Release* is a slower method of releasing the pressure from the pot. When you use *Natural Release,* the food continues to cook inside the Instant Pot as the pot gradually releases the pressure.

TIP

In some recipes, we may call for only a *Natural Release.* In others, we may indicate both a *Natural Release* and a *Quick Release* to avoid overcooking the food. *Natural Release* can take anywhere from 10 minutes to an hour depending on the recipe. We indicate specific times to help you know what we tested. In either case, we've already added the *Natural Release* time to each recipe's cook time, so you can plan accordingly.

Here are the most common reasons we enlist the *Natural Release* function in this book:

- To complete cooking

- To keep food warm

- To prevent liquids from coming out the vent

- To allow foods to cool and thicken

- To keep foods tender

>> **Quick Release:** You likely purchased (or maybe were gifted) an Instant Pot in the spirit of saving time. In that case, the *Quick Release* function may be your new best friend! The *Quick Release* functions just the way you're imagining it does: You quickly release pressure from the pot by immediately pressing *Cancel* and then turning the valve to *Venting* when the cooking cycle completes.

TIP

If you're looking for a recipe that enlists this time-saving spirit, be sure to read the heading section of the recipe and make sure it says *Quick Release.*

Here are the most common reasons we enlist the *Quick Release* function in this book:

- To avoid overcooking the food

- To save time

- To prevent delicate ingredients from becoming mushy

- To save time

WARNING

Don't vary the release method for the recipes — follow the instructions we've provided. Trust us, there's a method to our recipe writing madness!

Chapter **3**

Kitchen Staples for Making Meals Come to Life

Stocking up on the essential ingredients to create quick meals is one of the best pieces of advice we can give you when it comes to ensuring you get the most out of your Instant Pot! Plus, a well-stocked kitchen helps you cut back on eating out, even when you think it's faster to go through a drive-thru. With the Instant Pot and a well-stocked pantry, we guarantee you'll create a meal in less time than it takes to get through the drive-thru line.

You need to figure out what you have on hand before making a trip to the store. Take a moment to check the expiration dates on your spices (throw out anything more than a year old), the flavor of your oils, and the color of your vinegars. When these items are their best condition, you're sure to make a delicious meal.

In this chapter, we fill you in on foods you'll frequently find throughout the recipes in this book.

Starting with the Pantry

Whether you have a large walk-in pantry or a few cupboards, you can always keep a few essentials on hand. Deciding on those essentials can be tricky, especially if you aren't so keen on cooking. Rest assured, as two ladies who literally have jobs that require our supply cupboard to be well stocked, we're letting you in on our pantry must-haves so you, too, can make mealtime a breeze.

Grains and pastas

Here are the typical grains you'll make in your Instant Pot:

>> Amaranth

>> Brown rice

>> Bulgur

>> Couscous

>> Farro

>> Oats (old-fashioned, steel-cut)

>> Polenta

>> Quinoa

>> White rice

And here are some pastas you'll want to have on hand for your Instant Pot cooking as well:

>> Bowtie

>> Fettuccine

>> Lasagna noodles

>> Lentil pasta

>> Macaroni

>> Orzo

>> Penne

>> Spaghetti

>> Ziti

If you've read somewhere that "grains are bad for you," rest assured: As two registered dietitian nutritionists, we're here to tell you that grains are good for you. We recommend choosing whole-grain pasta when it's available. Many grains are also naturally gluten-free, meaning you can enjoy them on a gluten-free diet.

Legumes and beans

When you own an Instant Pot, you can instantly make dried beans into ready-to-serve beans in a matter of minutes, with just a little forethought (soaking the beans for a few hours is still encouraged). We recommend batch-cooking legumes and beans and storing them in your freezer for a quick grab-and-defrost option to toss into your recipes.

Here are the legumes and beans you'll want to have on hand:

>> Black beans

>> Garbanzo beans

>> Lentils (red and green)

>> Pinto beans

>> Split peas

>> White weans

If preplanning isn't your jam and you want to have a few "cantry" items stocked just in case, pick up one can each of black, garbanzo, pinto, and white beans to have on hand. Just be sure to look for non-BPA-lined cans, meaning the cans are void of the potential chemicals that aren't so stellar for your lifelong health.

Nuts and seeds

Here's a list of nuts and seeds you'll want to have on hand in your pantry:

>> Almond butter

>> Almonds

>> Cashews

>> Chia seeds

>> Flaxseeds

>> Peanut butter

>> Peanuts

>> Sesame seeds

>> Walnuts

TIP

Shop what's on sale in this category. For example, we don't list pistachios, but if you see they're going for a steal this week at the market, pick them up and swap them into your favorite dishes! Store your nuts in an airtight container in the freezer for optimum freshness.

Shelf-stable fruits and vegetables

Besides having a well-stocked "cantry," we also recommend that you keep shelf-stable fruits and vegetables on hand. A few of the items on our list may surprise you! Many people don't recognize that apples, avocados, and tomatoes should actually be stored on the counter and not in the fridge! Here's a good place to start:

>> Apples

>> Avocados

>> Corn (canned)

>> Garlic

>> Green chilies (canned, diced)

>> Mango (canned in 100 percent juice)

>> Onions

>> Pasta sauce

>> Potatoes (russet, red, and purple)

>> Shallots

>> Sweet potatoes or yams

>> Tomato paste (canned)

>> Tomato puree (canned)

>> Tomatoes, diced (canned, fire roasted)

>> Tomatoes, fresh (cherry, grape, and roma)

Condiments and dried herbs and spices

If you're reading this book, you're a chef in our eyes, so take note of what the "top chefs" we've interviewed always keep on hand. Buying all these items is an investment upfront, but you'll save big in the long run by being able to re-create your favorite dishes from the comfort of your own home.

Start with the following condiments:

>> Apple cider vinegar

>> Avocado oil

>> Balsamic vinegar

>> Beef broth

>> Chicken broth

>> Coconut milk

>> Coconut oil

>> Cornstarch

>> Ketchup

>> Lemon juice

>> Mayonnaise

>> Mustard

>> Olive oil, extra-virgin

>> Red wine vinegar

>> Rice wine vinegar

>> Soy sauce, lite soy sauce, or tamari (gluten-free)

>> Sesame oil

>> Vegetable broth

And try the following dried herbs and spices:

>> Basil

>> Black pepper

>> Chili powder

>> Cinnamon sticks

>> Cinnamon (ground)

>> Coriander

>> Cumin

- » Garam masala

- » Garlic powder

- » Ginger (ground)

- » Italian seasoning

- » Mustard seed (ground)

- » Onion powder

- » Oregano

- » Paprika

- » Parsley

- » Salt

SALTY FACTS

Salt does a lot for food, from tenderizing to preserving to intensifying flavor to enhancing the ability to taste something sweet. Simply stated, salt makes food taste good!

That said, if you're just breaking from a diet built around overly processed foods and you're now using your Instant Pot, your overall sodium intake will decrease. The recipes in this book cue you to taste and adjust salt as needed. Why? Because not everyone has the same taste for salt, and that's okay!

Our best advice is to taste your food and use salt as needed. With pressure cooking, seasonings are driven into the food, so you may need less than you realize. We recommend salting at the end because it's always easier to add more salt than to make the food less salty. Plus, there may be salty items in a recipe, like bacon, cheese, or stock that intensify as the recipe cooks under pressure. Just remember: Less is more with pressure cooking.

Okay, but are all salts the same? No, definitely not. Just as you would taste a wine or olive oil before cooking with them, we recommend tasting your salt, too — but not by the spoonful! Instead, dip your finger in and taste a couple crystals. Some salts have a more metallic taste, which can alter the taste of your meal. You don't need to rush out and spend a pretty penny on salt, but taste testing a couple may go a long way toward enhancing a meal. Save the fancy salts, like pink Himalayan salt or black salt for finishing off a salad or adding in a final touch of salt on a steak. When cooking, sea salt and kosher salt are what we keep on hand for our Instant Pot recipes.

Baking supplies

If you haven't taken a sneak peek at the recipes in this book yet, you'll be glad to know that you can bake in the Instant Pot, too! Here are the basics you'll want on hand to get started baking:

>> All-purpose flour

>> Applesauce

>> Baking powder

>> Baking soda

>> Brown sugar

>> Cane sugar

>> Chocolate chips

>> Cocoa powder

>> Dried fruit

>> Honey

>> Maple syrup

>> Molasses

>> Powdered sugar

>> Pumpkin puree

>> Pure vanilla extract

>> Wheat bran

>> Whole-wheat flour

Focusing on the Fridge

From the dairy case to the produce patch, your refrigerator houses some of the main staples your kitchen needs to run smoothly! We have our own individual preferences when it comes to the brands and dietary types of certain products we buy, but we want you to feel comfortable experimenting with what you typically use in your house. Other than a few recipes in particular, you can confidently swap almond or soy milk for the cow's milk we use in multiple recipes.

Here's a list of dairy products to have on hand:

>> Butter

>> Cheddar cheese

>> Cotija cheese

>> Cottage cheese

>> Cream cheese

>> Eggs

>> Milk

>> Parmesan cheese

>> Ricotta cheese

Add the following produce to your shopping list:

>> Bell peppers

>> Broccoli

>> Butter leaf lettuce

>> Green beans

>> Kale

>> Lemons

>> Lettuce greens

>> Limes

>> Mangos

>> Peaches

>> Pears

>> Pineapple

>> Spinach

WHEN FRESH CITRUS IS BEST

You can find bottled citrus juice, but nothing beats the flavor of fresh citrus. If you don't have vinegar on hand, lemon or lime juice can easily be swapped in as the acid for a fast dressing, or use a squeeze to finish off a dish.

Citrus *zest* (the outer portion of the rind) is a star-studded flavor booster! We add a pop of fresh zest on almost all salads or to finish off a soup or main dish. When zesting your citrus, be sure to get the outer rind and leave the white part. The white part of the rind has a bitter taste you don't want added to your meal.

When the season is right (and you have freezer space), you can buy extra citrus and freeze the zest and juice to use later.

And don't forget the following fresh herbs:

» Basil

» Chives

» Cilantro

» Parsley

» Rosemary

Making the Most of Your Freezer

A huge time-saving hack is purchasing frozen, washed, pre-chopped and ready-to-use vegetables. If you're looking for the Instant Pot to provide you with an instant meal, stocking up on these essentials is critical. Buying meat or poultry in bulk and freezing it is an excellent way to make healthy eating more affordable, too!

We recommend keeping the following protein sources on hand in your freezer:

» Beef:
- Brisket
- Lean ground
- Short ribs

>> Poultry:

- Boneless, skinless chicken breast
- Chicken sausage
- Chicken thighs
- Chicken wings
- Lean ground chicken or turkey
- Whole chicken

>> Pork:

- Butt
- Canadian bacon
- Sausage
- Shoulder

You can freeze the following fruits and vegetables, too:

>> Bell peppers

>> Blackberries

>> Blueberries

>> Broccoli florets

>> Cauliflower (riced)

>> Mangos

>> Potatoes

>> Raspberries

>> Spinach

>> Strawberries

Chapter 4

Building Your Kitchen Arsenal

No kitchen is complete without a solid toolbox. And, lucky for you, we've pulled together our list of essentials to make stocking up for instant success a breeze!

Use this chapter to find out which Instant Pot accessories may benefit you, as well as which other kinds of accessories and kitchen tools will make your life easier as you become the master of your Instant Pot.

Accessorizing Your Instant Pot

Yes, your Instant Pot will make your life easier all on its own, but when you discover all the Instant Pot accessories, well, that's a game changer.

Here are some of our favorite accessories — the ones we think you'll want as you expand your culinary experiments with the Instant Pot:

» **Silicone accessories:** Silicone is a great addition to your Instant Pot accessory collection. From protective slings (to keep your precious hands safe as you remove pot-in-pot-style recipes) to steamer baskets, egg racks, roasting racks, and tongs, there is an accessory out there for you!

>> **Springform pan (7- or 7½-inch):** If you love a good cheesecake or lasagna, investing in a quality springform pan is wise. You can use oven-safe bakeware you have on hand, too!

>> **Round pan (7-inch):** Many of the casseroles and dips in this book are made using a simple round casserole dish. It helps when you want to bake or pressure cook without the fear of getting a *BURN* notification. You can use oven-safe bakeware you have on hand, too!

REMEMBER

>> **Tempered-glass lid:** The clear lid comes in handy for steaming or slow cooking. The lid has a steam vent. It's also dishwasher safe, which makes for easy cleanup!

>> **Egg steamer rack:** If you're like our European friends who eat boiled eggs almost daily, you'll definitely want to invest in this contraption! You can cook 18 eggs in mere minutes, pressure cooked to perfection.

REMEMBER

You don't need to run out and buy everything on this list. Find the items that speak to the style of cooking you like to do in your Instant Pot and start with those. You'll soon see many of the recipes throughout the book can be made by investing in just a 7-inch pan!

TIP

Buying the right tools for the job means you'll get the job done right, every time! You can search your favorite retailer to find Instant Pot–compatible accessories for the price point and need you're looking to fill!

Play it safe, especially when dealing with such a powerful appliance, and use the tools that were made for it.

WARNING

While you're stocking up on accessories, consider adding a couple extra basics to your list. For example, buy an extra sealing ring or an extra inner pot. These little extras aren't necessary, but they can be time-saving or valuable, especially if you use your Instant Pot as often as we use ours!

TIP

Stocking Up on Other Kitchen Tools

A well-stocked kitchen helps every home cook. If you're new in the kitchen, or your idea of cooking in the past has meant popping a frozen dinner in the microwave, you may not have all the tools you need. The following list is a great place to start:

- » **Box grater:** Grating cheeses, vegetables, or hard fruits is quick and simple with a box grater. You'll want this before you make our Dark Chocolate Zucchini Loaf Cakes (Chapter 18).

- » **Chef's knife:** This is, hands down, the most versatile and efficient knife to have on hand for all your basic cutting skills.

- » **Cutting board:** A small wooden cutting board can help keep your counters looking great and keep your knives sharp. We prefer keeping several cutting boards on hand — one for meats, one for vegetables and breads, and one for seafood.

- » **Hand mixer or stand mixer:** If you're a baker at heart, a hand mixer or stand mixer is essential.

- » **Mason jars:** You can make personalized cakes, breads, cheesecakes, or custards with ease using these famous tempered-glass jars. We like to meal prep with Mason jars, too!

- » **Measuring cups and spoons (both dry and liquid):** Measuring cups and measuring spoons are essential! Be sure to pick up versions for both liquid and dry ingredients.

- » **Microplane or zester:** The essence of citrus zest adds a pop to even the blandest of recipes. We use our microplanes for grating chocolate, garlic, Parmesan, and ginger, too! It's one of our favorite tools.

- » **Potato masher:** A potato masher can help mash up fruits and vegetables with ease — and you can do it directly in the pot! Use a potato masher to whip up Shepherd's Pie (Chapter 12) or All-Natural Applesauce (Chapter 8).

- » **Silicone spatulas:** Protect the surface of your pots by using silicone spatulas. If you scratch a nonstick pan, you should really throw it away, so prevent that from happening by using soft, gentle tools.

- » **Tongs:** If you're braising meat, it's nice to be able to lift the meat out with ease. Tongs are useful if you want to grab something out of a hot pan, too. You can even use tongs to lift Mason jars out of your pot if you don't have a set of wide-mouth tongs on hand.

- » **Whisk:** We often use a whisk in our recipes. Whether it's for whisking in cornstarch for a gravy or whisking eggs before you whip up a frittata, this tool is essential.

- » **Wide-mouth funnel:** Pouring into a Mason jar can be tricky without a wide-mouth funnel. When you make our Plain Yogurt recipe (Chapter 8), you'll be thankful you have this funnel for easy storage!

TIP

If you're totally new to cooking, consider picking up *Cooking Basics For Dummies*, 5th Edition, by Bryan Miller and Marie Rama.

Taking Your Instant Pot Kitchen on the Road

Are you a fan of the open road? We are, too! We even take our all-in-one cookware in our campervan or RV. The truth is, whether you prefer a hotel, an Airbnb, or an RV, you can take your Instant Pot along for the ride.

REMEMBER

Tourist traps are called tourist traps for a reason: They're expensive. From restaurants to grocery stores, all the prices seem to go up exponentially. Plan ahead and plan to cook. The most expensive meal while traveling is dinner, so plan for fun lunches and eat at your hotel room, guesthouse, or camper for dinner.

TIP

Before you leave for your trip, follow these tips:

>> **Prepare meals in advance.** We like to freeze in round containers, so we can plop them right into the Instant Pot nicely and start cooking. If you only have dry storage, consider placing spices and dry ingredients together. Premeasure the spices and store them in resealable plastic bags or Mason jars.

>> **Accessorize.** Grab an extra sealing ring, a trivet, and some bakeware before you pack up. Also, invest in a pack of 4-inch aluminum loaf pans — these are excellent for a mess-free cleanup! Plan your meals before you leave, so you'll know which accessories you need for the journey.

>> **Pack compactly.** Place the cord, trivet, and whatever else you can fit inside the inner pot for storing. The Instant Pot is quite a compact, tiny kitchen appliance!

>> **Grab an extension cord.** Pick up a 3-foot, three-pronged extension cord for the journey. This will help just in case an outlet isn't in a nearby spot.

>> **Keep it clean.** Not all accommodations have cleaning supplies, so it's a good idea to pack a couple travel-size items. We love microfiber cloths for cleaning, along with a small bottle of dish detergent.

>> **Bring extra spices.** You can take the boring and elevate it with simple spices, so we like to have travel-size spices for the job. You can also find spice blends at the grocery store to help! Bring a couple different spices in case taste buds shift and you want something different. We make our own blends of our favorite dishes and keep them in small airtight containers.

Now you're ready to save money and time by making a quick meal while traveling! Our favorites include boiled eggs, steel-cut oats, chili, and spaghetti with sausage.

Chapter 5

Instant Pot Tips, Tricks, and Hacks

I f you're only slightly sold on the Instant Pot, trust us, after you get through this chapter, you'll wonder why it took you so long to become a part of the Instant Pot fan club!

From tips to dealing with the *BURN* message, to creative tricks to using your Instant Pot accessories in multiple ways, to saving money, to gifting, we swear you won't walk away without something new and useful to try with your pot!

BURN, Baby, BURN: Dealing with a Burn Error Message

Trust us: We've been there. You're not alone in seeing a *BURN* error message. This section helps you avoid the message in the first place and resolve it if it does occur.

To prevent the *BURN* error message from appearing, always ask yourself the following questions before you get started:

>> **Is there enough water-based liquid for the size pot you're using?** Water and/or water-based liquids (like animal and vegetable broths) are essential for pressurized cooking. If you don't use enough, the pot can't come to pressure and/or whatever ingredients are on the bottom of the pot may signal the pot to show *BURN*. This is a great advantage, because it reminds you to add more liquid!

>> **Is your steam release valve set to *Sealing*?** If your valve is in the wrong position, like *Pressure Release* when it should be sealed for cooking, steam can release, causing pressure to become altered in the pot, resulting in a *BURN* notification. Double-check your valve, as well as the sealing ring on the lid, to make sure both are in the correct position.

>> **Are you using tomato products?** Tomato products are thick and require more liquid. If you're using tomato paste, add ¾ cup of liquid for every tablespoon of tomato paste. If you're using canned tomatoes, add 2 cups of liquid for every 1 cup of tomatoes.

No one is perfect and sometimes the *BURN* message happens. We've got you covered if it does! Just try the following:

>> **Press *Cancel,* perform a *Quick Release,* and remove the lid.** The recipe isn't ruined. You just need to get whatever is stuck to the bottom of the metal pot off so the cooker base stops signaling to the Instant Pot that something is burning. This method will help halt the cooking so you can figure out what's going on.

>> **Use a spatula and remove food particles from the bottom of the metal pot.** If *BURN* is reading because you may have forgotten to deglaze the pot before you started to pressure cook, don't sweat it. You can use a spatula and a little elbow grease to remove whatever is sticking, and then stir, ensuring you have enough water or water-based liquid in the pot, and start the cooking process again.

>> **Add more water or broth.** If you do this, do it in small portions, like ¼ cup at a time, to prevent a watery soup. If you do happen to have a bit too much water in your final recipe, you can fix this by allowing the recipe to cook over the *Sauté* function to help absorb some of the excess water.

>> **Use the pot-in-pot (PIP) cooking method.** If you can salvage whatever you have in the pot, take that and place it inside an Instant Pot–safe dish. Cover it with aluminum foil and resume cooking.

Trying Some Mind-Blowing Tricks with Your Instant Pot

TIP

We were late to the game on these tricks, and we've made it our mission to ensure *you* aren't! The beauty of having others walk the path ahead of you is that you can relish in the bounty of tricks that'll save you more time and frankly, are just really cool! Take a look at the following tricks and smile, knowing you've invested in a kitchen appliance that offers so many possibilities:

>> **The lid has two special holders — they're on the top sides cooker base.** Take a look at the top of your cooker base. See the symmetrical pot holders? Those aren't just for carrying your pot. Set the lid right into one of them so you can keep it out of the way while sautéing, especially if you're in a tight space!

>> **The rice spoon can rest on the side of the pot — there's a space just for it.** Keep your kitchen tidy and let the spoon rest right on the side of the pot. Not sure where it is? Just look on the cooker base — you'll find it right there!

>> **You can make muffins in the egg bites mold.** No need to buy premade muffins or order another piece of special equipment! If you have the silicone egg mold, it doubles as a mini muffin pan. Assemble muffins as the recipe states and portion by the spoonful into the mold. Repeat until all batter is used.

>> **If you don't own an egg bite mold, use silicone muffin liners to make muffins.** The silicone can withstand the high temperature achieved inside the Instant Pot and will result in a light and fluffy muffin under the *Pressure Cook* setting found on all pots.

>> **Mason jars can double as individual cheesecake pans or individual cake or muffin pans; they can also be used to make yogurt.** These multifunctional glass jars are a must with your Instant Pot.

>> **Freeze meal prep in round molds.** If you're a planner, you'll love this trick. Prep your meals in round bowls that can fit into your Instant Pot. Then, when it's time to cook, all you need to do is dump in the mix and lock in the pressure. No need to worry about whether the frozen contents will fit!

Saving on Your Energy Bill
with the Instant Pot

Did you know that pressure cooking can help save money on your electricity bill? The Instant Pot is one of the greenest kitchen appliances you can have in your arsenal. Compared to other kitchen appliances (like your oven or stove), the Instant Pot uses 70 percent less electricity.

Plus, the Instant Pot cooks food much quicker than other appliances, meaning less energy is used during the entire recipe process. The Instant Pot cooks most food in 70 percent less time!

The Instant Pot is designed specifically to focus on cooking the food under a specific pressure level programmed into the pot instead of heating the entire cooker base or using a higher pressure than is needed for the particular food. For instance, think about the last time you cooked soup in a large pot on the stove. Typically, the pot's outer surface is very hot to touch. But thanks to the design of the Instant Pot, and the dual layer of air pockets between the inner pot and the cooker base, the energy is concentrated on cooking the food and not the appliance.

Another important feature built into the Instant Pot is the sealing mechanism, which requires significantly less water for cooking (resulting in less steam produced as well). This is actually a double whammy because not only will you save from less energy being used for cooking, but it'll also help keep your house cooler versus using an oven and hopefully preventing have to turn on the air-conditioning!

Finally, peak energy usage hours are typically from 4 to 9 p.m., typically prime dinner hours. Enlisting the help of your Instant Pot, you can keep your costs down while still putting a homemade, delicious meal on the table in a matter of minutes.

Making Edible Gifts for Every Occasion

Nothing says "I appreciate you" more than a homemade gift, in our humble opinions. Plus, do it yourself (DIY) gifts are a budget-savvy way to spread a little cheer throughout the year. Whether you're making something for Teacher Appreciation Day or spreading the holiday spirit to your coworkers, we've got just the gift idea for you.

>> **Vanilla extract:** Unless you're buying the imitation kind, pure vanilla extract can cost a pretty penny. Spread the holiday baking magic by whipping up a batch of your own in the Instant Pot. To make it, you need the following:

- Four 3-ounce Mason jars, sanitized

- Two vanilla bean pods, cut in half

- 1½ cups of high-quality vodka

Place the vanilla bean pods into the Mason jars and pour 3 ounces of vodka over each one. Secure the lids and place the jars on the metal trivet in the Instant Pot with 1 cup of water. Pressure cook for 1 hour. Carefully remove and store in a cool, dark place.

>> **Limoncello:** Everyone wants to vacation in Italy, right? Bring the taste of Italia to your friends by surprising them with their own batch of limoncello! This is also perfect for a bridal party gift. To make it, you need the following:

- Four 8-ounce Mason jars, sanitized

- 32-ounces of vodka

- 2 cups of lemon rinds

- 4 tablespoons cane sugar (or sweetener of choice)

Pour 8 ounces of vodka into each Mason jar. Then put ½ cup of lemon rinds in each jar. Place the jars on the metal trivet in your Instant Pot with 1 cup of water. Pressure cook for 30 minutes. Carefully remove the jars. Add 1 tablespoon of sweetener to each jar, and store in the fridge.

>> **Coffee liqueur:** Share the spirit of a fun after-dinner drink with all your friends! This is the perfect holiday gift to spread joy. Serve over ice cream or with cream. To make it, you need the following:

- Six 8-ounce Mason jars, sanitized

- 4 cups of strong brewed coffee

- 2 cups of sugar

- 2 teaspoons of vanilla extract

- 2 cups of vodka

In the Instant Pot, sauté together the brewed coffee and sugar until it simmers and the sugar is dissolved, stirring every couple minutes. Turn off the *Sauté* function and whisk in the vanilla extract and vodka. Divide the coffee liqueur evenly among the Mason jars, and store in a cool, dark cabinet for at least two weeks before serving. It gets better with age!

» **Apple or pumpkin butter:** You can find a great Simple Fruit Jam in Chapter 8, but this variation is a bit more seasonal. Whip up a batch of pumpkin bread and put this beside it in the bag. Your friends will thank you later, we promise! To make it, you need the following:

- Two 8-ounce Mason jars, sanitized

- 1½ to 2 pounds of apples or pumpkin

- 1 teaspoon of ground cinnamon

- ½ teaspoon of ground nutmeg

- ¼ teaspoon of salt

Place the apples or pumpkin on the metal trivet inside the Instant Pot with ½ cup of water and steam for 5 minutes. Remove the lid and carefully discard the skins. Drain the excess water and return the apples or pumpkin to the inner pot. Using a potato masher or wooden spoon, mash the cooked apples or pumpkin. Using the *Sauté* function, heat the puree and stir in the spices. (If you're making pumpkin butter, you can stir in 2 teaspoons of pumpkin pie spice, too.) You can keep this free of added sugar or add a bit of brown sugar for a sweeter taste. Store the butter in Mason jars and refrigerate for up to 3 months.

» **Make your own dry mixes:** Make a few dry mixes and keep them on hand for when you need a last-minute hostess gift. To make a DIY gift with the Cinnamon Walnut Monkey Bread (Chapter 18), layer the dry ingredients for the recipe inside a sanitized Mason jar. Layer the flours on the bottom with baking agents, sugar, and spices on top. Omit the butter, yogurt, milk, vanilla extract, and water from the jar. Attach a note that reads how to assemble the recipe with the remaining ingredients that need to be added. You can even include the DIY vanilla extract (earlier in this list) as part of the gift bundle!

2

Planning Ahead with the Instant Pot

Explore the basics of meal planning using your Instant Pot.

Plan a seven-day menu using your Instant Pot.

Chapter **6**

Meal-Planning Basics

The Instant Pot is a fantastic tool for saving time in the kitchen. And if you're anything like us, you can use all the extra time you can get! Whether you have an Instant Pot or not, a great way to be efficient and save time cooking is by planning your meals a week at a time. And when you combine the Instant Pot with meal planning, well, you've got a winning combination!

In this chapter, we walk you through what's involved in planning your meals, how to plan meals your whole family will love, and how to batch-cool using your Instant Pot. We end with a bunch of tips and tricks for saving even *more* time with your Instant Pot!

If time is what you need, you've come to the right place.

The Essentials of Meal Planning

If you've spent some time surfing the web for meal-planning advice, no one would blame you if you were totally overwhelmed. We get it. That's why we like to break meal planning down into a one-week cycle menu that uses main items like meat and poultry multiple times in unique ways.

TIP

But before we get to the meal plan, you have to know how to actually plan a meal. Essentially, the best way to plan a meal is to take inventory of what you have on hand while also noting the sales this week at your favorite market. Build your weekly menu around those two considerations to help reduce food waste while sticking to your food budget as well.

TECHNICAL STUFF

You can find all kinds of food guide pyramids or images showing how to divide your plate (for example, www.choosemyplate.gov). But we prefer the Mediterranean diet pyramid as a basis for teaching meal planning. You can find a great version of this pyramid at https://oldwayspt.org/resources/oldways-mediterranean-diet-pyramid (where you can even print out a copy for free).

In the Mediterranean diet, nothing is off limits when it comes to enjoying all foods in moderation. The key is to base every meal around the following:

>> Fruits

>> Vegetables

>> Whole grains

>> Olive oil

>> Legumes (including beans)

>> Nuts and seeds

>> Herbs and spices

At least a couple times a week, add some fish and seafood. Anywhere from once a day to once a week, eat some poultry, eggs, cheese, and yogurt. And on occasion, eat other meats and sweets. Drink lots of water, and if you want, drink wine in moderation.

TIP

For more specifics on the Mediterranean diet, check out *Mediterranean Diet Cookbook For Dummies,* by Meri Raffetto and Wendy Jo Peterson (Wiley). Or check out the super-useful Oldways website at https://oldwayspt.org.

Foods for the Whole Family — Even Baby!

One of the best reasons we love so many of the recipes in this book is because you can serve the same dish to the entire family. No short-order cooks around here! (We told you the Instant Pot was time-saving for multiple reasons!)

Chapter 23 offers ten recipes you can modify for babies, but rest assured, there are certainly more than ten recipes in this book that you can make baby-friendly. The key is to look at spices and texture.

TIP

Here are some quick tips we use when looking at a recipe to ensure that it's suitable for the entire family:

>> **Vary the textures.** Kids get in a texture rut unless they're regularly offered foods of varying textures. Keep offering foods, from mushy to crunchy, to challenge their senses.

>> **Keep it balanced.** When you're filling a plate, imagine filling about half of it with fruits and vegetables, one-quarter of it with protein, and one-quarter with whole grains. This visual comes in handy when we serve kids.

>> **Make sure you're offering enough iron.** Iron is a key nutrient that needs to be emphasized. Meats are star players for heme iron, but if your family shies from eating meat, try pairing more meals with kidney beans, chickpeas, dried apricots, pumpkin, or baked potatoes. Then, to help bodies (big and small) absorb the iron, pair the meal with a vitamin C–rich food, like kiwi or oranges.

>> **Stick to meals that are easy to make.** Parenting is busy work. Lighten your load by making meals that are simple.

>> **Pay attention to plants.** We all need to eat more fruits and vegetables, and serving them regularly to children is one way to raise healthy adults. Even if your recipe isn't plant centered, it's all about how you serve it! Serve up a side of cauliflower rice, zucchini noodles, or a fruit salad, or just put out a tray of raw veggies and dip as you prep dinner! When they start smelling everything, they're hungry! Surprise them with a tray of veggies to hold them over.

>> **Watch the spice factor.** Spicy foods — the ones that will light your mouth on fire — may be best reserved for the adults until your kids have developed an affinity for them. Don't hesitate to use herbs and spices, like garlic, onion, cumin, and chili powder, but remember when meal planning that kids have a more sensitive tongue!

>> **Keep it fun!** Mealtime is meant to be enjoyable, not miserable. Focus less on what your child is or is not eating and more on the time you're spending together as a family. Laugh and love when sharing the meal — that's what your kids will remember. Plus, they'll relate mealtimes to enjoyment and be more likely to try new things.

Cook Once Eat Twice: Batch-Cooking and Freezing

Batch-cooking is preparing a larger volume of food — say, doubling a recipe — to save time later.

Some people batch-cook and freeze the second portion for later that month or the next. Others use batch-cooking to prepare a large staple, like a protein or grain, and then use it throughout the week in various recipes.

We do both! And we highly recommend you jump on the batch-cooking bandwagon with us! Whether you're cooking for one or ten, batch-cooking will come to the rescue to provide a nourishing, delicious meal in no time flat.

Many recipes throughout this book can be batch-cooked. The meats and poultry (Chapter 10), soups and stews (Chapter 14), and many of the global recipes (Chapter 15) are all great starting points to get comfortable with batch-cooking.

WARNING

Don't exceed the max fill line limits of your Instant Pot. You want to make sure that the size of your Instant Pot will work for the recipe you're preparing, and that you stay below the max fill line.

Time-Saving Hacks for Busy People

To put meal planning into practice successfully often takes patience and time. But don't worry, we won't leave you fending for yourself here. We've done the hard work for you and combined our top hacks in one list to help make meal planning a breeze because we get it: You're busy!

>> **Buy prechopped produce.** When time is tight, there's nothing like throwing a bag of prechopped bell peppers and onions from the freezer into your soup to create a quick meal within minutes. Often, you'll pay a slightly higher price for these prechopped items, but as we're sure you can appreciate, sometimes convenience wins the day.

If you're concerned whether frozen produce is as nutritious as fresh, the answer is yes! Sometimes they're even *more* nutritious because they retain more of the vitamins and minerals because they're packed and frozen at the peak of freshness whereas other vegetables may spend a longer time in transport or on store shelves, losing some of their nutrients over time.

>> **Freeze herbs and spices in ice cube trays.** Is your garden producing a bounty of herbs right now? Take advantage of that and chop them, mix them with olive oil, and freeze them into ice cube trays. They make an excellent addition to the base of many of the recipes throughout this book. Just be sure to label them so you know which tray contains which herb or spice!

>> **Batch-cook beans and store them in the freezer.** When you have some extra time, batch-cook the beans you use most often. Black beans and garbanzo beans are great choices! Portion them based on your eating habits and freeze them in airtight containers. On a busy night, it's so easy to grab a container of beans from the freezer and reheat them in your Instant Pot in less than 5 minutes.

>> **Never forget eggs at the market.** Eggs are a complete source of protein that cook in less than a minute under pressure. Whether you fix a simple Shakshuka with Spinach (Chapter 9) for dinner or hard-boil eggs for a quick snack throughout the week, eggs are, without question, a staple.

>> **Make extra rice.** Rice is a great food to have on hand. You can make rice pudding, fried rice, or rice balls with leftovers. Plus, rice freezes really well. Simply lay it out on a cookie sheet and put it into your freezer. After it's frozen, transfer it to a resealable freezer bag, and you have rice for any day of the week!

>> **Find your favorite frozen foods.** Freezer-ready vegetables, fruits, and meats can help complete a meal in minutes. Don't forget: You can cook frozen meats in your Instant Pot, too. Just be sure to allow extra time.

>> **Make a meal in a bowl.** We love a good bowl (see Chapter 11). A bowl can come together with ease if you have extras on hand, like grains, beans, canned or frozen vegetables, and dressings. Add your favorite leftover meats, and the sky is the limit on carry-over options!

>> **Don't feel like you have to make everything from scratch.** Yes, we love to cook, but even *we* embrace things that are premade, store-bought, or restaurant-ready. Give yourself a break from any preconceived notion that everything must be made from scratch. If you find yourself stressing out, set a goal to have one element from a meal from scratch and that's it. Pair it with a rotisserie chicken or a main course you picked up at your family's favorite restaurant. Add some sides and — *voilá!* — your meal is complete and your sanity is saved.
A win-win for all!

Chapter **7**

Seven-Day Meal Plans

I f like a set guide to follow, this chapter is for you! Here, we pull together sample seven-day meal plans to help guide you as you begin your meal-planning journey using your Instant Pot. Whether you're cooking for yourself or an entire family, these plans can be tailored to meet your needs.

REMEMBER

You can adjust a recipe yield by increasing or decreasing the ingredients. Most recipes serve four to six people, so if you're cooking for yourself and you'd prefer to only have leftovers for a couple days, just cut the ingredients in half. Likewise, double the recipe ingredients if you want to double the yield!

TIP

You can create your own meal plan template on a computer, tablet, or phone, or just jot it down on a piece of paper to hang on your fridge!

Note: Throughout this chapter, each recipe title is in bold, followed by the chapter where that recipe appears. Anything not in bold is not a recipe in this book.

A Family-Friendly Meal Plan

Whether you're a family of two or you have a baby, a teenager, and grandparents under one roof, this meal plan is for you.

TIP

Give children the reins when choosing how they top or plate their food. Whether it's a make-your-own-salad, bowl, or yogurt parfait, giving kids options empowers them to choose what they like and cook on their own someday. Keep meals joyful and not stressful, and you'll be well on your way to raising healthy, happy eaters.

TECHNICAL STUFF

As registered dietitian nutritionists, we believe in Ellyn Satter's "division of responsibility." Basically, this means that, as parents, we get to decide what foods to serve, when to serve the food, and where our kids will eat. It's our children's job to determine how much they eat and whether they eat at all. We know this can be unnerving and completely counterintuitive to how you may have been raised, but there's science backing this approach! It helps foster a positive meal environment and combat battles that can arise around the dinner table.

REMEMBER

Just because you have a baby doesn't mean you have to make baby food! Visit Chapter 23 for a quick reminder on how to modify your recipes for baby.

Table 7-1 provides a meal plan that'll work for any family.

REMEMBER

Empower your children by letting them build their own bowls, tacos, or sandwiches!

TABLE 7-1   **A Family-Friendly Meal Plan**

	Breakfast	Lunch	Dinner	Snack or Dessert
Monday	Fruit and yogurt parfait made with **Plain Yogurt (Chapter 8)**	**Minestrone Soup (Chapter 14)** with fresh bread	**Seasoned Pulled Pork (Chapter 10)** sandwiches with coleslaw	**Dark Chocolate Zucchini Loaf Cakes (Chapter 18)**
Tuesday	**Morning Glory Bundt Cake (Chapter 19)**	**Cilantro Lime Fish Tacos (Chapter 15)** with leftover coleslaw	**Mediterranean-Inspired Short Ribs (Chapter 10)** with **Basic Brown Rice (Chapter 8)** and steamed green beans	**Quick Rice Pudding (Chapter 18)**
Wednesday	**Hard-Boiled Eggs (Chapter 8)** and avocado toast	Leftover orange chicken and rice bowls (let them build their own with avocado, cabbage, and chopped broccoli)	**Texas Beef Chili with Beans (Chapter 14)** with cornbread and raw veggies	**Sautéed Peaches with Honey Ricotta (Chapter 18)**
Thursday	**Farmers Market Frittata (Chapter 9)**	Baked potatoes with chili on top	**Creamy Sausage and Ziti Pasta (Chapter 12)**	**Apple Pecan Maple Bread Pudding (Chapter 18)**

	Breakfast	Lunch	Dinner	Snack or Dessert
Friday	**Cinnamon Spice Steel-Cut Oats (Chapter 9)** with fruit	**Greek Meatballs (Chapter 15)** with cucumber and tomato salad	**Mediterranean Bowl with Feta and Herb Yogurt Dressing (Chapter 11)**	**Sugar Cookie Pizookie (Chapter 19)**
Saturday	**McKittrick's French Toast Casserole (Chapter 9)**	**Sofritas Burritos (Chapter 15)**	**Turkey and Mushroom Meatloaf (Chapter 12), Sara's Lightened-Up Macaroni and Cheese (Chapter 12)**, and **Garlic Green Beans and Tomatoes (Chapter 13)**	**Key Lime Cheesecake (Chapter 18)**
Sunday	**Lemon, Blueberry, and Chia Breakfast Cake (Chapter 9)**	**Lentil Soup (Chapter 14)** with French bread	**Nonna's Lasagna (Chapter 15)** and tossed salad with **Ranch Dressing (found with the Mexican Beans and Rice Bowl with Ranch Dressing recipe in Chapter 11)**	**Apple Crisp Under Pressure and Baked (Chapter 19)**

A Vegetarian Meal Plan

If you're a vegetarian, the meal plan in Table 7-2 is for you!

TIP

If you're a vegan, take a look at the recipes and see how you can modify them to meet your needs. You can modify many recipes that call for dairy by using a plant-based alternative product, such as an almond or soy milk, yogurt, or butter alternative.

TABLE 7-2   A Vegetarian Meal Plan

	Breakfast	Lunch	Dinner	Snack or Dessert
Monday	Fruit and yogurt parfait made with **Plain Yogurt (Chapter 8)**	**Frijoles Negros Plantain Bowl (Chapter 11)**	**Sesame Tofu Stir-Fry (Chapter 12)**	**Hard-Boiled Eggs (Chapter 8)** with fruit
Tuesday	**Hard-Boiled Eggs (Chapter 8)** with fruit and toast	**Sesame Tofu Stir-Fry (Chapter 12)**	**Minestrone Soup (Chapter 14)** with fresh bread	**Classic Banana Bread (Chapter 9)**
Wednesday	Fruit and yogurt parfait made with **Plain Yogurt (Chapter 8)**	**Minestrone Soup (Chapter 14)** with fresh bread	**Madras Lentils (Chapter 15)**	**H's Peanut Butter Hummus (Chapter 16)** with fresh-cut vegetables

(continued)

TABLE 7-2 *(continued)*

	Breakfast	Lunch	Dinner	Snack or Dessert
Thursday	**Classic Banana Bread (Chapter 9)** with **Plain Yogurt (Chapter 8)**	**Sara's Lightened-Up Macaroni and Cheese (Chapter 12)** with steamed broccoli	**Frijoles Negros Plantain Bowl (Chapter 11)**	**Hard-Boiled Eggs (Chapter 8)** with fruit
Friday	Smoothie with **Plain Yogurt (Chapter 8)**	**H's Peanut Butter Hummus (Chapter 16)** with fresh-cut vegetables and **Hard-Boiled Eggs (Chapter 8)**	Baked potato with **Madras Lentils (Chapter 15)**	**Classic Banana Bread (Chapter 9)**
Saturday	**Shakshuka with Spinach (Chapter 9)**	**Lentil Soup (Chapter 14)** with baguette	**Sara's Lightened-Up Macaroni and Cheese (Chapter 12)** with steamed broccoli	**Grandma's Simple Rhubarb Crisp (Chapter 18)**
Sunday	**Cinnamon Spice Steel-Cut Oats (Chapter 9)** with fruit	**Balsamic-Stuffed Portobello Mushrooms (Chapter 15)** with side salad	**Lentil Soup (Chapter 14)** with baguette	**Hot Cocoa (Chapter 17)**

A Modified Keto Meal Plan

We've created the meal plan in Table 7-3 with the understanding that not every recipe as it's written is 100 percent keto compliant. However, with a few modifications (like omitting the sugar and using an approved keto sweetener, like stevia or monk fruit, instead, or swapping out a grain for cauliflower or lettuce), you can tailor the recipes to a keto diet.

REMEMBER

Keto means high fat, so you need to increase the fat of many (if not all) of the recipes in this seven-day meal plan by adding an approved keto fat source. These fat sources include oils (like avocado and olive), as well as high-fat foods like nuts, avocados, and seeds.

TABLE 7-3   **A Modified Keto Meal Plan**

	Breakfast	Lunch	Dinner	Snack or Dessert
Monday	**Plain Yogurt (Chapter 8)** with nuts and seeds	**Korean Beef Bulgogi Bowl (Chapter 11)**	**Seasoned Pulled Pork (Chapter 10)** with **Cilantro Lime Cauliflower Rice (Chapter 13)**	**Spiced Walnuts and Cashews (Chapter 18)**
Tuesday	**Farmers Market Frittata (Chapter 9)** with sausage	**Seasoned Pulled Pork (Chapter 10)** with **Cilantro Lime Cauliflower Rice (Chapter 13)**	**Mediterranean-Inspired Short Ribs (Chapter 10)** with steamed broccoli	**Hard-Boiled Eggs (Chapter 8)**
Wednesday	**Plain Yogurt (Chapter 8)** with nuts and seeds	**Mediterranean-Inspired Short Ribs (Chapter 10)** over **Fried Rice (Chapter 13)** made with cauliflower rice	**Korean Beef Bulgogi Bowl (Chapter 11)**	**Spiced Walnuts and Cashews (Chapter 18)**
Thursday	**Farmers Market Frittata (Chapter 9)** with sausage	**Seasoned Pulled Pork (Chapter 10)** salad with oil and seeds	**Cilantro Lime Fish Tacos (Chapter 15)** with lettuce tortillas and extra avocado	**Hard-Boiled Eggs (Chapter 8)**
Friday	**Plain Yogurt (Chapter 8)** with nuts and seeds	**Cilantro Lime Fish Tacos (Chapter 15)** with lettuce tortillas and extra avocado	**Fried Rice (Chapter 13)** made with cauliflower rice with two extra-large eggs	**Spiced Walnuts and Cashews (Chapter 18)**
Saturday	**Poached Eggs (Chapter 9)** with ghee and bacon	**Salsa Verde Shredded Chicken (Chapter 10)** with **Cilantro Lime Cauliflower Rice (Chapter 13)**	**Carnitas (Chapter 10)** with **Cilantro Lime Cauliflower Rice (Chapter 13)**	**Low-Carb Cheesecake (Chapter 18)**
Sunday	Omelet made with **Carnitas (Chapter 10)**	**Salsa Verde Shredded Chicken (Chapter 10)** tacos in lettuce leaves with avocado	**Carne Guisada (Chapter 10)**	**Low-Carb Cheesecake (Chapter 18)**

Get Cooking!

IN THIS PART . . .

Make basics like yogurt, applesauce, broth, and more.

Start your day the Instant Pot way.

Prepare classic meats and poultry.

Behold the beauty of bowls.

Wow your family with one-pot wonders.

Use the Instant Pot to make delicious side dishes.

Keep your family warm with hearty soups and stews.

Delight in cuisines from around the world.

Prepare for your next party.

Make hot and cold beverages in your Instant Pot.

Savor delicious desserts.

Use the newest Instant Pot with the *Bake* and *Sous Vide* options.

Chapter **8**

Instant Pot Basics: Yogurt, Applesauce, Broth, and More

Knowing how to use the Instant Pot to make the basics will save you big bucks in the long run! By making your own basics, you can control what goes into your food, like the amount of added sugar and sodium. Plus, you'll shrink your environmental footprint by using less plastic from those individual yogurt and applesauce containers.

Fortunately, the recipes in this chapter don't require any fancy or expensive ingredients. Using a few quality kitchen staples, like whole milk, eggs, and frozen berries, you can create timeless classics like yogurt, which can be used throughout this book to increase protein and provide a healthy substitution for butter in baked goods like the Chocolate Chip Muffins (see Chapter 9).

Yogurt	N/A
8–10 hr	N/A

Plain Yogurt

Instant Pot function: Yogurt

Special tools: Instant-read thermometer, glass storage jars

Fits diets: Gluten-Free, Keto, Mediterranean, Vegetarian

PREP TIME: 35 MIN	COOK TIME: 8–10 HR	YIELD: 9 SERVINGS

INGREDIENTS

½ gallon whole milk

2 tablespoons cultured whole milk yogurt

DIRECTIONS

1 Add the whole milk to the Instant Pot, secure the lid, and press the *Yogurt* setting twice until the screen reads *Boil*.

2 When the Instant Pot beeps and reads *Yogt*, remove the lid and check the temperature; it should read at least 180 to 183 degrees. If it isn't hot enough, press *Sauté* and heat until the temperature reads 183 degrees, stirring constantly. Press *Cancel* and carefully remove the inner pot. For the temperature to reach 183 degrees will take about 30 minutes.

3 In your kitchen sink, make an ice bath full of ice and cool water, deep enough to fit your pot. Place the pot into the ice bath. Stir constantly until the milk gets to the temperature range of 110 to 115 degrees. After it has cooled to this range, whisk in the cultured whole milk yogurt.

4 Wipe the bottom of the pot dry and return to the Instant Pot. Secure the lid and set the valve to *Sealing*.

5 Press the *Yogurt* function again. Use the +/– button to set the time for 8 to 10 hours (8 for a thinner yogurt, 10 for a thicker yogurt) and press Start.

6 When the yogurt is finished fermenting, add boiling water to storage jars. Let sit for 5 minutes, and then dump the water and allow the jars to air-dry. Pour the yogurt into the jars, secure the lids, and store in the refrigerator up to 10 days or in the freezer up to 1 month.

NOTE: You can leave your inner pot inside the Instant Pot to cool instead of quickening things by cooling in an ice bath. It will take about an hour to cool.

Ricotta Cheese

Instant Pot function: Yogurt, Sauté (High)
Special tools: Instant-read thermometer, glass storage jars
Fits diets: Gluten-Free, Keto, Mediterranean, Vegetarian

PREP TIME: 2 MIN | **COOK TIME: 1 HR 45 MIN** | **YIELD: 9 SERVINGS**

INGREDIENTS

½ gallon whole milk

2 tablespoons lemon juice or 3 tablespoons lime juice

1 teaspoon salt

DIRECTIONS

1 Pour the milk into the Instant Pot and press the *Yogurt* setting twice, until the screen reads *Boil*. Secure the lid. When the machine beeps, check the temperature; it should be close to 180 degrees. Press *Cancel* and set to *Sauté (High)*. While whisking constantly, get the temperature to 190 degrees.

2 Remove the pot with oven-safe mitts and place on a heat-safe surface. Whisk in the lemon juice or lime juice and the salt. Stop stirring and allow the mixture to curdle for 10 minutes. Do not whisk while the curds form.

3 Meanwhile, line a colander with cheesecloth, coffee filters, or a tea towel over a slightly larger bowl to catch the whey. Pour the curdled milk into the prepared colander, allowing the whey to separate from the cheese curds. Allow the cheese to separate for at least 1 hour at room temperature. Then scrape the cheese curds into an airtight glass container and store in the refrigerator up to 1 week.

TIP: To make a lower-fat alternative, use 2 percent reduced-fat milk.

VARY IT! Mix in fresh, chopped herbs and garlic for an easy cheese spread.

Coconut Milk Kefir

Yogurt	N/A
17 hr	N/A

Instant Pot function: Yogurt

Special tools: Instant-read thermometer, glass storage jars

Fits diets: Gluten-Free, Keto, Vegan, Vegetarian

PREP TIME: 5 MIN	COOK TIME: 17 HR	YIELD: 9 SERVINGS

INGREDIENTS

Two 13.5-ounce cans unsweetened coconut cream

2 tablespoons coconut yogurt with live active cultures or 1 capsule (emptied) probiotic powder

2 tablespoons maple syrup

2 teaspoons unflavored gelatin

DIRECTIONS

1 Add the coconut cream to the Instant Pot, close the lid, and press the *Yogurt* setting twice, until the screen reads *Boil.* Secure the lid.

2 When the Instant Pot beeps, remove the lid and check the temperature; it should read at least 180 degrees. If it doesn't, set it to *Sauté* and continue heating until it reaches 180 degrees.

3 In your kitchen sink, make an ice bath that will fit your pot. Place the pot into the ice bath. Stir constantly until the milk gets to the temperature range of 105 to 110 degrees. Then whisk in the coconut yogurt or probiotic powder, the maple syrup, and the gelatin. Continue whisking for 1 minute.

4 Wipe the bottom of the pot dry. Return it to the Instant Pot and secure the lid.

5 Press the *Yogurt* setting, set the time for 16 hours, and press Start.

6 When the kefir is complete, add boiling water to the storage jars. Let sit for 5 minutes, and then dump the water out and allow the jars to air-dry. Pour the kefir into the jars, secure the lids, and store in the refrigerator up to 10 days or in the freezer up to 1 month.

NOTE: The longer you ferment the kefir, the more likely it will get to a thin, yogurt-like consistency.

NOTE: Avoid using honey as a sweetener. The bacteria in honey will compete with the probiotics.

Pressure | High
6 min | Quick Release

Simple Fruit Jam

Instant Pot function: Pressure Cook (High), Keep Warm (Off), Quick Release

Special tools: Potato masher or pastry blender, glass storage jar

Fits diets: Gluten-Free, Mediterranean, Vegan, Vegetarian

PREP TIME: NONE	COOK TIME: 6 MIN	YIELD: 14 SERVINGS

INGREDIENTS

1 cup strawberries

1 cup blueberries

1 cup raspberries

1 tablespoon brown sugar

1 teaspoon pure vanilla extract

1 tablespoon orange juice

1 teaspoon orange zest

3 tablespoons chia seeds

DIRECTIONS

1 Place the berries, brown sugar, vanilla extract, orange juice, and orange zest in the Instant Pot and stir. Close and secure the lid. Set the valve to *Sealing* and press *Pressure Cook (High)* and *Keep Warm (Off)*. Set the cook time to 6 minutes using the +/– button.

2 When finished, press *Cancel* and use *Quick Release* to remove the pressure. Remove the lid.

3 Using a potato masher or pastry blender while hot, mash the remaining whole berries and stir in the chia seeds.

4 When the jam is complete, add boiling water to the storage jar. Let sit for 5 minutes, and then dump the water out and allow the jar to air-dry. Pour the jam into the glass jar, seal the lid, and store in the refrigerator up to 3 weeks.

TIP: Use frozen berries to enjoy this jam year-round. If you're using frozen berries, add an additional 1 teaspoon of chia seeds.

NOTE: For a sweeter jam, add 2 teaspoons of sugar.

VARY IT! Swap out raspberries for blackberries or use 3 cups of your preferred fruit. Peaches make a wonderful jam.

All-Natural Applesauce

| Pressure | High |
| 10 min | Natural Release |

Instant Pot function: Pressure Cook (High), Keep Warm (On), Natural Release

Fits diets: Gluten-Free, Mediterranean, Vegan, Vegetarian

Special tools: Potato masher or pastry blender

PREP TIME: 10 MIN	COOK TIME: 10 MIN	YIELD: 6 SERVINGS

INGREDIENTS

3 Granny Smith apples, cored and sliced into sixths

3 Fuji apples, cored and sliced into sixths

¾ cup water

1 teaspoon vanilla extract

2 cinnamon sticks

DIRECTIONS

1 Place the apples, water, and vanilla extract into the inner pot. Stir and place the cinnamon stick inside. Secure the lid and select *Pressure Cook (High)* and *Keep Warm (On)*. Set the cook time to 10 minutes using the +/− button. Make sure the *Keep Warm* function is set to *ON*. When cooking completes, do a *Natural Release* of the pressure for 30 minutes.

2 Remove the lid and discard the cinnamon stick and apple skins. Use a potato masher or pastry blender to mix the apples together, creating the sauce-like consistency.

3 Store in the refrigerator up to 7 days or in the freezer up to 3 months.

NOTE: Make sure the apple slices are about the same size to ensure even cooking. If desired, keep the skins on for more fiber and a chewier texture.

VARY IT! Add 1 cup of frozen mangos, raspberries, or carrots for a flavorful twist.

Pressure	High
7 min	Quick Release

Hard–Boiled Eggs

Instant Pot function: Pressure Cook (High), Keep Warm (Off), Quick Release

Fits Diets: Gluten-Free, Keto, Mediterranean, Vegetarian

PREP TIME: NONE	COOK TIME: 7 MIN	YIELD: 6 SERVINGS

INGREDIENTS

1 cup water

6 large eggs

DIRECTIONS

1 Pour the water into the Instant Pot and place a trivet inside. Set the eggs on top of the trivet.

2 Secure the lid and set the pressure release valve to *Sealing*. Select *Pressure Cook (High)* and *Keep Warm (Off)* and set the cook time to 7 minutes using the +/− button.

3 When finished, press *Cancel* and use *Quick Release* to remove the pressure. Place in an ice bath in your kitchen sink for 5 minutes. Serve immediately or store in the refrigerator up to 7 days.

NOTE: For a soft-boiled egg, adjust the cook time to 5 minutes.

TIP: To make egg salad, mix 2 hard-boiled eggs with 4 teaspoons of plain Greek yogurt, ½ teaspoon fresh dill, and a dash of salt and pepper. Spread on top of your favorite toasted bread or serve alongside whole-grain crackers.

Pressure | High

2 hr | Natural Release

Beef Bone Broth

Instant Pot function: Pressure Cook (High), Keep Warm (On), Natural Release

Special tools: Glass storage jars

Fits diets: Gluten-Free, Keto, Mediterranean

PREP TIME: NONE	COOK TIME: 2 HR	YIELD: 10 SERVINGS

INGREDIENTS

3 pounds beef bones

3 large carrots, chopped

3 celery stalks, chopped

1 large onion, chopped

½ teaspoon dried thyme

¼ cup parsley

1 bay leaf

¼ teaspoon peppercorns

2½ quarts filtered water

DIRECTIONS

1 Combine the bones, carrots, celery, onion, thyme, parsley, bay leaf, and peppercorns in the Instant Pot; then pour the filtered water over the top.

2 Secure the lid and set to *Pressure Cook (High)* and *Keep Warm (On)* or use the *Soup/Broth* setting. Set the time for 120 minutes using the +/– button and press Start.

3 When cooking completes, do a *Natural Release* of the pressure for 30 minutes.

4 Carefully remove the pot from the Instant Pot with oven mitts. Strain the stock with a colander into a clean bowl, and discard the bones and vegetables. Store in the refrigerator up to 5 days or in the freezer up to 4 months.

TIP: You can use onion skins, celery stems, and the tops of celery in stock.

VARY IT! To make a rich and robust beef stock, roast the bones in the oven for an hour at 400 degrees.

Pressure	High
1 hr 30 min	Natural Release

Chicken or Turkey Stock

Instant Pot function: Pressure Cook (High), Keep Warm (On), Natural Release

Fits diets: Gluten-Free, Keto, Low-Carb, Low-Fat, Low-Sodium, Mediterranean

PREP TIME: NONE	COOK TIME: 1½ HR	YIELD: 10 SERVINGS

INGREDIENTS

3 pounds chicken wings

3 large carrots, chopped

3 celery stalks, chopped

1 large onion, chopped

½ teaspoon dried thyme

¼ cup parsley

1 bay leaf

¼ teaspoon peppercorns

2½ quarts filtered water

DIRECTIONS

1 Combine the chicken wings, carrots, celery, onion, thyme, parsley, bay leaf, and peppercorns in the Instant Pot; then pour the filtered water over the top.

2 Secure the lid and set to *Pressure Cook (High)* and *Keep Warm (On)* or use the *Soup/Broth* setting. Set the time for 90 minutes using the +/– button and press Start.

3 When cooking completes, do a *Natural Release* of the pressure for 30 minutes.

4 Using oven mitts, carefully lift the pot out of the Instant Pot. Strain the stock with a colander into a clean bowl, and discard the bones and vegetables. Store in the refrigerator up to 5 days or in the freezer up to 4 months.

VARY IT! Add ginger, garlic, and lemongrass for an Asian-inspired stock!

Vegetable Broth

Instant Pot function: Sauté (High), Pressure Cook (High), Keep Warm (On), Natural Release

Fits diets: Gluten-Free, Keto, Mediterranean, Vegan, Vegetarian

PREP TIME: NONE	COOK TIME: 44 MIN	YIELD: 10 SERVINGS

INGREDIENTS

1 tablespoon extra-virgin olive oil

1 large onion, quartered

2 large carrots, halved

4 celery stalks, halved

1 large bell pepper, halved

2 cloves garlic, crushed

4 rosemary sprigs

1 bay leaf

½ teaspoon peppercorns

¼ teaspoon salt

2½ quarts filtered water

DIRECTIONS

1 Press the *Sauté (High)* button and add the olive oil to the inner pot. Place the onions, cut side down, into the oil. *Sauté* for 4 minutes. Press *Cancel* and then add the remaining ingredients into the inner pot; stir. Press *Pressure Cook (High)* and *Keep Warm (On)*, setting the timer to 40 minutes using the +/− button. Secure the lid and set the vent to *Sealing*.

2 When cooking completes, use *Natural Release* for 10 minutes.

3 Remove the lid and strain the stock; discard the vegetables. Store in the refrigerator for up to 5 days or in the freezer for up to 4 months.

NOTE: Out of peppercorns? Use ½ teaspoon ground black pepper.

TIP: Use any leftover vegetable scraps and toss them in.

VARY IT! Add a jalapeño pepper, serrano pepper, and bunch of cilantro for a spicy vegetable broth.

Sauté/Pressure | High
52 min | Natural Release

Bolognese Sauce

Instant Pot function: Sauté (High), Pressure Cook (High), Keep Warm (On), Natural Release

Fits diets: Gluten-Free, Keto, Mediterranean

| PREP TIME: 25 MIN | COOK TIME: 52 MIN | YIELD: 8 SERVINGS |

INGREDIENTS

1 tablespoon extra-virgin olive oil

1½ pounds boneless beef short ribs

½ teaspoon salt

½ teaspoon pepper

1 yellow onion, diced

2 medium carrots, diced

2 celery stalks, diced

4 cloves garlic, thinly sliced

¼ cup whole milk

2 tablespoons tomato paste

One 14.5-ounce can chopped tomatoes

¼ cup red wine (see note below)

1 cup beef stock

1 bay leaf

¼ cup chopped parsley

¼ cup heavy whipping cream

Fresh parsley, for garnish

Grated Pecorino Romano, for garnish

DIRECTIONS

1 Warm the oil on *Sauté (High)* in a 6-quart Instant Pot. Season the short ribs with salt and pepper. Sauté half of the short ribs for 4 minutes on each side to brown the ribs. Remove the ribs to a plate. Cook the remaining ribs the same way.

2 Next, set to *Sauté (Medium/Normal)* and sauté the onion, carrots, and celery for 3 minutes. Add in the garlic and sauté for 1 minute. Add in the milk, tomato paste, chopped tomatoes, red wine, beef stock, bay leaf, and ribs back into the pot. Press *Cancel*.

3 Set your pot to *Pressure (High)* or *Meat/Stew (High)* for 40 minutes using the +/− button and *Keep Warm (On)*. When the cooking is complete, do a *Natural Release* of the pressure for 20 minutes (a good time to cook the pasta); then complete the release.

4 Remove the meat from the Instant Pot and serve directly over desired pasta or vegetable.

5 With a blender or an immersion blender, blend the sauce with the heavy whipping cream. Season with more salt and pepper as needed. Pour the sauce over the entree and garnish with fresh parsley and grated cheese.

| Pressure | High |
| 4 min | Natural Release |

Basic White Rice

Instant Pot function: Pressure Cook (High), Keep Warm (Off), Natural Release

Fits diets: Gluten-Free, Mediterranean, Vegan, Vegetarian

| PREP TIME: NONE | COOK TIME: 4 MIN | YIELD: 6 SERVINGS |

INGREDIENTS

1 cup Jasmine white rice

1 cup filtered water

¼ teaspoon salt

DIRECTIONS

1 Rinse the rice under cool running water until the water runs clear.

2 Add the rice, filtered water, and salt to the inner pot of the Instant Pot. Secure the lid, set the valve to *Sealing*, and press *Pressure Cook (High)* and *Keep Warm (Off)*. Using the +/− button, set the timer to 4 minutes.

3 Do a *Natural Release* of the pressure for 10 minutes when the cooking completes. Serve immediately.

Pressure | High
15 min | Natural Release

Basic Brown Rice

Instant Pot function: Pressure Cook (High), Keep Warm (Off), Natural Release

Fits diets: Gluten-Free, Mediterranean, Vegan, Vegetarian

PREP TIME: NONE	COOK TIME: 15 MIN	YIELD: 6 SERVINGS

INGREDIENTS

1 cup Jasmine brown rice

1 cup filtered water

DIRECTIONS

1 Add the rice and filtered water to the inner pot of the Instant Pot. Secure the lid, set the valve to *Sealing*, and press *Pressure Cook (High)* and *Keep Warm (Off)*. Using the +/− button, set the timer to 15 minutes.

2 Do a *Natural Release* of the pressure for 5 minutes when the cooking completes. Serve immediately.

Chapter 9

Jump-Start Your Day: Breakfast

R ise and shine! It's time to get your day started with a nourishing breakfast. The 7-inch springform pan will help you succeed at making frittatas, breakfast stratas, casseroles, breakfast cakes, and breads. Plus, you'll use silicone muffin cups to make the Chocolate Chip Muffins. The muffin cups can also be used in making single-serving frittatas or eggs, like our Poached Eggs recipe.

If your family prefers the basics, like hard-boiled eggs, be sure to check out Chapter 8. If you want to jazz up your oats, check out the Cinnamon Spice Steel-Cut Oats in this chapter. Many of these breakfast options can also be frozen for busy mornings, so be sure to check out the tips on storage.

Steam | High

4 min | Quick Release

Poached Eggs

Instant Pot function: Steam (High), Quick Release

Special tools: Silicone muffin cups

Fits diets: Gluten-Free, Keto, Mediterranean, Vegetarian

PREP TIME: NONE	COOK TIME: 4 MIN	YIELD: 4 SERVINGS

INGREDIENTS

4 large eggs

1 cup water

DIRECTIONS

1 Spray 4 silicone muffin cups with cooking spray and crack 1 egg into each muffin cup holder.

2 Place the muffin cups onto the trivet. Pour the water into the pot and lower the trivet gently into the pot. Secure the lid and set to *Steam (High)*. Set the time to 4 minutes.

3 When cooking is done, press *Cancel* and *Quick Release* for venting.

4 Using a spoon, carefully scoop the eggs from the liner.

TIP: For a firmer egg yolk, increase the cook time to 5 minutes. For a softer poached egg, decrease the cook time to 3 minutes.

Sauté/Pressure | High
10 min | Quick Release

Shakshuka with Spinach

Instant Pot function: Sauté (High), Pressure Cook (High), Keep Warm (Off), Quick Release

Fits diets: Gluten-Free, Keto, Mediterranean, Vegetarian

| PREP TIME: 5 MIN | COOK TIME: 10 MIN | YIELD: 4 SERVINGS |

INGREDIENTS

1 teaspoon extra-virgin olive oil

½ small onion, chopped

1 teaspoon minced garlic

1 teaspoon Italian seasoning

½ teaspoon black pepper

One 28-ounce cans no-added-salt diced tomatoes

2 cups baby spinach, rinsed

4 large eggs

¼ cup chopped fresh basil, divided

Salt, to taste

Grated Parmesan cheese, for garnish

DIRECTIONS

1 Set the Instant Pot to *Sauté (High)*.

2 Place the oil in the inner pot; add the chopped onion and sauté for 3 minutes. Mix in the garlic, Italian seasoning, pepper, and canned tomatoes and sauté another 3 minutes. Press *Cancel* and add the spinach.

3 Crack the eggs, one at a time and spaced apart, directly into the tomato mixture, keeping the yolks intact. Set to *Pressure Cook (High)* and *Keep Warm (Off)*, using the +/– button to set the time for 0 minutes (the initial pressure buildup will cook the egg). Secure the lid and set the vent to *Sealing*.

4 When cooking is done, press *Cancel* and *Quick Release* to remove pressure from the pot.

5 Portion one egg and tomato mixture into 4 serving bowls. Top with fresh basil and grated Parmesan cheese. Serve immediately.

NOTE: For a firmer egg yolk, increase the cook time to 2 minutes. You can decrease the recipe ingredients by half for a smaller portion.

TIP: Serve Shakshuka over a cooked whole grain for a complete meal.

VARY IT! Add in chopped bell peppers and spinach or kale for a more veggie-centered dish.

Farmers Market Frittata

| Sauté/Pressure | High |
| 34 min | Natural Release |

Instant Pot function: Sauté (High), Pressure Cook (High), Keep Warm (On), Natural Release

Special tools: 7-inch springform pan

Fits diets: Gluten-Free, Keto, Mediterranean, Vegetarian

PREP TIME: 5 MIN	COOK TIME: 34 MIN	YIELD: 4 SERVINGS

INGREDIENTS

1 teaspoon extra-virgin olive oil

½ small onion, chopped

1 teaspoon minced garlic

½ teaspoon black pepper

⅛ teaspoon salt

1 cup cremini mushrooms, chopped

2 cups fresh spinach, roughly chopped

6 large eggs

⅓ cup 2 percent cottage cheese

⅓ cup shredded cheddar cheese

1 cup water

¼ cup chopped fresh basil, divided

Avocado, for garnish

Hot sauce, for garnish

DIRECTIONS

1 Turn *Sauté (High)* function on and add the oil. Add the onion and sauté until translucent, about 4 minutes. Stir in the garlic, black pepper, salt, and mushrooms; sauté 5 minutes.

2 Mix in the chopped spinach and cook another minute. Press *Cancel.* Carefully remove the inner pot and drain the excess liquid. Set aside.

3 Crack the eggs in a mixing bowl, and whisk in the cottage cheese and cheddar cheese. Add in the sautéed mixture and stir.

4 Liberally spray a 7-inch springform pan with cooking spray. Pour the egg mixture into the pan and cover with aluminum foil.

5 Rinse the inner pot of the Instant Pot with water and dry the outside. Place back inside the Instant Pot and add the water into the base, placing the metal trivet on top.

6 Set the springform pan on the trivet, secure the lid, and set the valve to *Sealing.* Press *Pressure Cook (High)* and *Keep Warm (On)* and use the +/– button to set the timer to 14 minutes.

7 When cooking completes, do a *Natural Release* of the pressure for 10 minutes.

8 Remove from the springform pan and slice into 4 wedges. Before serving, top with avocado or hot sauce, if desired.

NOTE: Serve alongside a garden salad.

TIP: Place leftovers between a whole-grain English muffin for a quick grab-and-go breakfast for a busy morning.

VARY IT! Swap in your favorite in-season vegetables for a sustainable twist.

Green Chile Country Sausage Gravy

Sauté	High
10 min	N/A

Instant Pot Function: Sauté (High)

Fits Diets: Keto, Low-Carb

PREP TIME: 5 MIN	COOK TIME: 10 MIN	YIELD: 8 SERVINGS

INGREDIENTS

2 chicken sausage links (about 4 ounces each)

⅓ teaspoon ground garlic powder

½ teaspoon ground black pepper

¼ cup diced green chilies

3 cups milk

¼ cup all-purpose flour

Salt and pepper, to taste

DIRECTIONS

1 Press the *Sauté (High)* function on the Instant Pot. Remove the casing from the chicken sausage, and add the sausage to the inner pot. While cooking the sausage, add in the garlic powder, black pepper, and chilies; stir.

2 After the sausage appears to be cooked (about 8 minutes), press *Cancel.* Slowly pour in the milk and stir. Whisk in 1 tablespoon of flour at a time. Continue to whisk until all the flour has been added and the gravy begins to coat the back of a wooden spoon.

3 Using oven-safe mitts, remove the inner pot from the Instant Pot and let cool on a wire rack (or stovetop) and continue to stir so the gravy doesn't burn the bottom of the Instant Pot. Serve warm. Season with salt and pepper as desired.

TIP: Serve over Green Chile Cornbread (Chapter 13) or premade biscuits and top with an egg.

NOTE: The gravy should stick to the back of a spoon when stirred. If it's too liquidy, add a tablespoon more of flour at a time.

TIP: Substitute 2 tablespoons cornstarch for a gluten-friendly gravy.

VARY IT! Prefer pork sausage? Swap it in!

Mediterranean Sausage Breakfast Strata

Sauté/Pressure	High
35 min	Natural/Quick Release

Instant Pot Function: Sauté (High), Pressure (High), Keep Warm (On), Natural Release, Quick Release

Special Tools: 7-inch springform pan

Fits Diets: Mediterranean, Vegetarian

PREP TIME:10 MIN	COOK TIME: 35 MIN	YIELD: 6 SERVINGS

INGREDIENTS

½ pound ground sausage

1½ cups water

3 cups cubed French or Sourdough bread

¼ cup chopped black olives

½ cup chopped red bell pepper

6 large eggs, whisked

½ teaspoon salt

¼ teaspoon black pepper

¼ cup chopped parsley

1 cup milk

¼ cup goat cheese, crumbled

Chopped parsley, for garnish

DIRECTIONS

1 Put the sausage into the inner pot, set to *Sauté (High)*, and sauté for 5 minutes. Drain the sausage and give the pot a quick rinse and scrub. Return the inner pot to the Instant Pot base and fill with the water.

2 In a separate bowl, mix together the ground sausage, bread cubes, olives, bell pepper, eggs, salt, pepper, parsley, and milk.

3 Spray the springform pan with cooking spray or rub with oil. Pour the strata mixture into the springform pan. Top with crumbled goat cheese. Using the trivet, lower the springform pan into the pot. Secure the lid and set to *Pressure Cook (High)* and *Keep Warm (On)* and set the time for 20 minutes.

4 Do a *Natural Release* of the pressure for 10 minutes before doing a *Quick Release*. Run a knife gently around the edge of the pan to release the strata. Allow to cool for 10 minutes before releasing the springform. Top with fresh, chopped parsley and serve warm.

TIP: Rinse the cooked ground sausage to remove excess grease and sodium.

VARY IT! Go Mexican with black beans, cilantro, and cheddar cheese!

Cinnamon Spice Steel-Cut Oats

| Pressure | High |
| 8 min | Quick Release |

Instant Pot Function: Pressure Cook (High), Keep Warm (Off), Quick Release

Fits Diets: Gluten-Free, Mediterranean, Vegan, Vegetarian

| PREP TIME: NONE | COOK TIME: 8 MIN | YIELD: 4 SERVINGS |

INGREDIENTS

3 cups water

1 cup steel-cut oats

¼ teaspoon salt

2 cinnamon sticks

DIRECTIONS

1 Put the water, oats, salt, and cinnamon sticks into the inner pot of the Instant Pot. Secure the lid, set the valve to *Sealing* and press *Pressure Cook (High)* and *Keep Warm (Off)*. Set the timer to 8 minutes using the +/– button.

2 When cooking completes, press *Quick Release*. Remove the lid and take out the cinnamon sticks. Stir the oats and allow them to sit for 5 minutes to soak up any remaining water.

3 Portion into bowls and add a splash of milk, chopped nuts, and fresh fruit, if desired.

TIP: If you don't have cinnamon sticks on hand, you can use ½ teaspoon ground cinnamon instead.

NOTE: Opt for gluten-free oats if you're on a gluten-free diet.

TIP: If you're using old-fashioned oats, decrease the cooking time to 6 minutes.

VARY IT! Quinoa is an excellent addition to breakfast to amp up the protein while providing a unique twist. You can also omit the cinnamon stick and leave plain; top with a fried egg, salsa, and avocado for a savory twist!

McKittrick's French Toast Casserole

Pressure	High
25 min	Quick Release

Instant Pot Function: Pressure Cook (High), Keep Warm (Off), Quick Release

Special Tools: 7-inch springform pan

Fits Diets: Vegetarian

PREP TIME: 5 MIN	COOK TIME: 25 MIN	YIELD: 6 SERVINGS

INGREDIENTS

1 medium banana, halved

4 large eggs

¼ cup light coconut milk

1 teaspoon ground cinnamon

¼ teaspoon ground nutmeg

1 teaspoon vanilla extract

½ loaf challah bread, torn into 1-inch pieces

1 tablespoon butter

2 tablespoons brown sugar

2 tablespoons maple syrup

1 cup water

Chopped walnuts, for garnish

DIRECTIONS

1 Mash one-half of the banana and thinly slice the remaining half. Set aside the banana slices.

2 In a medium bowl, whisk the mashed banana with the eggs, milk, cinnamon, nutmeg, and vanilla extract. Add the challah bread pieces to the mixture and allow them to soak up the liquid.

3 Press *Sauté (High)* on the Instant Pot and add the butter, brown sugar, and maple syrup. Sauté for 3 minutes; then press *Cancel.*

4 Liberally spray a 7-inch springform pan with cooking spray and line the bottom with the sliced banana pieces. Top with the soaked bread pieces and pour the maple syrup mixture over the top. Rinse out the inner pot, and dry the outside. Return the inner pot to the Instant Pot and add the water. Place the metal trivet inside the pot.

5 Cover the pan with aluminum foil and set on the trivet. Cover and secure the lid. Set the Instant Pot to *Sealing.* Press *Pressure Cook (High)* and *Keep Warm (Off)* and use the +/− button to adjust the time to 25 minutes.

6 When the cooking completes, press *Cancel* and use *Quick Release* to allow the steam to escape. Carefully remove the cake pan from the Instant Pot and let cool 10 minutes on a wire rack. Invert the casserole onto a plate and release from the pan.

7 Garnish with chopped nuts and serve warm.

Lemon, Blueberry, and Chia Breakfast Cake

Pressure	High
35 min	Quick Release

Instant Pot function: Pressure Cook (High), Keep Warm (Off), Quick Release

Special tools: 7-inch springform cake pan

Fits diets: Mediterranean, Vegetarian

PREP TIME: 10 MIN	COOK TIME: 35 MIN	YIELD: 6 SERVINGS

INGREDIENTS

2 cups all-purpose flour

2 teaspoons baking powder

½ teaspoon salt

1 tablespoon lemon zest

6 ounces fresh blueberries

¼ cup sugar

1 cup buttermilk, kefir, or plain yogurt

2 large eggs

2 tablespoons fresh lemon juice

½ cup canola oil

1 teaspoon vanilla extract

1½ cups water

½ cup powdered sugar

2 tablespoons fresh lemon juice

DIRECTIONS

1 In a medium bowl, stir together the flour, baking powder, salt, lemon zest, and blueberries.

2 In a separate bowl, whisk the sugar; buttermilk, kefir, or yogurt; eggs; lemon juice; canola oil; and vanilla extract.

3 Make a well in the center of the dry ingredients and pour the wet ingredients into the center. Stir the batter for 1 minute or until most of the flour lumps are broken up.

4 Pour the cake mix into a nonstick 7-inch springform pan or cake pan. Pour the water into the bottom of the Instant Pot and place the rack in the bottom of the pan. Carefully place the cake pan on the rack.

5 Secure the lid into the locking position. Set to *Pressure Cook (High)* and *Keep Warm (Off)* and use the +/− button to adjust the time to 35 minutes.

6 When cooking completes, use *Quick Release* to remove the pressure.

7 With oven mitts, carefully remove the rack and place the cake pan on a cooling rack.

8 Prepare the sauce by whisking together the powdered sugar and lemon juice. Drizzle over the cake and serve warm or cooled.

TIP: For a smaller yield, decrease the recipe by half and modify the cooking time to 18 minutes.

VARY IT! Switch up flavors with orange juice/zest and lime juice/zest.

Pressure	**High**
45 min	**Natural Release**

Classic Banana Bread

Instant Pot function: Pressure Cook (High), Keep Warm (On), Natural Release

Special tools: 7-inch springform or baking pan

Fits diets: Mediterranean, Vegetarian

PREP TIME: 10 MIN	COOK TIME: 45 MIN	YIELD: 8 SERVINGS

INGREDIENTS

1½ cups water

½ cup oil

2 large eggs

3 medium ripe bananas, mashed

3 tablespoons milk

½ teaspoon vanilla extract

½ cup granulated sugar

2 cups all-purpose flour

1 teaspoon baking soda

½ teaspoon baking powder

½ teaspoon salt

½ cup chopped walnuts or pecans (optional)

DIRECTIONS

1 Spray a 7-inch springform pan with cooking spray. Pour the water into the Instant Pot and place the trivet into the pot. In a medium mixing bowl, whisk together the oil, eggs, bananas, milk, vanilla extract, and sugar.

2 In a separate bowl stir together the flour, baking soda, baking powder, salt, and nuts.

3 Make a well in the dry ingredients and pour the wet ingredients into the center of the dry ingredients. Quickly stir together for 1 minute (the batter can still be slightly lumpy).

4 Pour the banana bread batter into the springform or baking pan. Carefully place into the Instant Pot on the trivet.

5 Set the pot to *Pressure Cook (High)* and *Keep Warm (On)* and cook for 30 minutes.

6 When cooking completes, do a *Natural Release* of the pressure for 10 minutes.

7 Carefully remove the springform pan with oven mitts and allow the bread to cool on a cooling rack for 20 minutes. Using a butter knife, gently loosen the sides between the cake and the pan; then release the springform or baking pan.

8 Serve the bread warm or at room temperature.

Pumpkin Spice Bread

Pressure	High
45 min	Natural Release

Instant Pot function: Pressure Cook (High), Keep Warm (On), Natural Release

Special tools: 7-inch springform pan

Fits diets: Mediterranean, Vegetarian

PREP TIME: 10 MIN | **COOK TIME: 45 MIN** | **YIELD: 8 SERVINGS**

INGREDIENTS

1½ cups water

One 14.5-ounce can pumpkin puree

1½ cups granulated sugar

3 large eggs

½ cup vegetable oil

2½ cups plus 2 tablespoons all-purpose flour

1½ teaspoons baking soda

1 teaspoon cinnamon

1 teaspoon nutmeg

1 teaspoon salt

½ cup chopped walnuts or pecans

DIRECTIONS

1 Spray a 7-inch springform pan with cooking spray. Pour the water into the Instant Pot and place the trivet into the pot.

2 In a medium mixing bowl, whisk together the pumpkin, sugar, eggs, and vegetable oil.

3 In a separate bowl stir together the flour, baking soda, cinnamon, nutmeg, salt, and nuts.

4 Make a well in the dry ingredients and pour the wet ingredients into the center of the dry ingredients. Quickly stir together for 1 minute (the batter may still be slightly lumpy).

5 Pour the batter into the springform pan. Carefully place the pan into the Instant Pot on the trivet.

6 Set to *Pressure Cook (High)* and *Keep Warm (On)* and cook for 30 minutes.

7 When cooking completes, do a *Natural Release* of the pressure for 10 minutes.

8 Carefully remove the springform pan with oven mitts and allow the bread to cool on a cooling rack for 20 minutes.

9 Using a butter knife, gently loosen the sides between the cake and the pan; then release the springform.

10 Serve the bread warm or at room temperature.

TIP: You can replace half of the all-purpose flour with white whole-wheat flour to boost the fiber content.

Pressure	High
20 min	Quick Release

Chocolate Chip Muffins

Instant Pot function: Pressure Cook (High), Keep Warm (Off), Quick Release
Special tools: Silicone muffin liners
Fits diets: Mediterranean, Vegetarian

PREP TIME: 10 MIN	COOK TIME: 20 MIN	YIELD: 12 SERVINGS

INGREDIENTS

⅓ cup brown sugar

1 large egg

½ cup milk

⅓ cup plain whole milk yogurt

½ cup unsweetened applesauce

1 teaspoon vanilla extract

1 cup whole wheat flour

½ cup wheat bran

1 teaspoon baking powder

½ teaspoon baking soda

1 teaspoon cinnamon

¼ teaspoon sea salt

3 tablespoons chopped walnuts

¼ cup mini chocolate chips

1 cup water

DIRECTIONS

1 In a medium bowl, mix the brown sugar, egg, milk, yogurt, applesauce, and vanilla extract. Set aside.

2 In a small bowl, combine the flour, wheat bran, baking powder, baking soda, cinnamon, and sea salt. Fold the dry mixture into the wet, combining the walnuts and chocolate chips at the end.

3 Place the water into the inner pot and add the trivet. Using a 1-inch scoop, add the mixture to 6 silicone muffin liners and place the muffins inside the pot on the metal trivet.

4 Secure the lid. Set the valve to *Sealing* and press *Pressure Cook (High)* and *Keep Warm (Off)*. Set the timer to 10 minutes using the +/− button.

5 When the cooking completes, use *Quick Release* and remove the lid. Carefully lift the muffins out of the pot and let sit for 10 minutes.

6 Repeat Steps 2 to 4 with the remaining batter.

7 Serve warm with butter or nut butter if desired.

NOTE: Decrease the ingredients by half if you're short on time.

VARY IT! Swap the chocolate for dried fruit, like raisins! If you're allergic to nuts, you can swap them for seeds like pumpkin seeds.

Chapter 10

Classic Meats and Poultry

Where are our meat lovers out there? This chapter is for you! Filled with hearty, delicious, melt-in-your-mouth recipes, you won't regret flipping through and whipping up Bob's Baby Back Ribs or the Rosemary and Garlic Whole Chicken for your next gathering.

And, contrary to what you may have heard, animal proteins like meat and poultry can provide a great addition to a balanced diet. Not only are animal meats rich in important nutrients like vitamin B12, iron, and protein, but they're also great to batch cook and use in multiple recipes (like the Chicken Enchilada Casserole in Chapter 15), ultimately lowering your stress when it comes to the question "What's for dinner?"

TIP

Pay attention to weekly ads and make your menu based on what's on sale. For instance, if you notice pork loin is a steal, be sure to grab one or two. Meats freeze very well and allow you the opportunity to watch your budget and feed your family delicious and nutritious meals without breaking the bank.

Choose your favorite veggie-centered side (Chapter 13) to create a balanced, complete meal!

Pressure | High

1 hr 30 min | Natural Release

Seasoned Pulled Pork

Instant Pot function: Pressure Cook (Normal), Keep Warm (Off), Natural Release

Special tools: Meat thermometer

Fits diets: Gluten Free, Keto

PREP TIME: 5 MIN	COOK TIME: 1½ HR	YIELD: 12 SERVINGS

INGREDIENTS

2 tablespoons blackened seasoning

2 teaspoons garlic powder

1 teaspoon onion powder

1 teaspoon paprika

½ teaspoon ground black pepper

¼ teaspoon salt

4 pounds bone-in pork shoulder

2 cups chicken broth

1 bay leaf

DIRECTIONS

1 In a large bowl, mix together the blackened seasoning, garlic powder, onion powder, black pepper, and salt. Add the pork shoulder, and rub the spices into the pork shoulder, covering the entire surface area.

2 Place the seasoned pork shoulder into the inner pot of the Instant Pot. Top with the remaining spices from the bowl. Pour the chicken broth over the top, add in the bay leaf, and secure the lid.

3 Set the valve to *Sealing* and select *Pressure Cook (Normal)* and *Keep Warm (Off)*, using the +/− button to set the time to 90 minutes.

4 The final internal temperature of the pork should reach 145 degrees. When cooking completes, do a *Natural Release* of the pressure for 25 minutes.

5 Switch the valve to *Venting* and allow the remaining pressure (if any) to release. Remove the lid and discard the bone, bay leaf, and any excess visible fat from the inner pot.

6 Using two large forks, begin to shred the pork directly into the broth and spice mixture. Serve immediately.

NOTE: For a smaller pork shoulder, adjust the time accordingly with the estimate of 22 minutes per pound.

TIP: Serve with cabbage slaw on top of a Hawaiian sweet roll or on its own over a salad for a keto-friendly option.

VARY IT! Switch up your seasonings and add your favorite spice blend! If you're using barbecue sauce, wait until the final stages of serving to add.

Pork Tenderloin with Gravy

Instant Pot function: Sauté (High), Pressure Cook (High), Keep Warm (Off), Natural Release, Quick Release

Special tools: Meat thermometer

Fits diets: Gluten-Free, Keto, Mediterranean

PREP TIME: 5 MIN	COOK TIME: 33 MIN	YIELD: 8 SERVINGS

INGREDIENTS

2 teaspoons garlic powder

1 teaspoon dried thyme

1 teaspoon onion powder

½ teaspoon black pepper

¼ teaspoon salt

2½ pound pork tenderloin

2 teaspoons extra-virgin olive oil

2½ cups chicken broth

1 bay leaf

2 tablespoons cornstarch

DIRECTIONS

1 In a large bowl, mix together the garlic powder, thyme, onion powder, black pepper, and salt. Place the pork tenderloin on top. Using your hands, liberally rub the spice mixture into the pork tenderloin. Set aside.

2 Press *Sauté (High)* on the Instant Pot, and add the olive oil. Place the pork tenderloin in the oil, and brown on all sides (about 4 minutes each), flipping over using kitchen tongs. Press *Cancel*.

3 Add the chicken broth and bay leaf on top of the pork tenderloin. Use a spatula to remove any pieces of pork that may be stuck to the bottom of the metal pan (this will help prevent receiving a *Burn* notification). Place the lid on the Instant Pot and set the valve to *Sealing*.

4 Press *Pressure Cook* (High) and *Keep Warm (Off)* and set the timer to 25 minutes using the +/– button. The internal temperature of the pork tenderloin should reach 145 degrees.

5 When the cook time completes, do a *Natural Release* of the pressure for 10 minutes. Use *Quick Release* to remove any excess pressure. Remove the pork tenderloin from the pot and set aside to rest. Meanwhile, remove the bay leaf and any visible excess fat (which should be minimal).

6 Press *Sauté (High)* and use the +/– button to set the timer to 5 minutes. Whisk the cornstarch into the broth until combined and gravy thickens to the point that, when a spoon is inserted, it coats the back of the spoon. Press *Cancel*.

7 Slice the pork tenderloin and top with gravy. Serve immediately.

NOTE: Approximate cooking time is 8 minutes per pound.

VARY IT! Prefer a spicier pork? Add a sliced jalapeño or, if in season, Hatch chilies to the broth mixture.

Carnitas

Instant Pot function: Pressure Cook (High), Keep Warm (On), Natural Release

Fits diets: Gluten-Free, Keto

Pressure	High
45 min	Natural Release

PREP TIME: 10 MIN	COOK TIME: 45 MIN	YIELD: 8 SERVINGS

INGREDIENTS

1 teaspoon cumin

1½ teaspoons salt

2 teaspoons chili powder

2 teaspoons oregano

2 teaspoons garlic powder

1 teaspoon onion powder

3 pounds boneless pork shoulder, cut into 3-inch chunks

1 bay leaf

1 orange, juiced

1 lime, juiced

2 cups chicken stock

2 tablespoons olive oil

Chopped cilantro, for garnish

Lime wedges, for garnish

Sliced jalapeño, for garnish

Corn tortillas, for garnish

Pico de gallo, for garnish

DIRECTIONS

1 In a small bowl, mix together the cumin, salt, powder, oregano, garlic powder, and onion powder. Place the pork shoulder into the Instant Pot and thoroughly rub the spices on the meat.

2 Place the bay leaf, orange juice, and lime juice into the pot, and pour the chicken stock over the top of the meat. Secure the lid and set the valve to *Sealing.*

3 Press *Pressure Cook (High)* on the Instant Pot, adjust the time to 40 minutes using the +/– button, with *Keep Warm (On).* Do a *Natural Release* of the pressure for 15 minutes.

4 Remove the meat from the pot onto a cutting board. Using two forks, shred the meat.

5 In a cast iron or stainless steel skillet, heat the olive oil on medium-high heat. Add in 2 cups of meat at a time and cook until the meat gets a crust or browned edges. Repeat in batches until all the meat has been browned. Alternatively, this can be done on a baking sheet and the meat broiled for 5 minutes.

6 Top the meat with chopped cilantro, lime wedges, and sliced jalapeño. Serve the meat with heated corn tortillas and *pico de gallo.*

| Pressure/Sauté | High |
| 39 min | Natural Release |

Carne Guisada

Instant Pot function: Pressure Cook (High), Keep Warm (On), Natural Release, Sauté (High)

Fits diets: Gluten-Free, Keto

PREP TIME: 10 MIN	COOK TIME: 39 MIN	YIELD: 8 SERVINGS

INGREDIENTS

3 pounds beef stew meat, cubed

2 cups beef stock

2 tablespoons tomato paste

1 tablespoon dried oregano

1 teaspoon cumin

4 garlic cloves, chopped

1 large onion, chopped

1 large green bell pepper, chopped

1½ teaspoons salt

2 tablespoons cornstarch

2 tablespoons cold water

DIRECTIONS

1 Place the cubed stew meat into the Instant Pot and add the beef stock, tomato paste, oregano, cumin, cloves, onion, bell pepper, and salt. Stir to combine the ingredients, and secure the lid.

2 Press *Pressure Cook (High)* on the Instant Pot, adjust the time to 35 minutes using the +/− button, with *Keep Warm (On)*. Do a *Natural Release* of the pressure for 15 minutes.

3 Using a slotted spoon, remove the meat to a serving bowl.

4 In a small bowl, whisk together the cornstarch and water.

5 Press *Sauté (High)* and, while whisking, add in the cornstarch slurry. Bring the sauce to a low simmer about 4 minutes; then ladle over the meat and serve.

TIP: If you prefer a smoother gravy, use an immersion blender or regular blender to blend the gravy before serving. Work in small batches with a towel over the top of the blender. Serve with flour tortillas or over rice, mashed potatoes, or cauliflower rice.

Mediterranean-Inspired Short Ribs

| Sauté/Pressure | High |
| 44 min | Natural Release |

Instant Pot function: Sauté (High), Pressure Cook (High), Keep Warm (On), Natural Release, Sauté (High)

Fits diets: Gluten-Free, Keto

PREP TIME: 15 MIN   **COOK TIME: 44 MIN**   **YIELD: 6 SERVINGS**

INGREDIENTS

3 pounds bone-in beef short ribs

1 teaspoon salt

½ teaspoon black pepper

¼ cup extra-virgin olive oil

1 large onion, finely chopped

2 large carrots, finely chopped

2 celery stalks, finely chopped

2 tablespoons tomato paste

½ cup red wine

1 cup beef stock

¼ cup balsamic vinegar

1 tablespoon sugar

1 tablespoon dried rosemary

1 bay leaf

1 teaspoon dried thyme

2 teaspoons dried oregano

2 tablespoons cornstarch

2 tablespoons cold water

Chopped parsley, for garnish

DIRECTIONS

1 Season the short ribs with the salt and pepper. Press *Sauté (High)* and place the olive oil in the pot. Working in batches, brown the short ribs for 6 minutes while flipping to brown all sides. Set the ribs aside on a plate.

2 Next, add the onion, carrots, celery, and tomato paste, and sauté for 3 minutes. Pour in the wine, beef stock, balsamic vinegar, sugar, rosemary, bay leaf, thyme, and oregano. Press *Cancel.*

3 Secure the lid and press *Pressure Cook (High)*. Adjust the time to 35 minutes using the +/− button, with *Keep Warm (On)*. Do a *Natural Release* of the pressure for 10 minutes. Using a slotted spoon, remove the ribs to a serving bowl.

4 In a small bowl, whisk together the cornstarch and water.

5 Press *Sauté (High)* and, while whisking, add in the cornstarch slurry. Bring the sauce to a low simmer; ladle over the meat.

6 Serve with chopped parsley over the top.

TIP: Serve over polenta or mashed potatoes if you like.

Pressure | High
30 min | Natural Release

Bob's Baby Back Ribs

Instant Pot function: Pressure Cook (High), Keep Warm (On), Natural Release
Special tools: Grill or oven (optional)
Fits diets: Gluten-Free, Keto

PREP TIME: 35 MIN	COOK TIME: 30 MIN	YIELD: 4 SERVINGS

INGREDIENTS

¼ cup brown sugar

1 tablespoon chili powder

1 teaspoon cumin

½ teaspoon coriander

1 teaspoon dried oregano

½ teaspoon black pepper

2 teaspoons salt

1 tablespoon garlic powder

2 teaspoons onion powder

One 3-pound pork baby back ribs rack

1 cup beef stock

½ cup apple cider vinegar

1 cup barbecue sauce

DIRECTIONS

1 In a small bowl, mix together the brown sugar, chili powder, cumin, coriander, oregano, black pepper, salt, garlic powder, and onion powder. Using your hands, liberally rub the spice mixture onto the ribs on all sides. Let the meat rest for 30 minutes at room temperature.

2 Place the trivet into the inner pot. Pour the beef stock and apple cider vinegar into the pot. Curve the rib rack like a C and lower it into the pot, with the ribs standing upright.

3 Secure the lid and seal the venting. Press *Pressure Cook (High)* and adjust the time to 25 minutes using the +/− button, with *Keep Warm (On)*. Do a *Natural Release* of the pressure for 10 minutes.

4 Remove the ribs from the pot with tongs and lay flat, meaty side up, onto a baking sheet lined with foil. Brush the barbecue sauce on the ribs. Set the oven to broil and broil the ribs for 3 to 5 minutes to heat the barbecue sauce and slightly brown the ribs. Another option is to heat a grill to 400 degrees and grill the ribs for 3 to 4 minutes and baste with the barbecue sauce.

NOTE: Most rib racks have 13 to 14 ribs per rack, so plan on one rack serving 3 to 4 people and adjust as needed. You can cook two baby back rib racks at the same time in a 6- or 8-quart Instant Pot.

Pressure/ Sauté	High
15 min	Quick Release

Pineapple Teriyaki Burgers

Instant Pot function: Pressure Cook (High), Keep Warm (Off), Quick Release, Sauté (High)

Fits diets: Mediterranean

PREP TIME: 5 MIN	COOK TIME: 15 MIN	YIELD: 4 SERVINGS

INGREDIENTS

1 pound lean ground turkey

1 teaspoon ground ginger

¾ teaspoon garlic powder

½ teaspoon onion powder

¾ teaspoon ground black pepper, divided

⅜ teaspoon salt, divided

1½ cups water

1 tablespoon extra-virgin olive oil

½ small onion, thinly sliced

⅓ cup teriyaki sauce

4 Hawaiian sweet buns

4 leaves butter leaf lettuce

1 cup diced pineapple

DIRECTIONS

1 In a large bowl, mix the ground turkey, ginger, garlic powder, onion powder, ½ teaspoon of the black pepper, and ¼ teaspoon of the salt. Divide the mixture into four 4-ounce patties. Wrap each patty individually with aluminum foil, securely folding over the edges.

2 Add the water to the inner pot of the Instant Pot. Place the trivet over the water and lay 3 of the patties on the trivet and 1 patty on top.

3 Secure the lid and set the valve to *Sealing*.

4 Press *Pressure Cooker (High)* and *Keep Warm (Off)*, and use the +/− button to set the timer for 10 minutes.

5 When cooking completes, press *Cancel* and use *Quick Release* to release the pressure. Carefully remove the trivet with the patties and let sit 5 minutes.

6 Meanwhile, discard the water from the pot and return the inner pot to the Instant Pot. Press *Sauté (High)*, add the olive oil, and sauté the onion with the remaining ¼ teaspoon pepper and ⅛ teaspoon salt until cooked, about 5 minutes. Press *Cancel* and stir in the teriyaki sauce.

7 Assemble the burgers by placing each burger patty on top of a Hawaiian bun with lettuce, diced pineapple, and the onion teriyaki sauce. Serve immediately.

NOTE: To make this recipe gluten-free, buy a teriyaki sauce that is gluten-free and use a gluten-free bun.

VARY IT! Use lean ground beef, chicken, or pork for a different twist.

Rosemary and Garlic Whole Chicken

| Sauté/ Pressure | High |
| 31 min | Quick Release |

Instant Pot function: Sauté (High), Pressure Cook (High), Keep Warm (Off), Quick Release

Special tools: Thermometer

Fits diets: Gluten-Free, Keto, Mediterranean

PREP TIME: 10 MIN	COOK TIME: 31 MIN	YIELD: 10 SERVINGS

INGREDIENTS

2 sprigs fresh rosemary

One 5-pound whole chicken, giblets removed

1 tablespoon minced garlic

¼ teaspoon salt

½ teaspoon black pepper

1 tablespoon extra-virgin olive oil

1 cup water

DIRECTIONS

1 Insert the rosemary into the cavity of the chicken, and rub the outside with garlic, salt, and pepper. Press *Sauté (High)* and add the olive oil and place the chicken into the pot. Sauté 3 minutes per side to get a nice crust on the outer skin.

2 Press *Cancel.* Using tongs and a large fork, remove the chicken and set aside. Add the water to the pot (do not rinse out the pot — this will create a great stock to use in another recipe like the soups in Chapter 14). Insert the metal trivet into the pot and place the chicken back onto the trivet, breast side up.

3 Secure the lid and set the valve to *Venting.* Press *Pressure Cook (High)* and set the timer to 25 minutes using the +/– button.

4 When the cooking completes, use the *Quick Release.* Remove the whole chicken and let rest 10 minutes. Store the chicken broth in a Mason jar for later use.

5 Pull off the chicken and serve.

NOTE: Buying an organic chicken will help control the sodium of this recipe. Many conventional chickens undergo a process called plumping that can increase the sodium content of the bird (even before preparing it) to over 400 milligrams per serving.

TIP: Save the chicken bones and use them in the Chicken or Turkey Stock recipe in Chapter 8.

VARY IT! Switch up the herbs! Sage, parsley, and lemon are also great options.

Salsa Verde Shredded Chicken

Pressure	High
10 min	Natural Release

Instant Pot function: Pressure Cook (High), Keep Warm (Off), Natural Release

Fits diets: Gluten-Free, Keto, Mediterranean

PREP TIME: NONE	COOK TIME: 10 MIN	YIELD: 8 SERVINGS

INGREDIENTS

One 16-ounce jar *salsa verde*

2 tablespoons filtered water

2 pounds bone-in chicken thighs

DIRECTIONS

1 Pour the *salsa verde* into the inner pot of the Instant Pot. Place the water inside the salsa jar and shake. Pour back into the pot. Place the chicken thighs into the salsa. Cover with the lid, set to *Sealing*, and press *Pressure Cook (High)* and *Keep Warm (Off)*. Using the +/– button, set the timer to 10 minutes.

2 When cooking completes, do a *Natural Release* of the pressure for 5 minutes. Use *Quick Release* to remove the remaining pressure.

3 Remove the chicken thighs from the pot. Allow them to cool 10 to 15 minutes. Shred with a fork and place back into the *salsa verde* sauce.

NOTE: Serve on a salad or with tortillas and garnish with chopped cilantro and cheese.

NOTE: Bone-in chicken thighs are a great option to boost the flavor of the broth.

TIP: Tight on time? Use boneless chicken thighs so you can shred straight in the pot.

VARY IT! Try a red salsa for a fun twist!

Chapter **11**

The Beauty of Bowls

The simplicity of a beautiful bowl never disappoints, and neither will the recipes you find in this chapter! The bowl concept has been around for some time, but here we've taken it up a notch to provide you eight delicious, nutritious, and culturally inspired bowls.

Bowls are a beautiful canvas that not only allow you to customize them to your preferences (they're the easiest and best way to satisfy a crowd with multiple dietary preferences), but they also can be an excellent way to add in more vegetables to your daily diet. Plus, by building your own bowl from the comfort of your own home, you can be in charge of what you add (or don't add) to the mix, creating a low-sodium, low-carb, or, heck, keto friendly bowl depending on your particular preference.

But we didn't stop just with the bowls! We wanted to show you how you can dress up your beautiful bowls with homemade dressings. You'll see some dressings combined with bowl recipes (for example, the Mediterranean Bowl with Feta and Herb Yogurt Dressing); you can use that dressing recipe on a salad or as a dip or with the Mediterranean Bowl, where it's featured.

Frijoles Negros Plantain Bowl

Pressure/Sauté	High
20 min	Quick Release

Instant Pot function: Pressure Cook (High), Sauté (High), Keep Warm (Off), Quick Release

Fits diets: Gluten-Free, Mediterranean, Vegan, Vegetarian

PREP TIME: NONE	COOK TIME: 20 MIN	YIELD: 4 SERVINGS

INGREDIENTS

1 cup dried black beans, soaked and rinsed

1 cup quinoa, uncooked

1 cup frozen mixed bell peppers

1 jalapeño, diced and seeds removed

2 cups vegetable broth

1 teaspoon minced garlic

1 teaspoon cumin

1 teaspoon chili powder

1 bay leaf

1 tablespoon coconut oil

1 ripe plantain, sliced on the bias into ¼-inch pieces (see Figure 11-1)

¼ cup fresh chopped cilantro, for garnish

⅓ medium avocado, sliced, for garnish

¼ cup fresh salsa, for garnish

Salt and pepper, to taste

4 tortillas, for serving

DIRECTIONS

1 Place the black beans, quinoa, bell peppers, jalapeño, and vegetable broth in the inner pot of the Instant Pot. Stir in the garlic, cumin, and chili powder, and add the bay leaf. Secure the lid and set the valve to *Sealing*. Press *Pressure Cook (High)* and *Keep Warm (Off)*, and set the timer for 10 minutes using the +/− button.

2 When cooking completes, press *Cancel*, using *Quick Release* to remove the pressure from the pot. Remove the bay leaf and stir. Carefully remove the bean and quinoa mixture and set aside. Rinse the pot and dry the outside.

3 Insert the pot back inside the Instant Pot and add the coconut oil. Press *Sauté (High)*, add the plantain slices. Sauté on both sides until a fork can easily be inserted into the plantain, about 10 minutes. Press *Cancel*.

4 Assemble the bowls by placing ¼ of the black bean and quinoa mixture into the bottom of each bowl. Top with the sautéed plantains, and garnish with fresh cilantro, avocado, and salsa. Serve with tortillas and garnish with salt and pepper, if desired.

NOTE: Plantains are cousins of the banana, but they aren't nearly as sweet and must be cooked before eaten. They're rich in fiber and comparable nutritionally to a potato.

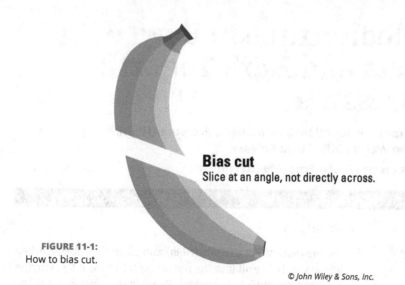

Bias cut
Slice at an angle, not directly across.

FIGURE 11-1:
How to bias cut.

© John Wiley & Sons, Inc.

Mediterranean Bowl with Feta and Herb Yogurt Dressing

Sauté/Pressure	High
25 min	Quick Release

Instant Pot function: Sauté (High), Pressure (High), Keep Warm (Off), Quick Release

Fits diets: Gluten-Free, Mediterranean

PREP TIME: 20 MIN	COOK TIME: 25 MIN	YIELD: 4 SERVINGS

INGREDIENTS

2 small chicken breasts, cubed

¼ cup extra-virgin olive oil

Salt and pepper, to taste

1 cup dried garbanzo beans, soaked overnight and drained

¼ cup farro

½ small onion, chopped

2 cups chicken stock

2 garlic cloves, chopped

1 teaspoon oregano

½ teaspoon salt

¼ teaspoon black pepper

1 avocado, peeled and sliced, for garnish

½ cup black or green olives, for garnish

1 medium bell pepper, thinly sliced or ½ cup chopped, canned red bell pepper, for garnish

1 medium tomato, chopped, for garnish

½ cup fresh grated carrot, for garnish

½ cup fresh basil, chiffonade (see Figure 11-2), for garnish

½ cup chopped walnuts, for garnish

Feta and Herb Yogurt Dressing (see the following recipe)

DIRECTIONS

1 Set the Instant Pot to *Sauté (High)* and place the cubed chicken breasts and olive oil into the pot. Sauté for 10 minutes, stirring occasionally until fully cooked. Remove the chicken from the pot, season with salt and pepper to taste, and set aside.

2 Place the garbanzo beans, farro, onion, chicken stock, garlic, oregano, salt, and pepper in the inner pot of the Instant Pot. Secure the lid and set the valve to *Sealing*. Press *Pressure Cook (High)* and, using the +/− button, set the timer to 15 minutes and *Keep Warm (On)*. When cooking has completed, allow do a *Natural Release* for 10 minutes.

3 Press *Cancel*, using *Quick Release* to remove any additional pressure from the pot. Carefully remove the bean and farro mixture and set aside.

4 Assemble the bowls by placing ¼ of the bean and farro mixture on the bottom of each bowl. Add a single line of cooked chicken cubes down the center of each bowl. Decorate the bowls with avocado, olives, bell pepper, tomatoes, and grated carrot. Top each bowl with basil and walnuts.

5 To serve, drizzle with Feta and Herb Yogurt Dressing or a quick squeeze of fresh lemon and olive oil.

Feta and Herb Yogurt Dressing

Fits diets: Gluten-Free, Mediterranean, Vegetarian

PREP TIME: 3 MIN	COOK TIME: NONE	YIELD: 8 SERVINGS

INGREDIENTS

1 cup plain yogurt

¼ cup crumbled feta

2 tablespoons chopped dill

2 tablespoons chopped parsley

½ teaspoon salt

½ cup grated cucumber

1 garlic clove, chopped

1 green onion, chopped

DIRECTIONS

Place all the ingredients in a bowl and whisk together. Serve immediately.

VARY IT! If you prefer a smoother dressing, you can skip the chopping and just blend all the ingredients in a blender.

1. Stack several leaves.

2. Roll the leaves lengthwise.

3. Slice in narrow strips crossways across the stems.

The result should look like this:

FIGURE 11-2: How to chiffonade.

© John Wiley & Sons, Inc.

Mexican Beans and Rice Bowl with Ranch Dressing

Sauté/ Pressure	High
35 min	Quick Release

Instant Pot function: Sauté (High), Pressure (High), Keep Warm (Off), Quick Release

Fits diets: Gluten-Free, Mediterranean, Vegetarian

PREP TIME: 20 MIN	COOK TIME: 35 MIN	YIELD: 4 SERVINGS

INGREDIENTS

1 pound chicken thighs, cubed

¼ cup plus 1 tablespoon extra-virgin olive oil, divided

Salt and pepper, to taste

1 cup dried black beans

1 cup white rice

½ small onion, chopped

3 cups chicken stock

2 garlic cloves, chopped

1 teaspoon cumin

½ teaspoon coriander

½ teaspoon salt

¼ teaspoon black pepper

1 avocado, peeled and sliced, for garnish

½ cup chopped cilantro, for garnish

1 medium tomato, chopped, for garnish

1 large carrot, grated, for garnish

½ cup chopped red onion, for garnish

¼ cup crumbled cotija cheese, for garnish

Ranch Dressing (see the following recipe)

DIRECTIONS

1 Set the Instant Pot to *Sauté (High)* and place the cubed chicken and ¼ cup of the olive oil into the pot. Sauté for 10 minutes, stirring occasionally. Make sure the chicken is fully cooked by cutting into a few pieces. Remove from the pot, season with salt and pepper to taste, and set aside.

2 Place the beans, rice, onions, chicken stock, garlic, cumin, coriander, and the remaining 1 tablespoon of olive oil inside the Instant Pot and stir. Secure the lid and set the valve to *Sealing*. Press *Pressure Cook (High)* and *Keep Warm (Off)*, and set the timer to 25 minutes using the +/– button.

3 When cooking completes, press *Cancel*, using *Quick Release* to remove the pressure from the pot. Carefully remove the bean and rice mixture and set aside.

4 Assemble the bowls by placing ¼ of the bean and rice mixture on the bottom of each bowl. Add a single line of cooked chicken cubes down the center of each bowl. Decorate the bowls with the avocado, cilantro, tomatoes, carrots, onion, and cheese.

5 To serve, drizzle with the Ranch Dressing.

VARY IT! Add in or exchange any of the bowl toppings with hummus, grated or sliced cucumbers, or shredded cabbage. For a simple dressing, use fresh squeezed lemon and extra-virgin olive oil.

Ranch Dressing

Fits diets: Gluten-Free, Mediterranean, Vegetarian

PREP TIME: 3 MIN	COOK TIME: NONE	YIELD: 8 SERVINGS

INGREDIENTS

1 garlic clove, minced

1 shallot, minced

2 tablespoons fresh parsley

1 tablespoon fresh dill

1 tablespoon fresh chives

½ teaspoon salt

½ teaspoon ground black pepper

1½ cups plain yogurt

1 tablespoon red or white wine vinegar

DIRECTIONS

Place all the ingredients in a bowl and whisk together. Serve immediately.

Southern-Inspired Sautéed Kale Bowl with Spicy Peanut Dressing

Sauté/Pressure	High
25 min	Quick Release

Instant Pot function: Sauté (High), Pressure Cook (High), Keep Warm (Off), Quick Release

Fits diets: Gluten-Free

PREP TIME: 10 MIN	COOK TIME: 25 MIN	YIELD: 4 SERVINGS

INGREDIENTS

1 teaspoon extra-virgin olive oil

4 slices thick-cut uncooked bacon, chopped

2 ounces Canadian bacon, chopped

½ small onion, chopped

1 teaspoon minced garlic

2¾ cups vegetable broth, divided

2 tablespoons apple cider vinegar

4 teaspoons brown sugar

¾ teaspoon red pepper flakes

1 pound collard greens, stems removed, roughly chopped

½ cup polenta

½ teaspoon black pepper

¼ teaspoon salt

2 teaspoons butter

Crispy onion strips, for garnish

Spicy Peanut Dressing (see the following recipe)

DIRECTIONS

1 Press *Sauté (High)* on the Instant Pot.

2 Add the oil to the inner pot and stir in both bacons, the onion, and the garlic. Sauté for 5 minutes or until the bacon is crispy and the onions are translucent. Press *Cancel*.

3 Stir in ¾ cup of the vegetable broth, the apple cider vinegar, the brown sugar, and the red pepper. Add the collard greens and secure the lid. Set the valve to *Sealing* and press *Pressure Cook (High)* and *Keep Warm (Off)*. Set the timer for 5 minutes using the +/− button.

4 When cooking completes, press *Cancel* and use *Quick Release* to release the pressure.

5 Move the greens and bacon into a dish and cover with foil to keep warm. Meanwhile, prepare the grits. Rinse the inner pot and wipe down any water on the outside of the pot.

6 Return to the Instant Pot and liberally spray the bottom and sides with cooking spray. Pour the polenta, the remaining 2 cups of vegetable broth, and the pepper and salt into the pot. Stir, secure the lid, and set to *Sealing*.

7 Press *Pressure Cook (High)* and *Keep Warm (Off)* and set the timer for 10 minutes using the +/− button.

8 When cooking completes, press *Cancel*. Use *Quick Release* to allow pressure to be removed and take off the lid.

9 Fluff the polenta with a fork and stir in the butter. Portion into 4 bowls and top with collard greens and the crispy onion strips. Top with the Spicy Peanut Dressing and serve immediately.

NOTE: If you can find collard greens, use them in place of the kale to maintain more of the flavor of the South.

TIP: Tight on time? Purchase bagged collard greens that are precut and washed.

Spicy Peanut Dressing

Fits diets: Gluten-Free, Mediterranean, Vegan, Vegetarian

PREP TIME: 5 MIN	COOK TIME: NONE	YIELD: 10 SERVINGS

INGREDIENTS

½ cup creamy peanut butter

½ lime, juiced

2 tablespoons rice vinegar

1 tablespoon cane sugar

2 tablespoons low-sodium soy sauce or tamari

¼ teaspoon ground ginger

¼ cup water

1 teaspoon Sriracha

1 tablespoon canola oil

1 garlic clove, minced

DIRECTIONS

Place all the ingredients in a bowl. Using a fork, whisk. Add more water if you prefer your dressing to be thinner. Serve immediately.

VARY IT! If you prefer coconut sugar, substitute that for the cane sugar.

Parmesan Pancetta Polenta Bowl

Sauté/Pressure	High
16 min	Quick Release

Instant Pot function: Sauté (High), Pressure Cook (High), Keep Warm (Off), Quick Release

Fits diets: Gluten-Free

PREP TIME: NONE	COOK TIME: 16 MIN	YIELD: 4 SERVINGS

INGREDIENTS

4 ounces pancetta, chopped

½ teaspoon minced garlic

¼ cup chopped onion

1 cup polenta

2 cups vegetable broth

2 cups filtered water

2 tablespoons butter

⅓ cup Parmesan cheese

Salt and pepper, to taste

1 cup marinara sauce, for garnish

½ fresh chopped basil, for garnish

DIRECTIONS

1 Press *Sauté (High)* on the Instant Pot. Add the pancetta, garlic, and onion to the inner pot. Sauté until the pancetta is crisp and the onions are translucent, about 6 minutes. Press *Cancel*. Remove and keep warm in a covered dish.

2 Do not rinse the pot. Spray the bottom and sides of the pot with cooking spray and add the polenta to the pot. Add in the vegetable broth and water. Secure the lid, set the valve to *Sealing*, and press *Pressure Cook (High)* and *Keep Warm (Off)*. Set the timer for 10 minutes using the +/− button.

3 When cooking completes, press *Cancel*. Use *Quick Release* to allow the pressure to be removed, and take off the lid.

4 Whisk the polenta and stir in the butter and cheese.

5 Divide into 4 bowls, top with the pancetta mixture, and season with salt and pepper to taste. Garnish with the marinara sauce and chopped basil.

NOTE: If pancetta is hard to locate, you can substitute with bacon. For a vegetarian version, omit the pancetta.

VARY IT! Try the Sautéed Balsamic Mushrooms (Chapter 13) or Italian Bell Peppers and Onions (Chapter 13) on top!

| Sauté/Pressure | High |
| 13 min | Quick Release |

Korean Beef Bulgogi Bowl

Instant Pot function: Sauté (High), Pressure Cook (High), Keep Warm (Off), Quick Release

PREP TIME: 5 MIN | **COOK TIME: 13 MIN** | **YIELD: 4 SERVINGS**

INGREDIENTS

⅓ cup filtered water

¼ cup low-sodium soy sauce

2 tablespoons rice wine vinegar

2 tablespoons packed brown sugar

2 teaspoons sesame oil

1 teaspoon ground ginger

2 tablespoons cornstarch

1¼ pounds lean ground beef

½ small onion, chopped

1 teaspoon minced garlic

2 cups chopped bell peppers

2 cups cooked brown rice, divided

2 cups Basic Brown Rice (see Chapter 8)

1 stalk of green onion, chopped, for garnish

½ teaspoon red pepper flakes, for garnish

4 teaspoons Sriracha, for garnish

DIRECTIONS

1 In a small bowl, whisk together the water, soy sauce, rice wine vinegar, brown sugar, sesame oil, ginger, and cornstarch. Set aside.

2 Press *Sauté (High)* on the Instant Pot and add the ground beef. When the beef begins to brown (about 3 minutes), add in the onion, garlic, and bell peppers. Continue to cook for 5 minutes. When finished, press *Cancel*.

3 Stir in the sauce and select *Pressure Cook (High)* and *Keep Warm (Off)*, adjust the timer to 5 minutes using the +/− button, and secure the lid. Ensure the vent is set to *Sealing*.

4 When the cooking completes, press *Cancel*, remove the lid, stir, and portion into 4 bowls, served over ½ cup of Brown Jasmine Rice. Garnish as desired with green onion, red pepper flakes, and Sriracha.

TIP: To make the recipe keto compliant, substitute a sugar replacement for the brown sugar. Because sugar substitutes are sweeter than sugar, use half the amount. Then serve with cauliflower rice.

TIP: Use a tamari sauce in place of soy to make the recipe gluten-free.

Chapter **12**

One-Pot Wonders

RECIPES IN THIS CHAPTER

Busy weeknights have you pulling out your hair and stressing to get a complete meal on the table? We're both busy moms, and we understand the need to get a nourishing meal on the table fast. Before you race off to the drive-thru, give these all-in-one recipes a whirl!

One of the main benefits of the Instant Pot is its ability to use just one pot to feed your family in a matter of minutes. That's why we've taken timeless classics and put them in this chapter. These recipes are our way of gifting you time! Although the recipes vary in preparation and cook time, we're certain you'll find a few that fit nicely into your schedule.

All these recipes pair beautifully with a simple salad using your refrigerator staples (see Chapter 3). Plus, a good salad will help balance out some of the cheesy goodness from the more decadent dishes you'll enjoy in this chapter. Enjoy!

Shepherd's Pie

Sauté/Pressure | High
26 min | Quick Release, Natural Release

Instant Pot function: Sauté (High), Pressure Cook (High), Keep Warm (On), Quick Release, Natural Release

Special tools: Pot-in-pot 3-inch-deep Instant Pot–friendly baking dish

PREP TIME: 10 MIN	COOK TIME: 26 MIN	YIELD: 6 SERVINGS

INGREDIENTS

2½ cups water, divided

½ pound new potatoes or baby Yukon Gold potatoes

4 ounces cream cheese

1½ teaspoons salt, divided

¼ teaspoon pepper

1 pound lean ground beef or lamb

½ medium onion, finely chopped

1 medium carrot, finely diced

1 teaspoon thyme

1 teaspoon Worcestershire sauce

1 tablespoon tomato paste

1 cup beef stock or chicken stock

2 tablespoons cornstarch

½ cup frozen peas

½ cup chopped parsley

DIRECTIONS

1 Place 1 cup of the water in the bottom of the pot. Place the trivet in the bottom of the pot. Add the potatoes to the pot. Set the Instant Pot to *Pressure Cook (High)* and set the timer to 7 minutes using the +/– button, with *Keep Warm (On)*. Do a *Quick Release*, and remove the potatoes from the pot and place them in a mixing bowl. Using a potato masher, mash the potatoes with the cream cheese, ½ teaspoon of the salt, and the pepper.

2 Dump the water out of the Instant Pot, and place the trivet to the side.

3 Select *Sauté (High)* and add the ground beef, onion, and carrot. Brown the mixture, about 8 minutes. Stir in the thyme, Worcestershire sauce, and tomato paste; stir for 1 minute.

4 In a small bowl, mix together the stock and cornstarch; then stir this mixture into the meat mixture and cook for 1 minute. Season with the remaining 1 teaspoon of salt, and add the frozen peas. Press *Cancel*.

5 Pour the beef mixture into the bottom of an Instant Pot–friendly casserole baking dish. Spread the mashed potatoes over the top, and cover the pan loosely with foil.

6 Add the remaining 1½ cups of water to the pot and insert the trivet. Lower the casserole dish onto the trivet (see Figure 12-1) and secure the lid. Set the valve to *Sealing*. Press *Pressure Cook (High)* and use the +/− button to set the timer to 10 minutes with *Keep Warm (On)*.

7 Do a *Natural Release* of the pressure for 10 minutes; then do a *Quick Release*. Sprinkle with chopped parsley and serve.

NOTE: If you prefer a crunchy top, sprinkle with grated cheddar cheese and broil for 3 to 5 minutes.

FIGURE 12-1: Pot-in-pot cooking.

© John Wiley & Sons, Inc.

Nancy's Stuffed Bell Peppers

| Sauté/Pressure | High |
| 16 min | Natural Release, Quick Release |

Instant Pot function: Sauté (High), Pressure Cook (High), Keep Warm (On/Off), Natural Release, Quick Release

Special tools: Pot-in-pot 3-inch-deep Instant Pot baking dish

Fits diets: Mediterranean

PREP TIME: 15 MIN	COOK TIME: 16 MIN	YIELD: 6 SERVINGS

INGREDIENTS

2 cups water, divided

3 medium red bell peppers, sliced in half across the equator

½ pound lean ground beef

1 cup jasmine rice

1 egg

2 cloves garlic, chopped

¼ cup chopped onion

¼ cup chopped celery

¼ cup chopped carrots

2 cups spaghetti sauce, divided

1 teaspoon Worcestershire sauce

½ teaspoon salt

¼ teaspoon pepper

DIRECTIONS

1 Place 1 cup of the water in the bottom of the Instant Pot. Place the trivet in the bottom of the pot. Place the bell peppers in the pot and set to *Pressure Cook (High)* and *Keep Warm (Off)* and set the timer to 0 minutes using the +/ button. Do a *Quick Release* when finished and place the peppers in a large bowl full of ice water to halt the cooking process.

2 In a large mixing bowl, thoroughly mix together the ground beef, rice, egg, garlic, onion, celery, carrots, 1 cup of the spaghetti sauce, Worcestershire sauce, salt, and pepper. Divide and stuff the filling into the 6 bell pepper halves.

3 Add the remaining 1 cup of water into the pot. Position the stuffed peppers into an Instant Pot–friendly casserole dish, standing upright. Pour the remaining 1 cup of spaghetti sauce over the tops of the stuffed bell peppers. Lower the casserole dish onto the trivet. Secure the lid and set to *Sealing*.

4 Press *Pressure Cook (High)* and use the +/− button to set the time to 15 minutes, with *Keep Warm (On)*.

5 When it's finished, do a *Natural Release* of the pressure for 10 minutes; then do a *Quick Release*.

NOTE: Leftover cooked rice can be used in place of uncooked rice, but don't adjust the time.

VARY IT! For a low-carb version of this recipe, opt for cauliflower rice in place of jasmine rice.

Sloppy Joes

Instant Pot function: Sauté (High), Pressure Cook (High), Keep Warm (Off), Quick Release

Fits diets: Keto

PREP TIME: NONE	COOK TIME: 15 MIN	YIELD: 8 SERVINGS

INGREDIENTS

2 teaspoons extra-virgin olive oil

½ small onion, finely chopped

1 tablespoon minced garlic

1 pound lean ground beef

2 cups frozen riced cauliflower

1 jalapeño, seeded and diced

2 teaspoons oregano

½ teaspoon black pepper

One 28-ounce can tomato puree

¼ cup tomato paste

2 tablespoons low-sodium soy sauce

3 tablespoons red wine vinegar

1 tablespoon packed brown sugar

1 tablespoon yellow mustard

¼ teaspoon salt

½ cup beef broth

8 buns, for serving

2 cups shredded cabbage, for garnish

DIRECTIONS

1 Press *Sauté (High)* on the Instant Pot. Add the olive oil, onion, and garlic, and sauté 3 to 4 minutes. Add the ground beef and begin to brown for 6 minutes. Add the remaining ingredients and stir. Scrape the bottom of the inner pot to ensure no ingredients stick to it (this will help prevent a *BURN* error message). Press *Cancel.*

2 Secure the lid, set the valve to *Sealing*, and press *Pressure Cook (Normal)* and *Keep Warm (Off)*. Use the +/− button to set the timer for 5 minutes.

3 When cooking completes, use *Quick Release*, and remove the lid.

4 Stir and serve on a bun. Garnish with shredded cabbage if desired.

TIP: For a gluten-free version, substitute tamari sauce for the soy sauce.

VARY IT! Not a fan of cauliflower? Substitute diced mushrooms to increase the fiber!

Turkey and Mushroom Meatloaf

Sauté/ Pressure	High
45 min	Natural Release

Instant Pot function: Sauté (High), Pressure Cook (High), Keep Warm (Off), Natural Release

Special tools: Three 4-inch loaf pans

Fits diets: Gluten-Free, Keto, Mediterranean

PREP TIME: 10 MIN	COOK TIME: 45 MIN	YIELD: 6 SERVINGS

INGREDIENTS

1 teaspoon extra-virgin olive oil

¼ small onion, chopped

1 teaspoon minced garlic

3 large white mushrooms, finely diced

1 pound lean ground turkey

1 large egg

1 teaspoon Italian seasoning

½ teaspoon ground black pepper

⅛ teaspoon salt

1 tablespoon fresh chopped basil

½ cup whole-wheat breadcrumbs

6 tablespoons barbecue sauce

1 cup water

DIRECTIONS

1 Press *Sauté (High)* on the Instant Pot, and place the oil in the inner pot. Add the onion, garlic, and mushrooms. Sauté for 10 minutes, until the mushrooms are tender. Press *Cancel.*

2 In a large bowl, combine the mushroom mixture with the ground turkey. Add in the egg, Italian seasoning, pepper, salt, basil, and breadcrumbs. Mix until uniformly combined. Liberally spray three 4–inch aluminum loaf pans with cooking spray. Divide the turkey mixture evenly into the loaf pans and top each loaf with 2 tablespoons of barbecue sauce.

3 Cover the loaf pans with aluminum foil. Rinse the inner pot and dry the outside. Place the insert back into the Instant Pot, and pour the water in. Position the metal trivet on the bottom and place 2 loaf pans on top; place the remaining loaf pan horizontally across the bottom pans. Close the lid and set to *Sealing.*

4 Press *Pressure Cook (High)* and *Keep Warm (Off)*, and use the +/− button to set the timer to 35 minutes. When cooking completes, do a *Natural Release* of the pressure for 5 minutes, and then use *Quick Release* to remove the remaining pressure.

5 Remove the foil from the loaf pans, slice, and serve.

NOTE: Serve with the Cream Cheese and Chive Mashed Potatoes (Chapter 13) or on top of a salad for a low-carb option.

TIP: These make an excellent freezer-friendly meal to enjoy later. Just reheat until the internal temperature of the meatloaf is 165 degrees.

Chicken Sausage and Ancient Grain Casserole

Instant Pot function: Sauté (High), Pressure Cook (High), Keep Warm (Off), Quick Release

Fits diets: Gluten-Free, Mediterranean

Sauté/Pressure	High
21 min	Quick Release

PREP TIME: 5 MIN	COOK TIME: 21 MIN	YIELD: 6 SERVINGS

INGREDIENTS

1 tablespoon extra-virgin olive oil

½ medium onion, chopped

1 tablespoon minced garlic

2 red bell peppers, chopped

3 cooked chicken sausages, thinly sliced

3 cups spinach leaves, washed

3 cups low-sodium vegetable broth

1 cup dry ancient grain blend

Red pepper flakes, for garnish

Parmesan cheese, for garnish

Chopped parsley, for garnish

DIRECTIONS

1 Press *Sauté (High)* on the Instant Pot, and add the olive oil. When the oil begins to simmer, add the onions and sauté for 4 minutes. Add in the garlic, and sauté another 1 minute. Stir in the bell peppers, and sauté another 1 minute. Press *Cancel*.

2 Stir in the chicken sausage, spinach, and vegetable broth. Close and lock the lid. Set the valve to *Sealing*. Press *Pressure Cook (High)* and *Keep Warm (Off)*, and set the timer to 15 minutes using the +/− button.

3 When cooking is finished, press *Cancel*. Use *Quick Release* and remove the lid.

4 Portion into 6 bowls and serve hot. Garnish as desired.

NOTE: This recipe uses cooked chicken sausages, but you can use raw if you prefer, and the high pressure will cook it properly.

TIP: Save money and buy ancient grains in bulk to create your own ancient grain mix! Place 1 cup quinoa, 1 cup amaranth, 1 cup whole-grain orzo, and 1 cup brown rice in a Mason jar; shake and store in your pantry.

VARY IT! Substitute your favorite grains or omit the sausage for a vegetarian option.

| Sauté/
Pressure | High |
| 7 min | Quick
Release |

Sesame Tofu Stir-Fry

Instant Pot function: Sauté (High), Steam (High), Keep Warm (Off), Quick Release

Fits diets: Gluten-Free, Mediterranean, Vegan, Vegetarian

PREP TIME: 5 MIN	COOK TIME: 7 MIN	YIELD: 4 SERVINGS

INGREDIENTS

One 16-ounce package firm tofu, pressed (see Figure 12-2) and cut into ½-inch pieces

2 tablespoons tamari sauce

¾ teaspoon ground ginger

½ teaspoon garlic powder

¼ teaspoon black pepper

2 tablespoons cornstarch

3 tablespoons sesame oil, divided

1 clove garlic, minced

2 cups broccoli florets

1 cup chopped carrots

1 cup shredded purple cabbage

One 8-ounce can sliced water chestnuts

½ cup filtered water

1 tablespoon rice wine vinegar

1 tablespoon fresh grated ginger

1 teaspoon cane sugar

¼ teaspoon salt

1 tablespoon sesame seeds, divided

DIRECTIONS

1 In a medium bowl, toss the tofu with the tamari sauce; set aside. In a separate medium bowl, combine the ginger, garlic powder, black pepper, and cornstarch; gently toss the tofu pieces in the dry seasoning mix.

2 Press *Sauté (High)* on the Instant Pot, and add 1 tablespoon of the sesame oil to the inner pot. Add the minced garlic and tofu pieces to the pot; sauté until browned (about 6 minutes). Press *Cancel*, remove from the heat, and keep warm.

3 Add the vegetables and water to the pot, select *Steam (High)* and *Keep Warm (Off)*, and set the timer for 1 minute using the +/− button. Secure the lid and set the valve to *Sealing*.

4 While the vegetables are cooking, make the dressing. In a medium bowl, whisk the remaining 2 tablespoons of sesame oil, the rice wine vinegar, the fresh ginger, the cane sugar, and the salt; set aside.

5 When the steaming completes, press *Cancel* and use *Quick Release*. Use a slotted spoon to remove the vegetables from the pot and portion into 4 bowls. Top with tofu and homemade sesame dressing. Garnish with sesame seeds and serve immediately.

NOTE: Tamari sauce is the gluten-free version of soy sauce. Feel free to substitute low-sodium soy sauce if you aren't looking for a gluten-free recipe.

FIGURE 12-2: Press tofu by placing a large pot on top of a baking sheet with cut tofu pieces.

Creamy Sausage and Ziti Pasta

Sauté/ Pressure	High
20 min	Quick Release

Instant Pot function: Sauté (High), Pressure Cook (High), Quick Release

Fits diets: Mediterranean

PREP TIME: 10 MIN	COOK TIME: 20 MIN	YIELD: 6 SERVINGS

INGREDIENTS

1 pound Italian sausage, casings removed

1 medium onion, finely chopped

2 cloves garlic, chopped

2 cups frozen, chopped spinach

2 cups spaghetti sauce

One 14.5-ounce can fire-roasted diced tomatoes

2 teaspoons dried oregano

1 cup red wine

1 cup beef stock

1 bay leaf

1 pound dried ziti or rigatoni pasta

8 ounces fresh mozzarella, drained and cubed

½ cup chopped, fresh basil

Grated Parmesan cheese, for garnish

Cracked black pepper, for garnish

Sea salt, for garnish

DIRECTIONS

1 Press *Sauté (High)* on the Instant Pot, and brown the Italian sausage, crumbling the meat as it cooks, about 8 minutes. Add in the onion and garlic and continue sautéing for 5 minutes.

2 Add in the spinach, spaghetti sauce, tomatoes, oregano, wine, beef stock, and bay leaf and stir, about 2 minutes. Press *Cancel.* Stir in the pasta and mozzarella, ensuring the pasta is completely covered. Add water if needed to cover the pasta.

3 Secure the lid and set the valve to *Sealing.* Press *Pressure Cook (High)* and *Keep Warm (On)* and set the timer to 5 minutes using the +/– button. When finished, press *Quick Release.* Stir in the fresh basil. Season with grated Parmesan, black pepper, and sea salt, as desired.

NOTE: If you receive a *BURN* error message, release pressure, add in 1 cup of water, and continue cooking.

NOTE: Fresh pasta is also referred to as "buffalo mozzarella" and is stored in water.

VARY IT! Don't love sausage? Swap out 4 ounces sliced mushrooms and ½ pound lean ground beef instead.

Shrimp Scampi Bowtie Pasta

Instant Pot function: Sauté (High), Pressure Cook (High), Keep Warm (Off), Quick Release

Fits diets: Mediterranean

PREP TIME: 5 MIN	COOK TIME: 8 MIN	YIELD: 4 SERVINGS

INGREDIENTS

8 ounces dried farfalle pasta or bow-tie pasta

3½ cups cold water

1 tablespoon plus ½ teaspoon salt

2 tablespoons unsalted butter

2 tablespoons extra-virgin olive oil

6 cloves garlic, chopped

1 shallot, chopped

1 cup parsley, divided

1 cup white wine

⅛ teaspoon crushed red pepper flakes

½ teaspoon salt

1 pound raw shrimp, peeled and deveined

½ lemon, juiced

¼ cup crushed croutons

DIRECTIONS

1 Place pasta inside the Instant Pot; cover with the water and sprinkle in 1 tablespoon of the salt. Stir the pasta, ensuring that all the pasta is covered with water. Secure the lid and set the valve to *Sealing*. Press *Pressure Cook (High)* and *Keep Warm (Off)*, and set the timer to 6 minutes using the +/− button. After the pasta has finished cooking, do a *Quick Release* and drain the pasta. Place the pasta in a large serving bowl.

2 Press *Sauté (High)* and add in the butter, olive oil, garlic, and shallot. Sauté for 1 minute, stirring frequently. Press *Cancel*. Add in ½ cup of the parsley, the white wine, the crushed red pepper flakes, the remaining ½ teaspoon of salt, and shrimp. Secure the lid and set the valve to *Sealing*. Press *Pressure Cook (High)* and *Keep Warm (Off)*, and set the timer to 1 minute using the +/− button. After the cooking has finished, do a *Quick Release*.

3 Add the pasta to the pot and stir to coat the pasta with sauce. Pour the shrimp scampi pasta into a serving bowl, squeeze the fresh lemon over the top, and top with croutons and the remaining ½ cup of chopped parsley. Serve immediately.

NOTE: If using frozen shrimp, defrost under cold running water first.

TIP: This dish is best eaten the day it's made. Reheating isn't recommended.

VARY IT! For a lower-carbohydrate dish, opt for raw zucchini noodles or cooked spaghetti squash to toss in at the end.

Georgia's Chicken and Dumplings

Sauté/ Pressure	High
30 min	Quick Release

Instant Pot function: Sauté (High), Pressure Cook (High), Keep Warm (Off), Quick Release, Sauté (High)

Fits diets: Mediterranean

PREP TIME: 10 MIN	COOK TIME: 30 MIN	YIELD: 6 SERVINGS

INGREDIENTS

1 tablespoon extra-virgin olive oil

1 medium onion, diced

2 large carrots, diced

1 green bell pepper, diced

2 cups diced boneless, skinless chicken breasts

2 quarts chicken broth, divided

3 teaspoons black pepper, divided

1 tablespoon allspice

3 large eggs

1 teaspoon poultry seasoning

2 teaspoons paprika

1 teaspoon ground garlic powder

1½ cups all-purpose flour

Shredded cabbage slaw, for garnish

DIRECTIONS

1 Press *Sauté (High)* on the Instant Pot and add the olive oil. Sauté the onions, carrots, and bell peppers for 5 minutes. Add in the chicken and ½ cup of the chicken broth; cook for another 5 minutes. Stir in 2½ cups of the chicken broth, 2 teaspoons of the black pepper, and the allspice.

2 Secure the lid, set the valve to *Sealing*, select *Pressure Cook (High)* and *Keep Warm (Off)*, and set the timer to 10 minutes using the +/− button.

3 While the chicken and vegetables are cooking, make the dough. In a large bowl, whisk the eggs. In a small bowl, combine the remaining 1 teaspoon of black pepper, the poultry seasoning, the paprika, the garlic powder, and the flour.

4 Slowly add the flour mixture into the eggs, creating a dough. Divide in half and roughly roll out the dough until it's about ¼-inch thick, adding flour as needed to prevent sticking. Cut the rolled dough with a pizza roller into squares (about 1 to 1½ inches); set the dumplings aside.

5 When cooking completes, press *Cancel* and use *Quick Release* to remove the pressure from the pot. Remove the lid and press *Sauté (High)*; set the timer for 10 minutes using the +/− button. Add the remaining chicken broth to the pot and begin to slowly mix in the dumplings, stirring frequently so they don't end up in one large chunk. If needed, add in an extra ¼ cup of chicken broth to make sure the entire recipe is covered and still below the maximum fill line labeled on the inner pot. Dumplings should take no longer than 10 minutes to cook in the broth. When the sauté timer completes, the recipe has completed cooking.

6 Portion into 6 bowls and garnish with a vinegar-based cabbage slaw, if desired.

TIP: Tight on time? You don't have to roll out the dough and drop by the teaspoon into the broth.

Sara's Lightened-Up Macaroni and Cheese

Pressure	High
5 min	Quick Release

Instant Pot function: Pressure Cook (High), Keep Warm (Off), Quick Release

Fits diets: Vegetarian

PREP TIME: NONE	COOK TIME: 5 MIN	YIELD: 4 SERVINGS

INGREDIENTS

8 ounces dry macaroni pasta

2 cups vegetable broth

1 tablespoon butter

½ cup milk

1½ cups shredded cheddar cheese

½ teaspoon cayenne pepper

¼ teaspoon black pepper

Salt, to taste

Parmesan cheese, for garnish

Fresh chopped parsley, for garnish

DIRECTIONS

1 Place the macaroni, broth, and butter inside the inner pot of the Instant Pot. Secure the lid, set the valve to *Sealing*, and press *Pressure Cook (High)* and *Keep Warm (Off)*. Set the timer to 5 minutes using the +/− button.

2 When cooking completes, press *Cancel* and use *Quick Release*. Remove the lid.

3 Sir in the milk, cheddar cheese, cayenne pepper, black pepper, and salt until the cheese has melted and the macaroni is coated with cheese sauce.

4 Portion into 4 bowls and garnish with Parmesan cheese and chopped parsley.

TIP: Increase the fiber by using whole-wheat macaroni noodles. Have a picky group? Start with a 50/50 white and wheat blend.

VARY IT! For a southwestern twist, add in bell peppers, green chilies, and black beans.

Chapter 13

Star-Studded Side Dishes

Main dishes may be the talk of most parties, but when you see the recipes in this chapter, you'll have a new respect for sides! The Instant Pot cuts your prep dramatically, with sweet potatoes cooking in less than 10 minutes and corn getting pressure-cooked in just 1 minute! Next time someone asks, "When will dinner be ready?" you can honestly reply with, "In just a minute!"

We've got you covered with some amped-up versions of traditional holiday fare like Cream Cheese and Chive Mashed Potatoes and Sourdough Stuffing, while walking you through some classics like Sautéed Balsamic Mushrooms, Mexican Corn on the Cob, and Italian Bell Peppers and Onions.

Plus, you'll see that sides don't have to mean high-calorie and void of nutrients. We've enhanced these recipes using fresh herbs and spices and healthy fats, such as extra-virgin olive oil. Vegetables need a fat to be paired with them in order to absorb all their fat-soluble vitamins — gone are the days when you need to fear that *F* word!

Cream Cheese and Chive Mashed Potatoes

Pressure	High
14 min	Quick Release

Instant Pot function: Pressure Cook (High), Keep Warm (Off), Quick Release

Special tools: Potato masher

Fits diets: Gluten-Free, Vegetarian

PREP TIME: 5 MIN	COOK TIME: 14 MIN	YIELD: 8 SERVINGS

INGREDIENTS

1½ cups filtered water

1 pound russet potatoes, skinned and cut into quarters

⅓ cup vegetable broth

2 tablespoons butter

4 ounces Neufchâtel cheese (light cream cheese)

2 tablespoons fresh chives

½ teaspoon black pepper

¼ teaspoon salt

DIRECTIONS

1 Add the water to the inner pot of the Instant Pot, and place the potatoes on top. Secure the lid, set the valve to *Sealing*, and press *Pressure Cook (High)* and *Keep Warm (Off)*. Use the +/– button to set the timer for 10 minutes.

2 When cooking completes, press *Cancel* and use *Quick Release*. Remove the lid, strain the potatoes, and transfer them to a large bowl. Add the vegetable broth and mash thoroughly.

3 Using a hand mixer, add the butter, Neufchâtel cheese, chives, pepper, and salt. Mix together until the desired consistency is reached, usually 3 to 4 minutes.

4 Serve immediately.

NOTE: Neufchâtel cheese is a French-inspired cheese that is lower in fat that regular cream cheese but imparts the same creamy, slightly tangy yet spreadable taste and texture. You'll find it right next to cream cheese in the grocery store.

TIP: You can also use a pastry blender or the backside of a large fork to help mash the potatoes.

Mexican-Inspired Roasted Sweet Potatoes

Instant Pot function: Sauté (High), Pressure Cook (High), Keep Warm (On), Quick Release

Fits diets: Gluten-Free, Vegetarian

PREP TIME: 5 MIN	COOK TIME: 8 MIN	YIELD: 6 SERVINGS

INGREDIENTS

2 tablespoons olive oil

2 tablespoons butter

1 pound sweet potatoes, peeled and sliced ¼-inch-thick rounds

½ cup vegetable stock

½ lime, zested and juiced

¼ cup cilantro, chopped

¼ teaspoon ground cumin

¼ teaspoon salt

DIRECTIONS

1 Set the Instant Pot to *Sauté (High)*. Heat the olive oil and butter until melted. In small batches, add the sweet potatoes and sauté for 3 minutes on each side. Transfer the browned sweet potatoes to a plate while you cook the remaining rounds.

2 Return all the sweet potatoes to the pot and pour the vegetable stock over the top. Set to *Pressure Cook (High)* and *Keep Warm (On)*. Set the timer to 2 minutes using the +/− button.

3 When finished, do a *Quick Release*. Add the lime zest, lime juice, cilantro, cumin, and salt. Toss and serve.

VARY IT! Looking for a festive Thanksgiving side dish? Use sage and orange instead of lime, cilantro, and cumin.

Pressure	High
1 min	Natural Release, Quick Release

Mexican Corn on the Cob

Instant Pot function: Pressure Cook (High), Keep Warm (Off), Natural Release, Quick Release

Fits diets: Gluten-Free, Vegetarian

PREP TIME: 5 MIN	COOK TIME: 1 MIN	YIELD: 4 SERVINGS

INGREDIENTS

1 cup water

4 medium corn cobs, husked

2 tablespoons butter, melted

1 lime, zested and juiced

¼ cup chopped cilantro

¼ cup Greek yogurt

1 teaspoon hot sauce or ¼ teaspoon chipotle powder

¼ teaspoon garlic powder

¼ teaspoon salt

¼ cup crumbled Cotija cheese or feta cheese

DIRECTIONS

1 Place the water into the inner pot of the Instant Pot. Place the corn on the cob upright in the pot. Secure the lid and seal the venting. Select *Pressure Cook (High)* and *Keep Warm (Off)*. Using the +/− button, set the timer to 1 minute.

2 Meanwhile, in a small bowl, whisk together the butter, lime juice, lime zest, cilantro, yogurt, hot sauce or chipotle powder, garlic powder, and salt.

3 When cooking is finished, do a *Natural Release* of the pressure for 3 minutes. Then do a *Quick Release* to release the remaining pressure. Toss the corn with the sauce and place on a serving platter. Top with the remaining sauce and crumbled cheese and serve.

TIP: If you can't find Cotija cheese, you can use grated Parmesan or crumbled feta instead.

Plain Yogurt (Chapter 8)

Pork Tenderloin with Gravy (Chapter 10)

Korean Beef Bulgogi Bowl (Chapter 11)

Shrimp Scampi Bowtie Pasta (Chapter 12)

Mexican Corn on the Cob (Chapter 13)

Chicken Tortilla Soup (Chapter 14)

Beef and Barley Stew (Chapter 14)

Morning Glory Bundt Cake (Chapter 19)

Simple Fruit Jam (Chapter 8)

Grandma's Simple Rhubarb Crisp (Chapter 18)

Sweet Potato Casserole with Pecans

Pressure	High
25 min	Quick Release

Instant Pot function: Pressure Cook (High), Keep Warm (Off), Quick Release

Fits diets: Gluten-Free, Mediterranean, Vegetarian

PREP TIME: 10 MIN	COOK TIME: 25 MIN	YIELD: 6 SERVINGS

INGREDIENTS

1 cup water

3 medium orange sweet potatoes, halved and rinsed, with skin left on

2 tablespoons butter

3 tablespoons pure maple syrup

1 teaspoon vanilla extract

2 teaspoons ground cinnamon

½ teaspoon ground nutmeg

¼ teaspoon salt

1 tablespoon brown sugar

⅓ cup chopped pecans

Plain yogurt, for garnish

DIRECTIONS

1 Pour 1 cup of water into the insert of the Instant Pot, and place the metal trivet on top. Place the sweet potatoes on top of the trivet and secure the lid, setting the valve to *Sealing*. Press *Pressure Cook (High)* and *Keep Warm (Off)*. Set the timer to 25 minutes using the +/– button.

2 When cooking completes, use *Quick Release* to release the pressure. Using tongs, remove the potatoes from the pot; set aside to cool. After the potatoes have cooled, remove the skins and add the potatoes to a large bowl. Using a potato masher or whisk, mash the potatoes. Use a hand mixer or stand mixer, and mix in the butter, maple syrup, vanilla extract, cinnamon, nutmeg, and salt.

3 Place the sweet potato mixture into a small baking dish and top with the brown sugar and pecans. Garnish with a dollop of plain yogurt if desired.

TIP: Don't have a potato masher? A pastry blender or the back side of a large fork will also work.

VARY IT! Swap in walnuts or your favorite crunchy topping of choice for the pecans. Granola also makes a fun addition!

Carrots with Maple and Thyme

| Pressure/ Sauté | High |
| 10 min | Quick Release |

Instant Pot function: Pressure Cook (High), Keep Warm (Off), Quick Release, Sauté (High)

Fits diets: Gluten-Free, Keto, Mediterranean, Vegetarian

| PREP TIME: NONE | COOK TIME: 10 MIN | YIELD: 4 SERVINGS |

INGREDIENTS

1 cup filtered water

1 pound carrots, sliced ¼ inch thick

2 teaspoons butter

1 tablespoon maple syrup

1 teaspoon fresh thyme

Salt and pepper, to taste

DIRECTIONS

1 Place the water into the inner pot of the Instant Pot. Add the carrots. Cover with the lid, set the valve to *Sealing*, and press *Pressure Cook (High)* and *Keep Warm (Off)*, adjusting the timer to 8 minutes using the +/– button.

2 When cooking completes, press *Cancel*. Use *Quick Release* to release the pressure. Remove the lid. Strain the carrots; set aside.

3 Place the inner pot back inside the Instant Pot. Add the butter and press *Sauté*.

4 Add the carrots back in, stir in the maple syrup and thyme, and sauté for 2 minutes.

5 Season as needed with salt and pepper. Serve immediately.

NOTE: If you want to use dried thyme, decrease the amount to ½ teaspoon.

VARY IT! Swap out the carrots for parsnips — they're an excellent vegetable to pair with maple and thyme!

Garlic Green Beans and Tomatoes

Pressure	High
1 min	Quick Release

Instant Pot function: Pressure Cook (High), Keep Warm (On), Quick Release

Fits diets: Gluten-Free, Mediterranean, Vegan, Vegetarian

PREP TIME: 5 MIN	COOK TIME: 1 MIN	YIELD: 6 SERVINGS

INGREDIENTS

½ cup water

1 pound fresh green beans, ends removed

2 cloves garlic, minced

1 lemon, zested and juiced

¼ cup extra-virgin olive oil

½ teaspoon salt

¼ teaspoon pepper

⅛ teaspoon onion powder

1 small red onion, thinly sliced

1 cup halved cherry tomatoes

DIRECTIONS

1 Place the water into the inner pot of the Instant Pot. Add the green beans. Cover with the lid, set the valve to *Sealing*, and press *Pressure Cook (High)* and *Keep Warm (Off)*. Adjust the timer to 0 minutes using the +/− button.

2 Meanwhile, in a small bowl, whisk together the garlic, lemon zest, lemon juice, olive oil, salt, pepper, and onion powder.

3 When the cooking completes, do a *Quick Release*, and immediately place the green beans in an ice bath for 1 minute. (This helps retain the bright green color and halts the cooking process.)

4 In a serving bowl, toss the green beans, red onions, and cherry tomatoes together. Drizzle with the dressing, toss, and serve.

VARY IT! Use fresh asparagus instead of green beans for a seasonal twist.

Cilantro Lime Cauliflower Rice

Instant Pot function: Pressure Cook (High), Keep Warm (On/Off), Quick Release

Special tools: Steamer basket

Fits diets: Gluten-Free, Keto, Mediterranean, Vegan, Vegetarian

PREP TIME: 5 MIN	COOK TIME: 3 MIN	YIELD: 4 SERVINGS

INGREDIENTS

1½ cups water

1 head cauliflower, stems removed, cut into florets

2 tablespoons avocado oil

1 fresh lime, juiced

½ teaspoon salt

½ teaspoon black pepper

½ cup fresh chopped cilantro

DIRECTIONS

1 Add the water to the inner pot of the Instant Pot, and place the cauliflower into the steamer basket. Secure the lid and set the valve to *Sealing*. Press *Pressure Cook (High)* and *Keep Warm (Off)*, and set the timer for 3 minutes using the +/− button.

2 When cooking completes, press *Cancel* and use *Quick Release*.

3 Remove the lid and drain the excess water. Add the cauliflower to a large bowl and use a potato masher to create a rice–like consistency.

4 Mix in the avocado oil, lime juice, salt, pepper, and cilantro. Serve immediately.

NOTE: To prepare this recipe with frozen cauliflower rice, add a 12-ounce package of cauliflower rice with 1 tablespoon of oil with 1 tablespoon of water to the inner pot. Use *Pressure Cook (High)* for 1 minute. Use *Quick Release* and mix with the remaining oil, spices, and cilantro.

TIP: Substitute olive or another oil if you don't have avocado oil on hand.

NOTE: Serve with Korean Beef Bulgogi Bowl (Chapter 11) or Buttered Chicken (Chapter 15) for a keto-friendly meal.

| Pressure/ Sauté | High |
| 21 min | Natural Release, Quick Release |

Fried Rice

Instant Pot function: Pressure Cook (High), Keep Warm (On), Natural Release, Quick Release, Sauté (High)

Special tools: Steamer basket

Fits diets: Gluten-Free, Mediterranean, Vegetarian

| PREP TIME: 5 MIN | COOK TIME: 21 MIN | YIELD: 4 SERVINGS |

INGREDIENTS

1 cup filtered water

1 cup basmati brown rice, uncooked and rinsed

2 tablespoons sesame oil

¼ cup diced onion

1 clove garlic, minced

2 medium carrots, finely diced

1 tablespoon tamari sauce

2 large eggs, whisked

½ teaspoon ground ginger

½ teaspoon black pepper

½ cup chopped green onion

Salt, to taste

DIRECTIONS

1 Add the water to the inner pot of the Instant Pot. Add the brown rice. Secure the lid and set the valve to *Sealing*. Press *Pressure Cook (High)* and *Keep Warm (On)*. Set the timer for 15 minutes using the +/− button.

2 When cooking completes, use *Natural Release* for 5 minutes. Then use *Quick Release* to remove the remaining pressure. Remove the rice from the pot; set aside.

3 Wipe the outside of the inner pot and return it to the Instant Pot. Press *Sauté (High)* and add the sesame oil. Stir in the onion, garlic, and carrots. Sauté for 4 minutes. Then add in the tamari sauce and rice. Pour in the eggs, and gently fold over the rice and vegetable mixture until cooked (about 2 minutes). Mix in the ginger and pepper.

4 Portion the rice into 4 bowls, garnish with green onion, and season with salt to taste. Serve immediately.

NOTE: To prepare this recipe with frozen cauliflower rice, add a 12-ounce package of cauliflower rice with 1 tablespoon of oil with 1 tablespoon of water to the inner pot. Use *Pressure Cook (High)* for 1 minute. Use *Quick Release* and follow Step 3 above.

NOTE: Serve with Korean Beef Bulgogi Bowl (Chapter 11) or Buttered Chicken (Chapter 15) for a keto-friendly meal.

TIP: Substitute soy sauce for the tamari if you do not have a gluten allergy.

Sautéed Balsamic Mushrooms

| Sauté/Pressure | High |
| 12 min | Quick Release |

Instant Pot function: Sauté (High), Pressure Cook (High), Keep Warm (Off), Quick Release

Fits diets: Gluten-Free, Keto, Mediterranean, Vegetarian

PREP TIME: 3 MIN	COOK TIME: 12 MIN	YIELD: 6 SERVINGS

INGREDIENTS

4 tablespoons unsalted butter, divided

2 tablespoons extra-virgin olive oil

4 cloves garlic, chopped

16 ounces small white button or baby portobello mushrooms, wiped clean and stems removed

½ teaspoon dried thyme

½ teaspoon dried oregano

2 tablespoons balsamic vinegar

½ cup white wine or vegetable stock

½ teaspoon salt

¼ teaspoon pepper

½ cup chopped parsley

DIRECTIONS

1 Select *Sauté (High)* on the Instant Pot. Add 2 tablespoons of the butter and the olive oil to the pot, and sauté for 1 minute. Add in the garlic and mushrooms, and sauté for 3 minutes. Press *Cancel.*

2 Add the thyme, oregano, vinegar, and white wine or vegetable stock to the pot. Stir to coat the mushrooms. Cover with the lid, set the valve to *Sealing,* and press *Pressure Cook (High)* and *Keep Warm (Off)*, adjusting the timer to 5 minutes using the +/− button.

3 When the cooking completes, do a *Quick Release.* Remove the mushrooms with a slotted spoon, and place into a serving bowl. Select *Sauté (High)* and whisk in the remaining 2 tablespoons of butter. Allow the sauce to slightly reduce, about 3 minutes, and add the salt and pepper. Stir in the parsley and press *Cancel.* Pour the hot sauce over the mushrooms. Serve immediately.

NOTE: To clean the mushrooms, wet a towel and squeeze it dry. Then place the mushrooms onto the towel and fold the towel to cover the mushrooms. Gently roll the mushrooms inside the towel to remove excess dirt. Don't immerse the mushrooms in water to clean them.

VARY IT! Have fresh herbs on hand? Marjoram or rosemary pair well. Leftover red wine? Feel free to swap out the white for a red!

Italian Bell Peppers and Onions

Sauté/Pressure | High
8 min | Quick Release

Instant Pot function: Sauté (High), Pressure Cook (High), Keep Warm (Off), Quick Release

Fits diets: Mediterranean, Vegetarian

PREP TIME: 5 MIN	COOK TIME: 8 MIN	YIELD: 6 SERVINGS

INGREDIENTS

2 tablespoons extra-virgin olive oil

3 red, yellow, or orange bell peppers, sliced ½-inch thick

1 large yellow onion, sliced ½-inch thick

4 cloves garlic, thinly sliced

½ cup chicken stock

½ cup white wine

½ teaspoon chicken bouillon

1 teaspoon dried thyme

¼ cup extra-virgin olive oil

¼ cup chopped basil or parsley

¼ teaspoon salt

DIRECTIONS

1 Select *Sauté (High)* on the Instant Pot. Place the olive oil, bell peppers, onions, and garlic into the pot. Sauté for 3 minutes, stirring occasionally. Add the chicken stock, white wine, bouillon, and thyme into the pot. Press *Cancel.*

2 Secure the lid and set the valve to *Sealing.* Select *Pressure Cook (High)* and *Keep Warm (Off).* Using the +/− button, set the timer to 5 minutes.

3 When finished, do a *Quick Release.* Drain the peppers and onions and place them into a serving bowl. Toss with olive oil and basil or parsley. Season with salt before serving.

TIP: When you drain the peppers and onions, you can freeze the sauce in ice cube trays and use it later in soups or stocks for an added flavor boost.

| Multigrain/Pressure | Low |
| 45 min | Quick Release |

Green Chile Cornbread

Instant Pot function: Multigrain (Low), Keep Warm (Off), Quick Release

Fits diets: Mediterranean, Vegetarian

PREP TIME: 5 MIN	COOK TIME: 45 MIN	YIELD: 8 SERVINGS

INGREDIENTS

1½ cups all-purpose flour

1 cup ground cornmeal

3 teaspoons baking powder

2 large eggs

2 cups reduced-fat milk

2 tablespoons butter, melted

3 tablespoons honey

¼ cup diced green chilies

DIRECTIONS

1 In a large bowl, combine the flour, cornmeal, and baking powder. Whisk in the eggs, milk, butter, honey, and chilies. Set aside.

2 Liberally spray the bottom and sides of the inner pot of the Instant Pot with cooking spray. Spoon the batter into the bottom of the inner pot and spread evenly with a spatula.

3 Secure the lid, set the valve to *Sealing*, and press *Multigrain (Low)* and *Keep Warm (Off)*. Use the +/– button to set the timer to 45 minutes.

4 When cooking completes, press *Cancel* and use *Quick Release* to remove the pressure. Remove the lid; set aside.

5 Let cool for 5 minutes. Then carefully remove the inner pot. Use a knife to loosen the sides of the cornbread from the inner pot. Invert the pot onto a large plate to remove the cornbread.

6 Slice and serve immediately with a teaspoon of honey butter.

NOTE: Be sure to liberally spray the inner pot with cooking spray so the cornbread comes out smooth when inverted.

TIP: Worried about the cornbread sticking? Use parchment paper and cut a circle to line the bottom and a 2-inch long strip to cover the sides of the inner pot before you pour the batter in.

VARY IT! Not a fan of chilies? No worries! Leave them out and add a cup of whole kernel corn if you want a fun texture.

| Sauté/ Pressure | High |
| 35 min | Natural Release, Quick Release |

Sourdough Stuffing

Instant Pot function: Sauté (High), Pressure Cook (High), Keep Warm (Off), Natural Release, Quick Release

Special tools: 7-inch pan

Fits diets: Mediterranean, Vegan, Vegetarian

| PREP TIME: 5 MIN | COOK TIME: 35 MIN | YIELD: 8 SERVINGS |

INGREDIENTS

1 tablespoon extra-virgin olive oil

½ small onion, chopped

1 teaspoon minced garlic

3 celery stalks, chopped

2 large carrots, chopped

1 teaspoon dried sage

1 teaspoon dried thyme

½ teaspoon black pepper

¼ teaspoon salt

2 cups vegetable broth

8 ounces of sourdough bread (half of a 16-ounce loaf), cut into 1-inch pieces

½ cup walnuts, chopped

1 cup water

Chopped parsley, for garnish

DIRECTIONS

1 Press *Sauté (High)* on the Instant Pot. Using the +/− button, set the timer to 10 minutes. Add the olive oil to the inner pot, and sauté the onions and garlic for 2 to 3 minutes. Add the celery and carrots, and cook for 7 to 8 minutes, or until soft. Stir in the sage, thyme, pepper, salt, and broth. Press *Cancel*.

2 Add the sourdough pieces to a large bowl, and pour the vegetable mixture over the top. Mix thoroughly with your hands and allow 5 minutes for the bread to absorb the liquid. Stir in the chopped walnuts.

3 Liberally spray a 7-inch pan and a large piece of aluminum foil with cooking spray. Add the sourdough stuffing into the pan. Cover with foil, placing the side sprayed with cooking spray down.

4 Rinse out the inner pot and dry the outside. Place the water inside the pot and set the metal trivet on top. Place the covered pan on top and secure the lid. Set the valve to *Sealing*.

5 Press *Pressure Cook (High)* and *Keep Warm (Off)*. Set the time to 25 minutes using the +/− button. Set the valve to *Sealing*.

6 When cooking completes, do a *Natural Release* of the pressure for 5 minutes. Then use *Quick Release* to remove any remaining pressure. Carefully remove the pan from the Instant Pot and discard the foil. Garnish with parsley and serve immediately.

NOTE: This recipe is made without butter to remain vegan, but if you prefer a richer flavor, you can add 2 tablespoons of butter when you add the vegetable broth.

Pressure | High

5 min | Quick Release

Dee's Macaroni Salad

Instant Pot function: Pressure Cook (High), Keep Warm (Off), Quick Release

Fits diets: Mediterranean, Vegetarian

| PREP TIME: 10 MIN | COOK TIME: 5 MIN | YIELD: 8 SERVINGS |

INGREDIENTS

3 cups filtered water

1 pound macaroni noodles

1 teaspoon salt

¼ cup white wine vinegar

1 teaspoon sugar

¼ cup finely diced onion

½ cup plus 2 tablespoons light mayonnaise, divided

2 celery stalks, finely diced

⅓ cup chopped green onion

½ teaspoon garlic powder

½ teaspoon salt, plus more, to taste

½ teaspoon black pepper

4 hard-boiled eggs, finely chopped

DIRECTIONS

1 Place the water, pasta, and salt in the inner pot of the Instant Pot. Select *Pressure Cook (High)* and *Keep Warm (Off)*, and set the timer for 5 minutes using the +/– button. Secure the lid and set the valve to *Sealing.*

2 In a medium bowl, whisk together the vinegar, sugar, and onion; set aside.

3 When cooking completes, use *Quick Release* to remove the pressure. Drain the pasta and pour into a bowl.

4 Add ½ cup of the mayonnaise, celery, onion, garlic powder, ½ teaspoon of the salt, and pepper to the bowl with the vinegar, sugar, and onion. Pour the sauce over the pasta. Stir in the hard-boiled eggs.

5 Refrigerate for at least 2 hours to develop the flavor. When ready to serve, remove from the refrigerator and stir with the remaining 2 tablespoons of mayonnaise. Season with salt, to taste.

NOTE: To increase the fiber and nutrient density, use a 100 percent whole-wheat or lentil-based pasta.

TIP: Use a vegan mayonnaise and omit the egg to create a vegan macaroni salad.

Chapter 14

Hearty Soups and Stews

The air is turning crisp and you find yourself dreaming about warm fires and cool evenings. Well, break out your Instant Pot because it's soup season! Actually, we enjoy a warm cup of soup any time of the year, but especially when the temperatures cool. The beauty of a delicious bowl of soup is that not only can you increase your daily intake of vegetables, but you can also easily modify them to suit whatever dietary preferences you have at your table. Take, for instance, the Minestrone Soup. Have a gluten-free guest? Sub the pasta for a gluten-free variety or swap for potatoes instead. We want you to feel comfortable making these recipes your own and encourage you to do so!

You'll notice throughout this chapter we have both vegan and meat friendly recipes. While we aren't vegan, we do enjoy eating plant-forward often! However, on those days we need a little more protein, we often will add some of the leftover Rosemary and Garlic Whole Chicken (Chapter 10) to the White Bean and Garden Vegetable Soup.

We hope you curl up with a nice book and a warm blanket after satisfying your tummy with these soups and stews!

Sauté/Pressure — High

11 min — Quick Release

Minestrone Soup

Instant Pot function: Sauté (High), Pressure Cook (High), Keep Warm (Off), Quick Release

Fits diets: Mediterranean, Vegan, Vegetarian

PREP TIME: 5 MIN	COOK TIME: 11 MIN	YIELD: 6 SERVINGS

INGREDIENTS

1 teaspoon extra-virgin olive oil

½ small onion, diced

1 teaspoon minced garlic

2 medium carrots, chopped

2 celery stalks, chopped

1 medium zucchini, quartered and thinly sliced

1 cup dry whole-wheat pasta

2 cups vegetable broth

1 cup cooked garbanzo beans

1 cup cooked red kidney beans

Salt and pepper, to taste

Parmesan cheese, for garnish

Fresh chopped basil, for garnish

Baguette

DIRECTIONS

1 Add the oil to the inner pot of the Instant Pot, and press *Sauté (High)*. Stir in the onion, garlic, carrots, and celery, and sauté for 8 minutes.

2 Press *Cancel*. Add in the zucchini, pasta, and vegetable broth, and stir. Secure the lid, ensuring the valve is set to *Sealing*. Press *Pressure Cook (High)* and *Keep Warm (Off)*, and set the timer to 3 minutes using the +/− button.

3 When cooking completes, use *Quick Release*. Add in the garbanzo beans and kidney beans, and stir. Add salt and pepper, to taste.

4 Serve immediately with Parmesan cheese, fresh basil, and a piece of baguette.

NOTE: If you're tight on time, substitute a 15-ounce can of red kidney or garbanzo beans in place of the garbanzo and kidney mixture.

VARY IT! Substitute gluten-free pasta like lentil pasta if you're on a gluten-free diet. Adjust the cooking time to 4 minutes if you go this route.

Creamy Tomato and Basil Soup

| Sauté/ Pressure | High |
| 8 min | Natural Release, Quick Release |

Instant Pot function: Sauté (High), Pressure Cook (High), Keep Warm (On), Natural Release, Quick Release

Fits diets: Mediterranean, Vegetarian

| PREP TIME: 3 MIN | COOK TIME: 8 MIN | YIELD: 4 SERVINGS |

INGREDIENTS

1 tablespoon extra-virgin olive oil

One 10-ounce bag frozen mirepoix (onions, carrots, and celery)

Two 14.5-ounce cans chopped fire-roasted tomatoes

1 tablespoon balsamic vinegar

3 cups vegetable stock or chicken stock

½ cup chopped basil

One 12-ounce can evaporated milk

¼ teaspoon baking soda

1 teaspoon sugar

½ cup grated Parmesan cheese, for garnish

¼ cup fresh chopped basil, for garnish

DIRECTIONS

1   Add the oil to the inner pot of the Instant Pot and press *Sauté (High)*. Stir in the frozen mirepoix mix, and sauté for 3 minutes. Press *Cancel.* Add in the tomatoes, vinegar, stock, basil, evaporated milk, baking soda, and sugar, and stir. Secure the lid, ensuring the venting is sealed, and press *Pressure Cook (High)* and *Keep Warm (Off)*, using the +/− button to set the timer to 5 minutes.

2   When cooking completes, do a *Natural Release* of the pressure for 3 minutes. Do a *Quick Release* to release the remaining pressure.

3   Using a blender, working in batches, blend the tomato soup to a creamy consistency, about 1 minute. Serve immediately with grated Parmesan cheese and chopped basil.

TIP: If you can't find frozen onions, carrots, and celery mix, or you prefer fresh, use 1 cup onions, ½ cup carrots, and ½ cup celery.

TIP: If you prefer a chunkier soup, only blend half of the soup.

NOTE: Baking soda may seem an odd addition, but trust us! Baking soda neutralizes the acid and leaves the soup with a creamy consistency.

VARY IT! Add a Mexican twist with ground cumin or a Spanish flare with paprika!

White Bean and Garden Vegetable Soup

Sauté/ Pressure	High
18 min	Quick Release

Instant Pot function: Sauté (High), Soup (High), Keep Warm (Off), Quick Release

Fits diets: Gluten-Free, Mediterranean, Vegan

PREP TIME: 5 MIN	COOK TIME: 18 MIN	YIELD: 6 SERVINGS

INGREDIENTS

1 tablespoon extra-virgin olive oil

½ small onion, chopped

1 teaspoon minced garlic

2 large carrots, chopped

2 celery stalks, chopped

2 teaspoons Italian seasoning

½ teaspoon ground black pepper

¼ teaspoon salt

4 cups vegetable broth

One 15-ounce can diced tomatoes, no salt added

1½ cups white beans, soaked and rinsed

3 cups baby kale

Shredded Parmesan cheese, for garnish

Croutons, for garnish

Chopped parsley, for garnish

DIRECTIONS

1 Add the olive oil to the inner pot of the Instant Pot, and press *Sauté (High)*. Add in the onions, garlic, carrots, and celery, and sauté for about 8 minutes.

2 When done, press *Cancel*. Stir in the Italian seasoning, black pepper, salt, vegetable broth, tomatoes, and white beans.

3 Secure the lid and set the valve to *Sealing*. Press *Pressure Cook (High)* and *Keep Warm (Off)*, and set the timer for 10 minutes using the +/- function. When cooking completes, press *Cancel* and use *Quick Release* to remove the pressure from the pot.

4 Portion into 6 bowls and top with Parmesan cheese, croutons, and chopped parsley. Serve immediately.

NOTE: You can make your own vegetable broth to keep the sodium lower. Check out Chapter 8 for a recipe.

TIP: Feel free to substitute fresh garden herbs for the Italian seasoning. Usually 1 tablespoon of fresh herbs to 1 teaspoon of dried is a great rule of thumb to follow.

Lentil Soup

Instant Pot function: Sauté (High), Pressure Cook (High), Keep Warm (On), Natural Release

Fits diets: Gluten-Free, Mediterranean

PREP TIME: 5 MIN	COOK TIME: 14 MIN	YIELD: 4 SERVINGS

INGREDIENTS

1 tablespoon extra-virgin olive oil

1 medium onion, finely chopped

1 large carrot, grated

2 celery stalks, thinly sliced

3 cloves garlic, chopped

One 14.5-ounce can chopped tomatoes

1 cup dried brown lentils

1 bay leaf

1 teaspoon dried thyme

6 cups vegetable stock or chicken stock

½ lemon, juiced, or 1 teaspoon red wine vinegar

2 cups raw baby spinach leaves

1 cup grated Parmesan cheese

½ teaspoon salt

¼ teaspoon pepper

DIRECTIONS

1 Select *Sauté (Hot)* on the Instant Pot. Add the olive oil and onion, and sauté for 3 minutes. Add in the carrots, celery, and garlic, and sauté for 1 minute. Press *Cancel*.

2 Add the tomatoes, lentils, bay leaf, thyme, and stock. Secure the lid and seal off the venting. Select *Pressure Cook (High)* and *Keep Warm (On)*. Using the +/− button, set the timer for 10 minutes. When finished, do a *Natural Release* of the pressure for 5 minutes; then do a *Quick Release* to remove the remaining pressure.

3 Discard the bay leaf. Stir in the lemon juice or vinegar, baby spinach, Parmesan cheese, salt, and pepper. Serve immediately.

NOTE: Don't skip the squeeze of fresh lemon or the vinegar. A touch of acid brightens the flavors of the soup!

TIP: For a great meal, serve with grilled cheese sandwiches or crusty French bread.

VARY IT! Craving a meatier dish? Add in sliced smoked sausage!

Broccoli Potato Cheese Soup

Instant Pot function: Sauté (High), Pressure Cook (High), Keep Warm (On), Natural Release

Fits diets: Gluten-Free, Vegetarian

PREP TIME: 10 MIN	COOK TIME: 10 MIN	YIELD: 6 SERVINGS

INGREDIENTS

1 tablespoon extra-virgin olive oil

1 tablespoon butter

1 cup chopped onion

½ cup chopped carrots

½ cup chopped celery

2 cups chopped broccoli with stems

½ teaspoon garlic powder

1 pound Yukon Gold potatoes, chopped

4 cups vegetable stock or chicken stock

¾ teaspoon salt

¼ teaspoon white pepper

1 cup grated cheddar cheese

½ cup Greek yogurt

8 slices cooked bacon, crumbled, for garnish

¼ cup chopped green onions, for garnish

DIRECTIONS

1 Place the olive oil, butter, onion, carrots, and celery into the Instant Pot and set to *Sauté (High)*. Sauté for 3 minutes, stirring occasionally. Press *Cancel*.

2 Add in the broccoli, garlic powder, potatoes, stock, salt, and pepper. Set to *Pressure Cook (High)* and *Keep Warm (Off)*, and use the +/− button to set the timer to 7 minutes. Secure the lid and set the valve to *Sealing*.

3 Do a *Natural Release* of the pressure for 10 minutes. Transfer the soup to a blender and add in the cheese and yogurt. Pulse the soup for 1 minute or until the desired consistency is reached.

4 To serve, garnish with bacon and onions.

TIP: Put a towel over the blender and keep it slightly vented as you begin to blend. Be sure to pulse and not turn it on, because hot contents could spill out. If you prefer a thinner soup, add more hot chicken stock or broth to reach your desired consistency.

VARY IT! Asparagus or cauliflower are great swaps for broccoli.

Corn and Potato Chowder

Instant Pot function: Sauté (High), Pressure Cook (High), Keep Warm (Off), Quick Release

Fits diets: Gluten-Free, Mediterranean, Vegetarian

| Sauté/Pressure | High |
| 14 min | Quick Release |

| PREP TIME: 10 MIN | COOK TIME: 14 MIN | YIELD: 6 SERVINGS |

INGREDIENTS

1 tablespoon extra-virgin olive oil

½ small onion, chopped

1 teaspoon minced garlic

12 ounces mini potatoes, quartered

2 cups sweet corn kernels

2 cups vegetable broth

½ teaspoon black pepper

1 cup plain whole milk yogurt

¾ cup medium cheddar cheese

Fresh chives, for garnish

Salt, to taste

DIRECTIONS

1 Add the oil to the inner pot and press *Sauté (High)*. Add the onions and garlic, and sauté for 4 minutes, or until the onions are translucent. Press *Cancel*.

2 Add the potatoes, corn, broth, and pepper to the pot. Stir. Secure the lid and set the valve to *Sealing*.

3 Press *Pressure Cook (High)* and *Keep Warm (Off)* on the Instant Pot; using the +/− button, adjust the timer to 10 minutes.

4 When cooking completes, press *Cancel* and use *Quick Release* to remove the pressure from the pot.

5 Remove the lid and stir in the yogurt and cheese. (The heat from the pressure cooking will melt the cheese as you continue to stir.)

6 Portion into 6 bowls and garnish with chives. Season with salt, to taste.

NOTE: For a lighter soup, use reduced-fat yogurt and cheese. Just don't use fat-free dairy — it won't result in a good soup!

TIP: Frozen corn works very well in this recipe.

Sausage, Potato, and Kale Soup

Sauté/Pressure	High
14 min	Natural Release

Instant Pot function: Sauté (High), Pressure Cook (High), Keep Warm (On), Natural Release

Fits diets: Mediterranean

PREP TIME: 10 MIN	COOK TIME: 14 MIN	YIELD: 6 SERVINGS

INGREDIENTS

1 tablespoon extra-virgin olive oil

½ pound Italian sausage links, casings removed

1 cup chopped onion

3 cloves garlic, chopped

1 pound Yukon Gold baby potatoes, cut into ¼-inch slices

4 cups vegetable stock or chicken stock

4 cups chopped kale, stems removed

½ cup chopped parsley

1 teaspoon dried oregano

½ cup heavy whipping cream

¾ teaspoon salt

¼ teaspoon pepper

⅛ teaspoon crushed red pepper flakes

DIRECTIONS

1 Place the olive oil, sausage, and onion into the Instant Pot, and set the pot to *Sauté (High)*. Sauté for 5 minutes, stirring occasionally and breaking up the sausage pieces into crumbles. Add in the garlic, and continue to sauté for 1 minute. Press *Cancel*.

2 Add the potato, stock, kale, parsley, and oregano; stir. Secure the lid and seal the venting. Press *Pressure Cook (High)* and *Keep Warm (On)*. Using the +/− button, set the timer to 5 minutes.

3 Do a *Natural Release* of the pressure for 8 minutes; then do a *Quick Release* to remove the remaining pressure. Select *Sauté (High)*, and stir in the heavy whipping cream and heat for 3 minutes. Season with salt, pepper, and crushed red pepper flakes, and adjust seasoning as needed.

NOTE: If you prefer more texture to your kale, stir it in when you add the cream. Kale is a heartier green and can withstand pressure cooking. Don't use baby kale under pressure, though — treat baby kale like spinach and stir it in at the end.

TIP: Serve with a wedge of crusty French bread to complete the meal.

VARY IT! Not a kale fan? You can replace the kale with baby spinach and stir it in with the cream instead of cooking it under pressure.

Chicken Tortilla Soup

Sauté/Soup or Pressure | High
17 min | Quick Release

Instant Pot function: Sauté (High), Soup (High), Keep Warm (Off), Quick Release

Fits diets: Gluten-Free, Mediterranean

PREP TIME: 5 MIN | **COOK TIME: 17 MIN** | **YIELD: 6 SERVINGS**

INGREDIENTS

1 tablespoon extra-virgin olive oil

½ small onion, chopped

1 teaspoon minced garlic

2 carrots, chopped

1 large bell pepper, chopped

1½ teaspoons dried oregano

¾ teaspoon cumin

½ teaspoon chili powder

½ teaspoon ground black pepper

2 cups chicken broth

One 28-ounce canned crushed tomatoes

One 15-ounce canned no-salt-added black beans, rinsed and drained

1 pound boneless, skinless chicken breasts (about 2 large breasts)

1 bay leaf

Salt, to taste

Crunchy tortilla strips, for garnish

Avocado slices, for garnish

Shredded cheese, for garnish

Plain yogurt, for garnish

DIRECTIONS

1 Place the oil in the inner pot of the Instant Pot, and press *Sauté (High)*. Add in the onion and garlic, and sauté 3 to 4 minutes (or until the onions appear translucent).

2 Stir in the carrots, bell peppers, oregano, cumin, chili powder, and pepper. Cook the 6 to 7 minutes. Press *Cancel*.

3 Stir in the broth, tomatoes, and beans. Place the chicken breasts on top, and add the bay leaf.

4 Press *Soup (High)* and *Keep Warm (Off)*, and set the timer for 7 minutes using the +/− button.

5 When cooking completes, press *Cancel*. Use *Quick Release* to remove the pressure.

6 Remove the lid and take out the chicken breasts. Shred the chicken using two forks and add the chicken back to the pot.

7 Divide among 6 bowls and garnish with tortilla strips, avocado slices, cheese, and a dollop of yogurt.

Texas Beef Chili with Beans

| Sauté/Pressure | High |
| 27 min | Natural Release |

Instant Pot function: Sauté (High), Pressure Cook (High), Keep Warm (On), Natural Release

Fits diets: Gluten-Free

| PREP TIME: 5 MIN | COOK TIME: 27 MIN | YIELD: 6 SERVINGS |

INGREDIENTS

1 pound lean ground beef

1 large onion, finely chopped

1 large green bell pepper, finely chopped

3 cloves garlic, chopped

Two 14.5-ounce can fire-roasted canned tomatoes

2 cups beef stock or chicken stock

One 14.5-ounce can pinto beans, drained and rinsed

One 14.5-ounce can kidney beans, drained and rinsed

3 tablespoons chili powder

1 teaspoon cumin powder

½ teaspoon coriander

½ teaspoon salt

Chopped cilantro, for garnish

Shredded cheddar cheese, for garnish

Chopped jalapeño peppers, for garnish

Sour cream, for garnish

DIRECTIONS

1 Select *Sauté (High)* on the Instant Pot, and add the ground beef to the pot. Sauté until fully cooked, around 8 to 10 minutes.

2 Add the onions, bell peppers, and garlic; sauté for 3 minutes. Press *Cancel.*

3 Add the tomatoes, stock, pinto beans, kidney beans, chili powder, cumin, coriander, and salt. Secure the lid and seal the venting. Press *Pressure Cook (High)* and *Keep Warm (On)*. Using the +/− button, set the timer to 15 minutes. When finished, do a *Natural Release* of the pressure for 10 minutes. Do a *Quick Release* to remove any remaining pressure.

4 Serve the chili with cilantro, cheddar cheese, jalapeño peppers, and a dollop of sour cream, if desired.

NOTE: Serve on top of corn bread or corn chips to complete this festive dish!

Sauté/ Pressure or Stew | High

40 min | Natural Release

Persian Stew

Instant Pot function: Sauté (High), Pressure Cook (High) or Stew, Keep Warm (On), Natural Release

| PREP TIME: 15 MIN | COOK TIME: 40 MIN | YIELD: 6 SERVINGS |

INGREDIENTS

¼ cup extra-virgin olive oil

1 pound beef round, cut into ½-inch or smaller pieces

1 teaspoon salt, divided

1 large yellow onion, chopped

½ cup dry split yellow peas, rinsed

½ teaspoon turmeric

1 teaspoon ground cumin

½ teaspoon ground coriander

¼ teaspoon ground cinnamon

1 lime, zested and juiced, divided

2 tablespoons tomato paste

⅛ teaspoon saffron

3 cups vegetable stock

6 cups cooked rice

¼ cup chopped parsley or cilantro, for garnish

DIRECTIONS

1 Pour the olive oil into the Instant Pot. Season the meat with ½ teaspoon of the salt. Set the Instant Pot to *Sauté (High)*, and sauté the meat for 4 to 5 minutes, turning over the pieces after 2 minutes.

2 Add the onions, peas, turmeric, cumin, coriander, cinnamon, lime zest, tomato paste, saffron, and vegetable stock. Press *Cancel* and change the setting to *Pressure Cook (Low)* and *Keep Warm (On)*. Using the +/− button, set the timer to 35 minutes.

3 Set the pot for *Natural Release* for 10 minutes; then do a *Quick Release*. Stir in the lime juice. Add the remaining ½ teaspoon of salt, as needed. Serve over rice and top with fresh chopped parsley or cilantro.

NOTE: Your use of salt may depend on how salty the stock is, as well as your personal preference. Be sure to season the meat before cooking and then season with the remaining salt at the end. Lime juice enhances the salt flavor as well.

Sauté/Pressure or Stew | High
1 hr 10 min | Natural Release

Pot Roast

Instant Pot function: Sauté (High), Pressure Cook (High) or Stew, Keep Warm (On), Natural Release

| PREP TIME: 10 MIN | COOK TIME: 1 HR 10 MIN | YIELD: 8 SERVINGS |

INGREDIENTS

3 pounds beef chuck roast

½ teaspoon salt

½ teaspoon pepper

1 tablespoon extra-virgin olive oil

1 large onion, sliced

2 carrots, cut lengthwise in half and in 2-inch pieces

2 celery stalks, cut in 2-inch pieces

1 pound new potatoes, halved

4 cloves garlic, chopped

3 cups beef stock

1 tablespoon Worcestershire sauce

1 tablespoon dried rosemary, chopped finely, or 2 fresh sprigs rosemary

1 bay leaf

2 tablespoons cold water

2 tablespoons cornstarch

¼ cup chopped fresh parsley, for garnish

DIRECTIONS

1 Season the chuck roast with salt and pepper. Select *Sauté (High)* on the Instant Pot, and add the oil to the pot. Sauté the pot roast on all sides, 2 to 3 minutes per side. Press *Cancel*.

2 Add the onions, carrots, celery, potatoes, garlic, beef stock, Worcestershire sauce, rosemary, and bay leaf to the pot. Stir to coat the meat with the broth. Secure the lid, and seal the venting. Select *Pressure Cook (High)* and *Keep Warm (On)* and use the +/− button to set the timer for 20 minutes per pound (60 to 80 minutes, depending on the size of your chuck roast). Do a *Natural Release* of the pressure for 20 minutes before releasing the pressure. Remove the meat and vegetables to a serving bowl.

3 In a small mixing bowl, stir together the water and cornstarch. Select *Sauté (High)* and whisk the cornstarch slurry into the broth. Allow the sauce to thicken, about 3 to 5 minutes. Pour the thickened sauce over the top of the pot roast. Top with chopped parsley and serve.

NOTE: Want to use a frozen chuck roast? You can! Simply adjust the time to 30 minutes per pound and skip the browning of the meat at the beginning. Put all the ingredients in the Instant Pot and beginning pressure cooking.

TIP: Keep the vegetables a uniform length and size for even cooking.

VARY IT! Add in rutabagas or turnips to use fall and winter vegetables.

Beef and Barley Stew

Instant Pot function: Sauté (High), Pressure Cook (High) or Stew, Keep Warm (On), Natural Release, Quick Release

PREP TIME: 10 MIN	COOK TIME: 23 MIN	YIELD: 6 SERVINGS

INGREDIENTS

1 pound beef stew meat, cubed

½ teaspoon salt

¼ teaspoon pepper

1 teaspoon garlic powder

2 teaspoons canola or vegetable oil

2 tablespoons tomato paste

1 large onion, thinly sliced

2 large carrots, thinly sliced

¾ cup pearled barley (not instant)

8 ounces cremini or button mushrooms, wiped clean and quartered

3 cups beef stock

12 ounces dark beer

2 tablespoons Worcestershire sauce

¼ cup chopped parsley, for garnish

2 tablespoons prepared horseradish, for garnish

DIRECTIONS

1 Season the stew meat with salt, pepper, and garlic powder. Select *Sauté (High)* on the Instant Pot, and add the oil to the pot. Sauté the meat for 2 minutes, stirring constantly. Add the tomato paste, and stir for 1 minute. Press *Cancel.*

2 Add the onions, carrots, barley, mushrooms, beef stock, beer, and Worcestershire sauce. Select *Pressure Cook (High)* and *Keep Warm (On)*. Use the +/− button to adjust the timer to 20 minutes. Do a *Natural Release* of the pressure for 10 minutes, then do a *Quick Release.* Ladle into 6 soup bowls.

3 In a small bowl, mix together the parsley and horseradish. Top each bowl with a dollop of horseradish and parsley.

NOTE: Skip the horseradish if you're sensitive to spicy foods.

VARY IT! Add in rutabagas or turnips to use fall and winter vegetables.

| Sauté/Pressure | High |
| 25 min | Quick Release |

Papa John's Gumbo

Instant Pot function: Sauté (High), Pressure Cook (High), Keep Warm (Off), Quick Release

| PREP TIME: 10 MIN | COOK TIME: 25 MIN | YIELD: 8 SERVINGS |

INGREDIENTS

½ cup roux

2 quarts chicken broth, divided

2 cups diced onions

2 cups diced carrots

2 cups diced celery

½ cup diced bell peppers

1½ cups sliced okra

2 tablespoons crushed minced garlic

2 Andouille chicken sausage links

2 boneless, skinless chicken breasts, diced

3 tablespoons Worcestershire sauce

1 teaspoon sugar

1 tablespoon gumbo file

2 tablespoons chicken bouillon

2⅔ cups cooked brown rice

Hot sauce, to taste

DIRECTIONS

1 Press *Sauté (High)* on the Instant Pot and add the roux. Mix using a spatula. After the roux has become viscous and hot (about 5 minutes), add in ½ cup of the chicken broth, onions, carrots, celery, peppers, okra, garlic, sausage, and chicken. Sauté for 5 minutes.

2 Add in the remaining chicken broth, Worcestershire sauce, sugar, gumbo file, and chicken bouillon, and stir. Press *Cancel*. Then select *Pressure Cook (High)* and *Keep Warm (Off)*. Set the timer to 15 minutes using the +/− button, secure the lid, and set the vent to *Sealing*.

3 When cooking completes, use *Quick Release* and remove the lid.

4 Portion ⅓ cup brown rice into each bowl, and top with 1 cup of gumbo. Add hot sauce to taste.

NOTE: For a spicier gumbo, add 1 diced jalapeño to the cup of peppers.

VARY IT! Serve on top of a scoop of brown rice or farro.

Chapter 15

Going Global

Have you always dreamed of traveling the Amalfi Coast, dining on the finest Italian fare, and sipping the best red wine around? If you're nodding your head yes, then you're our kind of person!

This chapter is designed for people who love a sense of culinary adventure and enjoy ethnic cuisine. We've taken some of the classics and transformed them to fit the Instant Pot. With a little time and a lot of love, you'll take your entire family on a tour of India with the Chana Masala in under an hour!

These recipes make stellar main meals, but you can also enjoy dishes like the Cilantro Lime Fish Tacos as simple appetizers to prepare for a big game or Oscars party! And, as if that weren't enough, you can certainly modify each recipe to your level of comfort, meaning if you prefer a less spicy dish, hold off on the peppers in the Madras Lentils. Or take it up a notch and add a habanero to the Chicken Enchilada Casserole!

Go big or go home as you go global in this chapter!

Nonna's Lasagna

Sauté/ Pressure	High
32 min	Natural Release, Quick Release

Instant Pot function: Sauté (High), Pressure (High), Keep Warm (On), Natural Release, Quick Release

Special tools: Casserole dish or Instant Pot–friendly baking dish, at least 3 inches deep

Fits diets: Mediterranean

PREP TIME: 15 MIN	COOK TIME: 32 MIN	YIELD: 6 SERVINGS

INGREDIENTS

½ pound ground beef

8 ounces mushrooms, chopped

1 clove garlic or ½ teaspoon garlic powder

1 tablespoon fresh chopped parsley or 1 teaspoon dried parsley

1 teaspoon salt

2 cups jarred spaghetti sauce

1½ cups water

1 large egg, beaten

1 cup ricotta cheese

¼ cup grated Parmesan cheese

½ teaspoon salt

¼ teaspoon pepper

1 tablespoon parsley

1 tablespoon fresh chopped basil or 1 teaspoon dried basil

4 ounces dried lasagna noodles, uncooked

1 medium zucchini, thinly sliced

1 cup grated mozzarella cheese

DIRECTIONS

1 Set the Instant Pot to *Sauté (High)* and add the beef, mushrooms, and garlic to the pot. Sauté for 4 minutes. Add the parsley, salt, and spaghetti sauce, and stir to combine. Turn off *Sauté* and set to *Pressure Cook (Low)*. Set the timer to 3 minutes using the +/− button, and secure the lid.

2 *Quick Release* the sauce and transfer to a mixing bowl for assembly. Quickly wash and dry the pot, and return it to the Instant Pot. Add the water into the bottom of the pot.

3 In a medium bowl, combine the egg, ricotta cheese, Parmesan cheese, salt, pepper, parsley, and basil.

4 Begin assembling the lasagna in the springform pan. First, pour ¼ cup of the sauce onto the bottom of the pan. Break up the lasagna noodles, and using the broken pieces, fit onto the sauce in a single layer, reserving the remainder of the noodles for other layers. Don't allow the noodles to overlap. Next, add ⅓ of the sauce mixture over the top of the noodles. Then, in a single layer, arrange the zucchini slices over the top of the sauce. Layer ½ of the ricotta mixture thinly over the zucchini. Add another layer of lasagna noodles, then ⅓ of the sauce mixture, another layer of zucchini, the ricotta mixture, the noodles, and the meat. Top with mozzarella.

5 Using aluminum foil, make an X with the foil and place the springform pan in the center. Cover the springform pan and place onto the trivet. Gently lower the trivet into the pot and secure the lid.

6 Set to *Pressure (High)* and *Keep Warm (On)* and set the timer to 25 minutes using the +/− button. Do a *Natural Release* of the pressure for 10 minutes. Then do a *Quick Release* or allow to hold warm until you're ready to serve.

NOTE: If you want, you can broil the lasagna for 4 minutes to get a browned surface or allow the lasagna to rest for 10 minutes before removing from the springform pan.

VARY IT! Replace the zucchini with 1 cup of defrosted frozen spinach that has been squeezed dry.

Balsamic–Stuffed Portobello Mushrooms

Instant Pot function: Pressure Cook (High), Keep Warm (Off), Quick Release, Sauté (High)

Fits diets: Gluten-Free, Mediterranean, Vegetarian

PREP TIME: 5 MIN	COOK TIME: 20 MIN	YIELD: 4 SERVINGS

INGREDIENTS

1 medium bell pepper, diced

¼ cup diced onion

½ cup cherry tomatoes, quartered

2 tablespoons extra-virgin olive oil

1 teaspoon minced garlic

¼ teaspoon red pepper flakes

1 teaspoon Italian seasoning

4 portobello mushrooms, cleaned, caps, stems and gills removed (see Figure 15-1)

½ cup shredded Italian cheese blend

1½ cups filtered water

¼ cup balsamic vinegar, divided

¼ cup fresh basil, finely chopped

DIRECTIONS

1 In a small bowl, toss the bell peppers, onion, and tomatoes with olive oil, garlic, red pepper flakes, and Italian seasoning.

2 Spray 4 squares of aluminum foil with cooking spray. Place each mushroom cap on a separate aluminum foil square, stem side up. Evenly portion the zucchini mixture into the mushroom caps. Sprinkle with cheese and loosely seal the foil packets so the cheese doesn't touch the top of the foil.

3 Add the water to the bottom of the metal pot and place the metal trivet on top. Place the foil packets stem side up on the trivet, positioning them so each packet is resting on the other.

4 Cover and secure the lid. Set the valve to *Sealing* and press *Pressure Cook (High)*. Use the +/− button to set the timer for 15 minutes.

5 When cooking completes, press *Cancel* and use *Quick Release* to remove the pressure from the pot.

6 Carefully lift the metal trivet out and let the mushrooms sit for a few minutes to cool.

7 Meanwhile, discard the water, dry the outer metal pot, and return it to the Instant Pot. Add the balsamic vinegar and press *Sauté (High)*.

8 Slowly stir the vinegar with a spatula so it doesn't burn but begins to become reduced and thickens to the point that it coats the back of a wooden spoon, about 5 minutes. When this happens, press *Cancel*.

9 Prepare the mushrooms by removing the foil and placing the mushrooms in a bowl. Top with balsamic glaze and fresh basil. Serve immediately.

NOTE: To remove the mushroom gills, take a spoon and gently press under the cap.

TIP: To save time, you can buy a premade balsamic glaze.

VARY IT! Use whatever vegetables and Italian cheese blend you have on hand!

FIGURE 15-1:
Cleaning a portobello mushroom.

© *John Wiley & Sons, Inc.*

Creamy Butternut Squash Orzo Risotto

Instant Pot function: Sauté (High), Pressure Cook (High), Quick Release

Fits diets: Mediterranean, Vegetarian

PREP TIME: 5 MIN	COOK TIME: 15 MIN	YIELD: 6 SERVINGS

INGREDIENTS

1 teaspoon extra-virgin olive oil

½ small onion, chopped

1 teaspoon minced garlic

1 pound ground chicken sausage

2 cups cubed butternut squash

3 cups chicken broth

2 teaspoons dried sage

1 teaspoon dried rosemary

1 teaspoon parsley

½ teaspoon black pepper

1 cup dried whole-wheat orzo

1 bay leaf

4 ounces reduced-fat cream cheese

Salt, to taste

Fresh chopped parsley, for garnish

DIRECTIONS

1 Press *Sauté (High)* on the Instant Pot, and set the timer to 6 minutes using the +/− button. Add the olive oil to the metal pot insert, and toss in the onions and garlic. Cook for 3 to 4 minutes. Stir in the chicken sausage and brown the remaining few minutes. Press *Cancel*.

2 Place the butternut squash, chicken broth, sage, rosemary, parsley, pepper, and orzo into the pot, and stir. Add in the bay leaf and secure the lid.

3 Set the valve to *Sealing*, and press *Pressure Cook (High)* and *Keep Warm (Off)*. Use the +/− button to set the timer to 5 minutes.

4 When cooking completes, use *Quick Release* to remove the pressure from the pot.

5 Remove the lid and stir in the cream cheese until uniformly combined.

6 Portion the orzo into bowls, salt as desired and garnish with fresh parsley. Serve immediately.

NOTE: You can use the homemade Chicken or Turkey Stock (Chapter 8) to keep the sodium in check for this recipe.

VARY IT! Omit the chicken sausage and use a vegetable broth if you're looking for a vegetarian option. This dish tastes wonderful with asparagus, too — feel free to add in a cup of chopped asparagus before you secure the lid.

| Pressure | High |
| 15 min | Quick Release |

Red Lentil Curry

Instant Pot function: Pressure Cook (High), Keep Warm (Off), Quick Release

Fits diets: Gluten-Free, Mediterranean, Vegan, Vegetarian

| PREP TIME: NONE | COOK TIME: 15 MIN | YIELD: 4 SERVINGS |

INGREDIENTS

1 tablespoon extra-virgin olive oil

½ small onion, chopped

2 celery stalks, chopped

2 teaspoons minced garlic

1 pound chopped root vegetables (such as red, purple, or sweet potatoes, or parsnips)

1 tablespoon curry powder

2 teaspoons ground turmeric

1 teaspoon red pepper flakes

¾ teaspoon ground mustard seeds

1 cup red lentils, rinsed and drained

One 15-ounce can crushed tomatoes in puree

One 13.5-ounce canned coconut milk

⅓ cup filtered water

1 bay leaf

Plain yogurt, for garnish

Chopped cilantro, for garnish

DIRECTIONS

1 Press *Sauté (High)* on the Instant Pot. Add the oil, onions, celery, and garlic. Cook for 7 minutes. Press *Cancel*.

2 Add in the root vegetables, curry powder, turmeric, red pepper flakes, mustard seeds, lentils, tomatoes, coconut milk, water, and bay leaf, and stir. Scrape the bottom of the metal pot insert to ensure no ingredients are sticking to the bottom.

3 Secure the lid and set the valve to *Sealing*. Press *Pressure Cook (Low)* and *Keep Warm (Off)* and set the timer to 8 minutes using the +/– button.

4 When cooking completes, press *Cancel*. Use *Quick Release* to remove the pressure.

5 Remove the lid and stir. Portion into bowls and garnish with yogurt and cilantro, as desired. Serve immediately.

TIP: Check out the freezer produce section! You can find a variety of root vegetable blends that are precut and washed for easy use in recipes.

VARY IT! Use green lentils instead of red, if you prefer.

Beefy Green Curry

Sauté/Pressure	Medium, High
6 min	Quick Release

Instant Pot function: Sauté (Medium), Pressure Cook (High), Keep Warm (On), Quick Release

PREP TIME: 5 MIN	COOK TIME: 6 MIN	YIELD: 4 SERVINGS

INGREDIENTS

2 tablespoons canola or vegetable oil

1 pound sirloin steak, thinly sliced

1 small onion, thinly sliced

2 cloves garlic, chopped

1 inch ginger, minced

½ teaspoon ground turmeric

½ teaspoon pepper

¼ teaspoon ground cumin

¼ teaspoon ground coriander

1 tablespoon fish sauce

1 tablespoon brown or palm sugar

One 14-ounce can coconut milk

½ cup vegetable stock

2 tablespoons green curry paste

½ cup canned bamboo shoots

½ cup sliced basil leaves

2 cups zucchini zoodles

1 lime, juiced

2 cups white rice

DIRECTIONS

1 Select *Sauté (Medium)* on the Instant Pot. Add the oil, steak, onions, garlic, ginger, and turmeric to the pot and sauté for 1 minute, stirring constantly. Press *Cancel*.

2 Add in the pepper, cumin, coriander, fish sauce, brown or palm sugar, coconut milk, vegetable stock, green curry paste, and bamboo shoots. Secure the lid and seal the venting.

3 Select *Pressure Cook (High)* and set the timer to 5 minutes using the +/− button. When the cooking has completed, do a *Natural Release* of the pressure for 8 minutes; then do a *Quick Release* to remove the remaining pressure.

4 Stir in the basil, zucchini noodles, and lime juice. Divide the white rice among 4 bowls and ladle the beef and green curry sauce over the top to serve.

NOTE: If you like curry to have a little kick of spice, add a jalapeño or a Thai pepper into the mix and finish off with a squirt of Sriracha.

VARY IT! For a low-carb version, replace the white rice with cauliflower rice or double the zucchini noodles.

Chana Masala

| Sauté/Pressure | High |
| 41 min | Natural Release |

Instant Pot function: Sauté (High), Pressure Cook (High), Keep Warm (Off), Natural Release

Fits diets: Gluten-Free, Mediterranean, Vegan, Vegetarian

| PREP TIME: 5 MIN | COOK TIME: 41 MIN | YIELD: 4 SERVINGS |

INGREDIENTS

2 teaspoons extra-virgin olive oil

½ medium onion, chopped

2 celery stalks, chopped

1 teaspoon minced garlic

1½ cups mini potatoes, quartered

1 jalapeño, seeded and diced

¼ cup tomato paste

¾ teaspoon ground turmeric

¾ teaspoon ground ginger

¾ teaspoon ground mustard seed

¾ teaspoon ground black pepper

1½ teaspoons ground coriander

1½ teaspoons garam masala

¼ teaspoon salt

3 cups filtered water

1 cup dried chickpeas, soaked and rinsed

Cucumber yogurt sauce, for garnish

Chopped cilantro, for garnish

DIRECTIONS

1 Press *Sauté (High)* on the Instant Pot. Add the oil, onion, celery, garlic, and potatoes to the metal pot insert. Cook 6 minutes, stirring frequently. Press *Cancel* when the cooking completes.

2 Stir in the jalapeño, tomato paste, turmeric, ginger, mustard seed, pepper, coriander, garam masala, salt, water, and chickpeas. Secure the lid and set the valve to *Sealing*. Press *Pressure Cook (High)* and *Keep Warm (Off)*, and set the timer for 35 minutes using the +/− button.

3 When cooking completes, do a *Natural Release* of the pressure for 10 minutes. Use *Quick Release* to remove any remaining pressure, and remove the lid.

4 Portion into bowls and garnish, if desired, with cucumber yogurt sauce and chopped cilantro.

TIP: Tight on time? Use canned chickpeas and adjust the time to 20 minutes on Pressure Cook (High), using a Quick Release. Stir in the canned chickpeas at the end and allow 5 minutes for them to warm from the temperature of the pot.

Sauté/Pressure | High
38 min | Quick Release

Madras Lentils

Instant Pot function: Sauté (High), Pressure Cook (High), Keep Warm (Off), Quick Release

Fits diets: Gluten-Free, Mediterranean, Vegetarian

PREP TIME: NONE	COOK TIME: 38 MIN	YIELD: 6 SERVINGS

INGREDIENTS

1 tablespoon extra-virgin olive oil

½ small onion, chopped

2 teaspoons minced garlic

1 tablespoon cumin

1 teaspoon garam masala

½ teaspoon cayenne pepper

One 14.5-ounce canned diced tomatoes

¼ cup tomato paste (chipotle in adobo)

1 cup lentils, rinsed, soaked, and drained

½ cup red kidney beans, rinsed, soaked, and drained

4 cups vegetable broth

Salt and pepper, to taste

Lavash squares, for garnish

Plain yogurt, for garnish

Chopped cilantro, for garnish

DIRECTIONS

1 Press *Sauté (High)* on the Instant Pot.

2 To the metal pot insert, add the oil, onions, and garlic. Sauté for 3 minutes. Then add in the cumin, garam masala, cayenne pepper, tomatoes, and tomato paste. Continue to stir. Press *Cancel.*

3 Stir in the lentils, kidney beans, vegetable broth, and water. Secure the lid and set the valve to *Sealing.* Press *Pressure Cook (High)* and *Keep Warm (Off),* and use the +/− button to set the timer to 35 minutes.

4 When cooking completes, use *Quick Release* to remove the pressure.

5 Portion into bowls and serve with lavash, yogurt, and cilantro, if desired.

TIP: These lentils make an excellent topping for baked potatoes, too.

VARY IT! If you prefer a spicier dish, use 2 finely diced canned chili peppers in adobo and 1 teaspoon of adobo sauce in place of the tomato paste.

| Sauté/Pressure | High |
| 9 min | Quick Release |

Buttered Chicken

Instant Pot function: Sauté (High), Pressure Cook (High), Keep Warm (Off), Quick Release

Fits diets: Gluten-Free, Keto

| PREP TIME: 5 MIN | COOK TIME: 9 MIN | YIELD: 4 SERVINGS |

INGREDIENTS

2 tablespoons butter

½ small onion, chopped

2 celery stalks, chopped

2 teaspoons minced garlic

1 pound boneless, skinless chicken breasts, thinly sliced

One 14-ounce canned tomato puree

2 tablespoons tomato paste

1 tablespoon garam masala

2½ teaspoons turmeric

2 teaspoons ground coriander

1 teaspoon chili powder

1 teaspoon ginger

½ teaspoon black pepper

¼ teaspoon salt

One 13.5-ounce can coconut milk

2 tablespoons cornstarch (optional)

1⅓ cups cooked brown rice, for serving

Fresh chopped cilantro, for garnish

Cucumber yogurt sauce, for garnish

DIRECTIONS

1 Press *Sauté (High)* on the Instant Pot. Add the butter to the metal pot and sauté the onion, celery, and garlic for about 3 minutes. Press *Cancel*.

2 Add the chicken, tomato puree, tomato paste, garam masala, turmeric, coriander, chili powder, ginger, pepper, salt, and coconut milk to the metal pot insert. Stir together. Secure lid and set the valve to *Sealing*.

3 Select *Pressure Cook (High)* and *Keep Warm (Off)*, and set the timer for 6 minutes using the +/– button.

4 When cooking competes, press *Cancel* and use *Quick Release* to remove the pressure.

5 Portion over brown rice and top with cilantro and yogurt sauce, if desired. Serve immediately.

NOTE: Refer to the Basic Brown Rice (Chapter 8) for a simple Instant Pot–friendly recipe to serve with the Buttered Chicken.

Chicken Tikka Masala

Sauté/Pressure	Medium, High
9 min	Natural Release

Instant Pot function: Sauté (Medium), Pressure Cook (High), Keep Warm (On), Natural Release

Fits diets: Gluten-Free

PREP TIME: 10 MIN	COOK TIME: 9 MIN	YIELD: 8 SERVINGS

INGREDIENTS

2 pounds boneless, skinless chicken thighs, cubed

1 cup whole-milk plain yogurt

2 tablespoons garam masala, divided

1 teaspoon cumin

¾ teaspoon ground turmeric, divided

½ lime, juiced and zested

1 teaspoon black pepper

¼ teaspoon ground ginger

1 tablespoon canola or vegetable oil

1 small onion, thinly sliced

3 cloves garlic, minced

¼ teaspoon paprika

1 cup chicken stock

One 15-ounce can tomato puree

½ cup heavy whipping cream

1 teaspoon salt

½ teaspoon pepper

Chopped cilantro, for garnish

DIRECTIONS

1 In a medium glass mixing bowl, stir together the chicken, yogurt, 1 tablespoon of the garam masala, cumin, ½ teaspoon of the turmeric, lime zest, lime juice, pepper, and ginger; set aside.

2 Select *Sauté (Medium)* on the Instant Pot, and add the oil and onions to the pot. Sauté for 3 minutes. Add in the garlic, the remaining 1 tablespoon of garam masala, paprika, and the remaining ¼ teaspoon of turmeric, and cook for 1 minute. Press *Cancel.*

3 Add in the chicken stock, tomato puree, and yogurt-marinated chicken, including all the yogurt marinade. Stir the chicken mixture. Secure the lid and seal the venting. Select *Pressure Cook (High)* and *Keep Warm (On).* Using the +/– button, set the timer to 5 minutes. When the cooking has completed, do a *Natural Release* of the pressure for 15 minutes before doing a *Quick Release* on the remaining pressure.

4 Stir in the heavy whipping cream and season with salt and pepper. Garnish with cilantro, if desired, and serve.

NOTE: If you receive a *BURN* message on your Instant Pot, release the pressure, add 1 cup of chicken stock, and try again.

TIP: Serve with steamed rice, roasted potatoes, flatbread, or naan plus a side salad or zucchini zoodles (spiralized raw zucchini).

| Sauté/
Pressure | High |
| 45 min | Natural
Release |

Beef Rouladen

Instant Pot function: Sauté (High), Pressure Cook (High), Keep Warm (On), Natural Release

| PREP TIME: 15 MIN | COOK TIME: 45 MIN | YIELD: 4 SERVINGS |

INGREDIENTS

1 pound top round, cut into 4 thin slices

1 teaspoon salt, divided

1 teaspoon black pepper, divided

½ teaspoon paprika

4 teaspoons Dijon mustard

4 slices bacon, cut into half across the center to make 8 slices

4 tablespoons dill pickle relish

2 tablespoons canola oil

1 large onion, diced

2 large carrots, diced

2 large celery stalks, diced

1 tablespoon tomato paste

1 cup beef stock

2 tablespoons cornstarch

2 tablespoons cold water

DIRECTIONS

1 Lay out slices of beef onto a cutting board. Using ½ teaspoon of the salt, ½ teaspoon of the pepper, and the paprika, season each piece of meat. Next, spread 1 teaspoon of Dijon mustard onto each piece. Top the mustard with 2 pieces of bacon on each. Next, place 1 tablespoon of pickle relish onto each rouladen. Roll up each rouladen like a burrito, tucking in the sides as you roll. Secure each rouladen with two toothpicks.

2 Set the Instant Pot to *Sauté (High)* and add in the canola oil. Brown the rouladens on all sides, about 2 minutes per side. Then remove the rouladens onto a plate.

3 Add in the onions, carrots, and celery, and sauté for 3 minutes, stirring constantly. Add the tomato paste and continue to sauté for 1 minute. Press *Cancel*.

4 Add in the beef stock and return the rouladens to the pan, nestling into the stock.

5 Secure the lid and set the valve to *Sealing*. Set the Instant Pot to *Pressure (High)* and *Keep Warm (On)*. Using the +/– button, adjust the timer to 20 minutes. Press *Hold Warm (On)*. When finished cooking, use *Natural Release* for 10 minutes before using *Quick Release*.

6 Remove the beef rouladens to a serving platter. Using a potato masher, mash up the cooked vegetables. Season with the remaining ½ teaspoon of salt and ½ teaspoon of pepper, to taste.

7 In a separate bowl, mix together the cornstarch and cold water. Stir the cornstarch slurry into the sauce, stirring for about 1 minute. Press *Sauté (High)* for an additional 3 minutes until bubbly. Serve the sauce over the rouladens.

Greek Meatballs

Pressure	High
15 min	Natural Release

Instant Pot function: Pressure Cook (High), Keep Warm (On), Natural Release

Fits diets: Gluten-Free, Low-Fat, Mediterranean

PREP TIME: 15 MIN	COOK TIME: 15 MIN	YIELD: 6 SERVINGS

INGREDIENTS

2 pounds lean ground beef

1 cup uncooked white rice

2 eggs, whisked

½ teaspoon cinnamon

1 teaspoon cumin

½ teaspoon coriander

1 teaspoon dried oregano

¼ cup chopped fresh mint leaves

4 cloves garlic, minced

1 teaspoon salt

1 cup chicken stock

4 cups spaghetti sauce

½ cup chopped parsley

½ cup green olives, chopped

Chopped parsley, for garnish

DIRECTIONS

1 In a large bowl, mix together the ground beef, white rice, eggs, cinnamon, cumin, coriander, oregano, mint leaves, garlic, and salt. Form into 1½-inch meatballs, about 24 meatballs.

2 Spray the bottom of the pan with cooking spray. Pour in the chicken stock. Place the trivet into the pot and arrange the meatballs on the trivet stacked on top of each other. (It's okay if they don't stay on the trivet.) Pour the spaghetti sauce over the meatballs and top with parsley and olives.

3 Secure the lid and seal the venting. Select *Pressure Cook (High)* and *Keep Warm (On)*. Using the +/– button, set the timer to 15 minutes. After the cooking has completed, do a *Natural Release* of the pressure for 10 minutes and do a *Quick Release* on any remaining pressure.

4 Pour out the contents into a serving bowl and remove the trivet. Top with chopped parsley and serve.

Sofritas Burritos

Sauté/ Pressure	High
7 min	Natural Release, Quick Release

**Instant Pot function: Sauté (High), Pressure Cook (High),
Keep Warm (Off), Natural Release, Quick Release**

Fits diets: Mediterranean, Vegan, Vegetarian

PREP TIME: 5 MIN	COOK TIME: 7 MIN	YIELD: 6 SERVINGS

INGREDIENTS

3 chipotle peppers in adobo sauce

1 tablespoon adobo sauce

2 tablespoons tomato paste

3 tablespoons extra-virgin olive oil, divided

1 tablespoon rice wine vinegar

½ cup filtered water

2 garlic cloves, roughly chopped

1 tablespoon ground oregano

2 teaspoons ground cumin

2 teaspoons smoked paprika

½ teaspoon ground black pepper

¼ teaspoon salt

16 ounces extra-firm tofu, pressed and cut into ½-inch squares

Six 8-inch whole-wheat tortillas

3 cups shredded lettuce

1 medium avocado, diced

DIRECTIONS

1 Add the chipotle peppers, adobo sauce, tomato paste, 2 tablespoons of the olive oil, rice wine vinegar, filtered water, garlic cloves, oregano, cumin, paprika, pepper, and salt to a food processor or blender. Pulse until smooth. Set aside.

2 Press *Sauté (High)* on the Instant Pot. Add the remaining 1 tablespoon of olive oil, and sauté the tofu for about 5 minutes. Press *Cancel*. Carefully mash the tofu using a potato masher directly in the metal pot until it has a crumbled consistency.

3 Pour the sauce from the blender over the tofu and stir. Cover and secure the lid. Set the valve to *Sealing*, and press *Pressure Cook (High)* and *Keep Warm (Off)*. Set the timer for 2 minutes using the +/– button.

4 When cooking completes, do a *Natural Release* of the pressure for 8 minutes. Then use *Quick Release* to remove any remaining pressure.

5 Assemble the burritos by placing tortillas down on a flat surface and topping with ⅓ cup sofritas, lettuce, and avocado. Fold the sides towards the center, roll, and serve.

TIP: Tight on time? Use 1½ cups of red enchilada sauce in place of the sauce in this recipe.

VARY IT! Prefer a less spicy sauce? Only use 2 chipotle peppers use ¼ cup tomato paste in place of the adobo sauce.

| Sauté/Pressure | High |
| 25 min | Quick Release |

Chicken Enchilada Casserole

Instant Pot function: Sauté (High), Pressure Cook (High), Keep Warm (Off), Quick Release

Special tools: 7-inch springform pan

Fits diets: Gluten Free, Mediterranean

| PREP TIME: 5 MIN | COOK TIME: 25 MIN | YIELD: 6 SERVINGS |

INGREDIENTS

2 teaspoons extra-virgin olive oil

½ small onion

1 teaspoon minced garlic

1 pound boneless, skinless chicken breasts, frozen

1 cup frozen chopped bell peppers

1 teaspoon ground cumin

½ teaspoon black pepper

One 28-ounce can mild red enchilada sauce

6 corn tortillas

1½ cups reduced-fat shredded Mexican cheese

1 cup filtered water

Avocado, for garnish

Greek yogurt, for garnish

Salsa, for garnish

Cilantro, for garnish

DIRECTIONS

1 Press *Sauté (High)* on the Instant Pot. Add the oil, onions, and garlic, and sauté for 3 minutes. Press *Cancel*. Stir in the chicken, bell peppers, cumin, and black pepper.

2 Select *Pressure Cook (High)* and *Keep Warm (Off)*, and set the timer for 10 minutes using the +/− button. Secure the lid and set the valve to *Sealing*. When cooking completes, do a *Quick Release* to release the pressure. Carefully pour the chicken and enchilada sauce mixture into a glass bowl and shred the chicken into the liquid. Set aside.

3 Rinse out the metal pot, dry the outside, and set back inside the Instant Pot. Spray a 7-inch springform pan with cooking spray.

4 Place 2 tablespoons of the enchilada sauce on the bottom of the springform pan, and then layer 1 tortilla and ¼ tortilla on the bottom so the entire base is covered. Top with ⅓ cup of the enchilada chicken mixture and cover with ¼ cup of cheese. Repeat 3 times until all the tortilla and enchilada chicken mixture is used. Pour the remaining enchilada sauce over the top and sprinkle with cheese. Cover with foil.

5 Add the water to the inner pot. Select *Pressure Cook (High)* and *Keep Warm (Off)* and set the timer for 12 minutes using the +/− function.

6 When cooking completes, use *Quick Release* to remove the pressure. Take off the lid and carefully remove the pan from the Instant Pot.

7 Let the casserole sit 20 minutes before releasing from the springform pan.

8 Slice and garnish with avocado, yogurt, salsa, and cilantro, as desired. Serve immediately.

TIP: Save extra enchilada sauce and make it a wet burrito by adding additional sauce to the top of your slice.

VARY IT! Prefer alternative meat? Try the Seasoned Pulled Pork (Chapter 10) for a new variety.

Sauté/Pressure | High
10 min | Quick Release

Cilantro Lime Fish Tacos

Instant Pot function: Sauté (High), Pressure Cook (High), Keep Warm (Off), Quick Release

Fits diets: Gluten-Free, Mediterranean

PREP TIME: 10 MIN	COOK TIME: 10 MIN	YIELD: 4 SERVINGS

INGREDIENTS

1 teaspoon garlic powder

1 teaspoon paprika

1 teaspoon salt, divided

¼ teaspoon ground black pepper

1 pound white fish (hoki), thinly sliced

1 bunch cilantro

2 limes, juiced

¼ cup extra-virgin olive oil, divided

¼ cup filtered water

Eight 4-inch corn tortillas

1 medium avocado, thinly sliced

1 cup shredded purple cabbage

½ cup fresh salsa

DIRECTIONS

1 In a medium bowl, mix the garlic powder, paprika, ½ teaspoon of the salt, and black pepper. Add in the fish. Use your hands to ensure the fish slices are nicely coated with the seasoning. Set aside and wash your hands.

2 To a blender, add the cilantro, lime juice, 3 tablespoons of the olive oil, the remaining ½ teaspoon of salt, and water. Pulse until smooth.

3 Press *Sauté (High)*. Add the remaining 1 tablespoon of oil to the metal pot insert and sauté the white fish for 2 minutes per side, or until lightly browned. Press *Cancel*.

4 Add in the cilantro sauce and mix, ensuring the fish is not stuck to the bottom of the pot.

5 Press *Pressure Cook (High)* and *Keep Warm (Off)*. Set the timer for 6 minutes using the +/− button.

6 When cooking completes, press *Cancel* and use *Quick Release* to remove the pressure from the pot.

7 Use tongs to remove the fish from the pot, and serve inside corn tortillas. Garnish with avocado, cabbage, and salsa.

NOTE: For a fun twist on a traditional white sauce, add a teaspoon of hot sauce to ½ cup of plain yogurt to make a spicy dressing for your tacos.

Simple Spanish Paella

Instant Pot function: Sauté (High/Medium), Pressure Cook (High), Keep Warm (On), Quick Release

Fits diets: Gluten-Free, Mediterranean

PREP TIME: 10 MIN	COOK TIME: 15 MIN	YIELD: 4 SERVINGS

INGREDIENTS

1 teaspoon paprika

½ teaspoon turmeric

½ teaspoon salt

¼ teaspoon pepper

¼ teaspoon saffron threads (a pinch)

¼ teaspoon cumin

2 tablespoons extra-virgin olive oil

1 small onion, finely chopped

1 medium red bell pepper, julienned or small dice

4 ounces Spanish chorizo, small dice

2 cloves garlic, minced

1 cup chicken stock

½ cup white wine

1 cup Arborio rice

1 pound raw shrimp, peeled and deveined

½ cup frozen peas

¼ cup green onions, thinly sliced

½ cup chopped parsley

DIRECTIONS

1 In a small bowl, mix together the paprika, turmeric, salt, pepper, saffron, and cumin; set aside.

2 Press *Sauté (High)* on the Instant Pot. Add the olive oil to the pot. Add the onion, bell pepper, and Spanish chorizo, and sauté for 3 minutes. Add the garlic and spice mixture, and continue to sauté for 1 minute. Add the stock and wine, stirring to scrape the bottom for 1 minute. Press *Cancel*.

3 Stir in the rice. Secure the lid and seal the venting. Select *Pressure Cook (High)* and *Keep Warm (On)*. Use the +/− button to set the timer to 6 minutes.

4 When cooking has finished, do a *Quick Release* to release the remaining pressure. Stir in the shrimp and peas. Select *Sauté (Medium)*, and cook until the shrimp turns pink, about 3 to 4 minutes. Press *Cancel*.

5 Top with green onions and parsley, and then serve.

VARY IT! You can use scallops instead of shrimp if you prefer. If you can't find Arborio rice, you can use basmati or jasmine instead.

Chapter 16

Getting the Party Started: Appetizers

Woo hoo! You have your Instant Pot, and now it's time to celebrate! Go ahead and throw a party, and make your Instant Pot the star. Instead of heading off to the grocery store for last-minute party food, you can pull together party favorites in just minutes!

This chapter is designed for those who love to throw a good party but can't spend all their time preparing food. As your guests arrive, set out a pot of Cheese Fondue with Jalapeños with fresh vegetables, or Southwestern Queso and chips. Then use another pot (because let's face it, you know you'll want to have two or three pots) for the Beefy Blue Cheese Sliders.

REMEMBER

These dishes aren't just meant for parties! You can enjoy them any time you want. But we encourage you to break out the party hats and celebrate your joy of the Instant Pot with all your favorite foodies!

Cheese Fondue with Jalapeños

Pressure	High
10 min	Quick Release

Instant Pot function: Pressure Cook (High), Keep Warm (Off), Quick Release

Special tools: Instant Pot–friendly casserole dish

Fits diets: Gluten-Free, Keto, Vegetarian

PREP TIME: 5 MIN	COOK TIME: 10 MIN	YIELD: 8 SERVINGS

INGREDIENTS

One 12-ounce can cheese soup

½ cup plain Greek yogurt

8 ounces shredded reduced-fat cheddar cheese

One 8-ounce canned diced jalapeño

½ teaspoon garlic powder

1 tablespoon yellow mustard

½ teaspoon paprika

¼ teaspoon ground black pepper

¼ teaspoon salt

1½ cups water

¼ cup chopped parsley, for garnish

Crusty bread, for serving

Tortilla chips, for serving

DIRECTIONS

1 In a medium bowl, mix the cheese soup, yogurt, cheddar cheese, jalapeño, garlic powder, yellow mustard, paprika, pepper, and salt. Pour into an Instant Pot–friendly casserole dish and cover tightly with foil.

2 Press *Pressure Cook (High)* and *Keep Warm (Off)*, and set the timer for 10 minutes using the +/− button.

3 Add the water to the base of the metal pot insert and place the metal trivet over the water. Position the pan on top of the trivet and secure the lid. Set the valve to *Sealing*.

4 When the cooking completes, press *Cancel*. Use *Quick Release* to remove the pressure.

5 Carefully remove the pan from the Instant Pot and discard the foil. Stir the cheese fondue one more time, and garnish with parsley.

6 Serve with crusty bread or tortilla chips, or use as a topping for tacos, nachos, or burgers.

TIP: If you prefer less-spicy foods, you can omit the jalapeños.

| Pressure | High |
| 15 min | Quick Release |

H's Peanut Butter Hummus

Instant Pot function: Pressure Cook (High), Keep Warm (Off), Quick Release

Special tools: Food processor or high-power blender

Fits diets: Gluten-Free, Mediterranean, Vegan, Vegetarian

PREP TIME: 5 MIN	COOK TIME: 15 MIN	YIELD: 8 SERVINGS

INGREDIENTS

1¼ cups filtered water, divided

½ cup garbanzo beans, presoaked and rinsed

3 tablespoons natural peanut butter

2 tablespoons extra-virgin olive oil

1½ tablespoons lemon juice

1 clove garlic, minced

¼ teaspoon ground black pepper

½ teaspoon salt

DIRECTIONS

1 Place 1 cup of the water and the garbanzo beans into the metal inner pot of the Instant Pot and secure the lid. Set the valve to *Sealing*.

2 Select *Pressure Cook (High)* and *Keep Warm (Off)*, and set the timer to 15 minutes using the +/– button.

3 When the cooking completes, press *Cancel* and use *Quick Release* to remove the pressure.

4 Carefully strain the water from the pot and add the garbanzo beans to a food processor or high-power blender.

5 Add the remaining ¼ cup of water, peanut butter, olive oil, lemon juice, garlic, pepper, and salt to the food processor or blender and pulse until smooth, about 1 minute. If the hummus is too thick to move the blade, add a teaspoon of water at a time.

6 Transfer to a serving bowl when ready to serve.

TIP: This hummus is great with apple slices, carrot ships, celery sticks, cucumber slices, and/or whole-grain crackers.

NOTE: Traditional hummus is made with tahini, a sesame seed paste that many often do not have in their pantries. This uses a pantry staple, natural peanut butter, to provide the creamy texture (and delicious taste) to the hummus!

Saute/Pressure — High

8 min — Quick Release

Southwestern Queso

Instant Pot function: Sauté (High), Pressure Cook (High), Keep Warm (On), Quick Release

Special tools: Pot-in-pot glass or metal 3-inch-deep Instant Pot–friendly baking dish

Fits diets: Vegetarian

PREP TIME: 5 MIN	COOK TIME: 8 MIN	YIELD: 10 SERVINGS

INGREDIENTS

2 tablespoons butter

2 tablespoons extra-virgin olive oil

One 10-ounce can tomatoes with green chilies

2 cloves garlic, chopped

1 cup water

1 pound American cheese, cubed

½ cup sharp cheddar cheese, grated

1 tablespoon lime juice

¼ teaspoon salt

¼ cup beer or chicken or vegetable stock

8 ounces cream cheese, cubed

Chopped cilantro, for garnish

Crumbled Cotija cheese, for garnish

Hot sauce, for garnish

DIRECTIONS

1 Select *Sauté (High)* on the Instant Pot, and add the butter, olive oil, and tomatoes with chilies. Sauté for 3 minutes. Add the garlic and sauté an additional 1 minute. Press *Cancel*. Place the mixture in an Instant Pot–friendly casserole dish.

2 Clean out the pot, rinsing and patting dry. Secure the pot and place the trivet in the bottom. Add the water to the pot.

3 Stir the American cheese cubes, grated cheddar cheese, lime juice, salt, beer or stock, and cream cheese into the casserole dish. Cover with foil and lower onto the trivet. Select *Pressure Cook (High)* and *Keep Warm (On)*. Adjust the timer to 4 minutes using the +/– button. Secure the lid and set the valve to *Sealing*.

4 After the cooking is complete, do a *Quick Release* and whisk the queso until smooth. Hold warm for serving and add hot water or beer as needed to thin out the sauce if it thickens.

NOTE: If you have fresh tomatoes on hand, you can use 4 medium tomatoes and a jalapeño instead of the canned variety.

| Pressure | High |
| 5 min | Quick Release |

Spinach and Artichoke Dip

Instant Pot function: Pressure Cook (High), Keep Warm (Off), Quick Release

Fits diets: Vegetarian

| PREP TIME: NONE | COOK TIME: 5 MIN | YIELD: 16 SERVINGS |

INGREDIENTS

One 13.75-ounce can quartered artichoke hearts in brine

One 10.5-ounce can reduced-sodium cream of chicken condensed soup

½ cup water

1 garlic clove, minced

½ teaspoon ground black pepper

8 ounces reduced-fat cream cheese

4 cups chopped spinach

6 ounces (about ⅔ cup) shredded Italian cheese blend

¼ cup fresh chopped parsley

DIRECTIONS

1 To the metal pot of the Instant Pot, add the artichoke hearts and cream of chicken soup. Add the water to the soup can, swirl to remove the soup from the side of the can, and add it to the pot.

2 Add the garlic, pepper, cream cheese, and spinach to the pot.

3 Secure the lid and set the valve to *Sealing*. Press *Pressure Cook (High)* and *Keep Warm (Off)*. Set the timer to 5 minutes using the +/– button.

4 When cooking completes, press *Cancel*. Use *Quick Release* to remove the pressure from the pot.

5 Add the cheese and stir. The heat from the pot will melt the cheese.

6 Carefully remove the pot and use a spatula to pour the dip into an oven-safe serving bowl. Serve immediately.

TIP: This dip goes well with tortilla chips, pita wedges, or crackers.

VARY IT! Use broccoli instead of spinach for a unique twist.

Pressure | **High**
10 min | **Quick Release**

Katie's Buffalo Chicken Dip

Instant Pot function: Pressure Cook (High), Keep Warm (Off), Quick Release

Special tools: 7-inch springform pan or Instant Pot–friendly casserole dish

Fits diets: Gluten-Free, Vegetarian

PREP TIME: 5 MIN | COOK TIME: 10 MIN | YIELD: 12 SERVINGS

INGREDIENTS

8 ounces reduced-fat cream cheese, softened

½ cup plain Greek yogurt

One 12-ounce canned chicken breast, drained

½ teaspoon garlic powder

¼ teaspoon ground black pepper

¼ cup buffalo hot sauce

4 ounces gorgonzola cheese

1½ cups water

½ cup chopped green onion

DIRECTIONS

1 In a large bowl, mix the cream cheese and yogurt. Add in the canned chicken, garlic powder, black pepper, and hot sauce; stir. Mix in the cheese and pour into a 7-inch springform pan. Cover tightly with foil.

2 Place the water on the bottom of the metal pot insert and insert the metal trivet. Position the pan on top of the trivet and secure the lid. Set the valve to *Sealing*.

3 Press *Pressure Cook (High)* and *Keep Warm (Off)*, and set the timer for 10 minutes using the +/– button.

4 When cooking completes, press *Cancel* and use *Quick Release* to remove the pressure. Remove the pan from the pot and let cool 5 minutes.

5 Discard the foil and portion the dip into a serving bowl. Garnish with chopped green onions.

TIP: This dip goes great with crackers and celery sticks.

NOTE: If you have leftover cooked chicken in the refrigerator, you can dice that up and use it in place of the canned chicken.

| Pressure | High |
| 20 min | Quick Release |

Smashed Potato Nachos

Instant Pot function: Pressure Cook (High), Keep Warm (Off), Quick Release

Special tools: Steamer basket, rimmed baking sheet

Fits diets: Gluten Free, Mediterranean, Vegetarian

| PREP TIME: 5 MIN | COOK TIME: 20 MIN | YIELD: 8 SERVINGS |

INGREDIENTS

1½ cups water

1 pound mini potatoes, washed

One 15-ounce can refried beans

8 ounces reduced-fat shredded cheddar cheese

1 medium avocado, mashed

½ teaspoon garlic powder

¼ teaspoon salt

¼ cup minced onion

½ cup diced tomatoes

½ cup fresh chopped cilantro

½ cup guacamole

½ cup plain Greek yogurt

½ cup salsa

1 jalapeño, thinly sliced

DIRECTIONS

1. Add the water to the metal inner pot of the Instant Pot, and place the steamer basket with the potatoes on top. Secure the lid and set the valve to *Sealing*. Press *Pressure Cook (High)* and *Keep Warm (Off)*, and set the timer for 12 minutes using the +/− button.

2. While the potatoes are cooking, preheat the oven to 425 degrees.

3. Press *Cancel* when the cooking completes and use *Quick Release* to remove the pressure.

4. Remove the potatoes from the pot and transfer to a rimmed baking sheet sprayed with cooking spray.

5. Using the back of a large fork or a meat tenderizer, smash each mini potato down vertically and then horizontally. Repeat until all potatoes are smashed on the baking sheet.

6. Top all the potatoes with refried beans and place the baking sheet inside the oven; bake for 8 minutes. After 6 minutes in the oven, remove the baking sheet and add the shredded cheese on top. Place the baking sheet back in the oven.

7. In a small bowl, mix the avocado, garlic powder, salt, onion, tomatoes, and cilantro. Set aside.

8. When the cooking completes, remove the baking sheet and top the potatoes with guacamole, yogurt, salsa, and jalapeño slices. Serve immediately from the baking sheet.

Potluck German Potato Salad

Instant Pot function: Sauté (High), Pressure (High), Keep Warm (On), Natural Release, Quick Release

PREP TIME: 4 HR 30 MIN	COOK TIME: 15 MIN	YIELD: 8 SERVINGS

INGREDIENTS

1½ cups water

2 pounds baby Yukon gold potatoes

1 cup beef stock

1 large onion, finely chopped

½ cup white wine vinegar or apple cider vinegar

2 tablespoons mustard

1 teaspoon salt

½ teaspoon pepper

¼ cup canola oil or sunflower oil

¼ cup chopped parsley, for garnish

DIRECTIONS

1   Place the water in the bottom of the Instant Pot, and then place the trivet in the bottom of the pot. Add the baby potatoes to the pot. Set to *Pressure Cook (High)* and set the timer using the +/– button to 8 minutes with *Keep Warm (On)*. Secure the lid and set the valve to *Sealing.* Allow a *Natural Release* for 10 minutes; then release the vent to do a *Quick Release* on the remaining pressure.

2   Drain off the water and allow the potatoes to cool just until safe to handle, about 10 minutes. Using a paring knife, peel the skins off the potatoes. Slice the potatoes into ¼-inch slices and place them into a large mixing or serving bowl.

3   Meanwhile, while the potatoes are cooling, start the beef stock. Place the beef stock, onions, vinegar, mustard, salt, and pepper into the Instant Pot. Press *Sauté (High)* and bring the stock to a boil, about 5 minutes; then turn off. Next, pour half of the stock mixture over the potatoes and stir to coat. Allow the potatoes to absorb the stock for 10 minutes. Then repeat with the remaining hot stock. Allow the potatoes to rest for 30 minutes.

4   Add in the oil and stir well. Allow the potato salad to refrigerate at least 4 hours before serving. Before serving, sample and add more vinegar and oil, as desired.

5   Garnish with fresh chopped parsley and serve at room temperature.

NOTE: Use potatoes about 2 inches in size, and try to keep the potatoes uniform in size so that they completely cook under pressure. If you're using slightly larger potatoes, check for doneness and, if needed, cook under pressure for an additional 2 minutes. This recipe won't work as well with new potatoes, so be sure to look for golden potatoes.

Sauté/ Pressure	High
1 hr 5 min	Natural Release, Quick Release

Beefy Blue Cheese Sliders

Instant Pot function: Sauté (High), Pressure Cook (High), Keep Warm (On), Natural Release, Quick Release

PREP TIME: 10 MIN	COOK TIME: 1 HR 5 MIN	YIELD: 16 SERVINGS

INGREDIENTS

3 to 4 pounds beef chuck roast

1½ teaspoons salt

1 teaspoon pepper

1 medium onion, chopped

1 teaspoon onion powder

1 teaspoon paprika

2 teaspoons garlic powder

1 teaspoon dried thyme

2 teaspoons dried oregano

2 teaspoons beef bouillon

2½ cups beef stock

1 cup Coca-Cola

2 tablespoons low-sodium soy sauce

2 tablespoons Worcestershire sauce

2 tablespoons cornstarch

2 tablespoons cold water

16 French bread rolls, sliced in half

4 ounces crumbled blue cheese

DIRECTIONS

1 Season the beef chuck roast with salt and pepper. Place the beef roast into the inner pot of the Instant Pot. Add the onions, onion powder, paprika, garlic powder, thyme, oregano, and beef bouillon. Then add the beef stock, Coca-Cola, soy sauce, and Worcestershire sauce.

2 Secure the lid and set the valve to *Sealing*. Set to *Pressure Cook (High)* and set the timer to 60 minutes using the +/– button, with *Keep Warm (On)*. Allow a *Natural Release* for 15 minutes; then release the vent to do a *Quick Release* on the remaining pressure.

3 Remove the meat from the pot using tongs. Allow the meat to rest on the cutting board while you thicken the sauce.

4 In a small bowl, whisk together the cornstarch and water. Press *Sauté (High)* and whisk in the cornstarch slurry. Continue whisking until thickened, about 5 minutes. Press *Cancel*.

5 Thinly slice the meat. Broil the open sandwich rolls for 3 to 5 minutes. Top the toasted rolls with sliced meat and crumbled blue cheese on each. Serve with thickened dip.

TIP: If dipping at a party is too much, you can add the meat back into the thickened sauce and allow your guests to top their rolls with meat and cheese, as desired.

Chapter **17**

Beverages

The Instant Pot can take your party to a whole new level with the beverages in this chapter. If you're like us, and you love a good reason to gather friends and family together over the holiday season, you'll enjoy the seasonal favorites like the Hot Cocoa and Mulled Wine. Whether you're in the mood for something hot or cold, we've got you covered with these classic beverages made from the comfort of your own home!

TIP

When making beverages in the Instant Pot, if you're doing a *Quick Release* and you notice liquid escaping from the vent, go back to a *Natural Release* and try again in a couple minutes. If you're serving a warm beverage for a party, set your pot to *Keep Warm (On)* to keep the temperature just right.

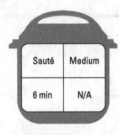

Sauté	Medium
6 min	N/A

Hot Cocoa

Instant Pot function: Sauté (Medium), Keep Warm (On)

Fits diets: Gluten-Free, Vegetarian

PREP TIME: 1 MIN	COOK TIME: 6 MIN	YIELD: 4 SERVINGS

INGREDIENTS

3 cups whole milk

1½ cups half-and-half

⅓ cup sugar

⅓ cup cocoa

1 teaspoon vanilla extract

Marshmallows, for garnish

Whipped cream, for garnish

DIRECTIONS

1 Pour whole milk, half-and-half, sugar, and cocoa into the Instant Pot, and select *Sauté (Medium)*. Whisk until the ingredients get hot, about 6 to 8 minutes. Press *Cancel*. Whisk in the vanilla extract.

2 Pour into 4 mugs and serve with marshmallows or whipped cream on top.

VARY IT! Add ⅛ teaspoon cinnamon for a Mexican-inspired cocoa.

| Pressure | High |
| 5 min | Natural Release |

Hot Apple Cider

Instant Pot function: Pressure Cook (High), Keep Warm (On), Natural Release

Fits diets: Vegan

| PREP TIME: 3 MIN | COOK TIME: 5 MIN | YIELD: 10 SERVINGS |

INGREDIENTS

8 cups unfiltered apple juice

1 orange, sliced in half around the equator

12 cloves

3 cinnamon sticks

¼ teaspoon ground cardamom

⅛ teaspoon grated nutmeg

1 inch fresh ginger

1 Granny Smith apple, quartered

Thinly sliced apples, for garnish

DIRECTIONS

1 Place the apple juice into the Instant Pot. Poke the cloves into the orange halves and place into the pot. Add the cinnamon sticks, cardamom, nutmeg, ginger, and quartered apple. Secure the lid and set the valve to *Sealing*. Select *Pressure Cook (High)* and *Keep Warm (On)*, and adjust the time to 5 minutes using the +/– button.

2 When the cooking is complete, do a *Natural Release* of the pressure for 3 minutes; then do a *Quick Release*.

3 Using a colander, strain the apple cider. Serve immediately or hold warm in the Instant Pot.

Warm White Russian

Instant Pot function: Pressure Cook (High), Keep Warm (Off), Quick Release

Fits diets: Gluten-Free, Vegetarian

PREP TIME: NONE	COOK TIME: 5 MIN	YIELD: 6 SERVINGS

INGREDIENTS

2 cups milk

½ cup half-and-half

1½ cups brewed coffee

1 teaspoon vanilla extract

4 ounces coffee liqueur

2 ounces vodka

Whipped cream, for garnish

DIRECTIONS

1 Add the milk, half-and-half, coffee, and vanilla extract to the metal inner pot of the Instant Pot. Whisk together. Then secure the lid and set the valve to *Sealing*. Press *Pressure Cook (High)* and *Keep Warm (Off)*, and set the timer to 5 minutes using the +/– button.

2 When cooking completes, press *Cancel* and use *Quick Release* to remove the pressure from the pot. Remove the lid and stir in the coffee liqueur and vodka.

3 Serve immediately with whipped cream, if desired. Keep warm by keeping the lid on top and turning the *Slow Cook* function on with a glass lid on top.

NOTE: If you prefer to use a plant-based milk, you can. Just make sure to use a coconut cream to replace the half-and-half so you still get the creamy fat.

Sauté	Medium
20 min	N/A

Mulled Wine

Instant Pot function: Sauté (Medium)

Fits diets: Vegetarian

PREP TIME: 3 MIN	COOK TIME: 20 MIN	YIELD: 10 SERVINGS

INGREDIENTS

12 cloves

1 orange, sliced in half around the equator

1 bottle (750 milliliters) red wine

2 cups apple juice

¼ cup honey or sugar

1 cup orange juice

2 cinnamon sticks

3 star of anise

Orange slices, for garnish

DIRECTIONS

1 Stick the cloves into the orange halves. Place the oranges, wine, apple juice, honey or sugar, orange juice, cinnamon sticks, and star of anise into the Instant Pot.

2 Select *Sauté (Medium)* and heat for 20 minutes, whisking occasionally.

3 Ladle the mulled wine into mugs and serve with an orange slice.

TIP: Use a bolder wine, like a Syrah or Malbec.

TIP: Hold mulled wine warm on the *Warm* setting.

Lemonade

Instant Pot function: Pressure Cook (High), Keep Warm (Off), Quick Release

Fits diets: Gluten-Free, Vegetarian

PREP TIME: 5 MIN	COOK TIME: 1 MIN	YIELD: 8 SERVINGS

INGREDIENTS

2 cups filtered water

6 lemons, zested and juiced

½ cup honey or sugar

2 cups ice

6 cups cold, filtered water

Lemon slices, for garnish

DIRECTIONS

1 Place the water, lemon zest, lemon juice, and honey or sugar into the Instant Pot and whisk. Secure the lid and set the valve to *Sealing*. Select *Pressure Cook (High)* and *Keep Warm (Off)* and, using the +/– button, set the timer to 1 minute.

2 When the cooking has completed, do a *Quick Release*. Whisk the concentrated lemonade. Using a cheesecloth or fine strainer, strain the lemon zest out of the lemonade concentrate.

3 Place the ice and cold water into a serving container. Next, add the lemonade concentrate to the water and ice, and stir to combine. Serve with fresh lemon slices.

VARY IT! Add a couple sprigs of lavender or rosemary for a fun spin on lemonade.

| Pressure | High |
| 1 min | Natural Release |

Herbal Tea

Instant Pot function: Pressure Cook (High), Keep Warm (On), Natural Release

Fits diets: Gluten-Free, Vegetarian

PREP TIME: 2 MIN	COOK TIME: 1 MIN	YIELD: 12 SERVINGS

INGREDIENTS

12 cups filtered water

8 herbal tea bags

½ cup honey or sugar

DIRECTIONS

1 Place the water, tea, and honey or sugar into the Instant Pot. Secure the lid and seal the venting.

2 Select *Pressure Cook (High)* and *Keep Warm (On)*. Using the +/− button, select 0 minutes. When the cooking has completed, do a *Natural Release* of the pressure for 5 minutes.

3 Pour into mugs and serve.

VARY IT! Use any variety or blend of herbal teas, such as chamomile, chai, raspberry, or mint.

Chapter **18**

Sweet Treats

However you feel about sweet treats, this chapter has a recipe that will work for you. Craving a slice of cheesecake, but watching your carbs? Check out the Low-Carb Cheesecake to satisfy that craving or stick with the carbs in our Key Lime Cheesecake with a spicy ginger crust. Or, do you want to simply enjoy a delicious, family favorite that uses your garden-fresh rhubarb? Grandma's Simple Rhubarb Crisp is for you!

We've put a whole lot of love into creating these recipes for you. And we believe good food becomes even better when you share it with those you care about, so consider spreading the wealth and sharing your creations with your loved ones! Life is better with dessert, and the Instant Pot helps deliver something sweet in just minutes.

Spiced Walnuts and Cashews

Sauté/Pressure	High
26 min	Quick Release

Instant Pot function: Sauté (High), Pressure Cook (High), Keep Warm (Off), Quick Release

Fits diets: Gluten-Free, Keto, Mediterranean, Vegan, Vegetarian

PREP TIME: NONE	COOK TIME: 26 MIN	YIELD: 12 SERVINGS

INGREDIENTS

¼ cup pure maple syrup

1 teaspoon vanilla extract

1 teaspoon ground cinnamon

1 teaspoon ground turmeric

½ teaspoon ground nutmeg

¼ teaspoon cayenne pepper

2 cups walnut halves, raw

1 cup cashews, raw

⅓ cup water

½ cup dried cranberries

2 tablespoons sesame seeds

½ teaspoon salt

DIRECTIONS

1 Press *Sauté (High)* on the Instant Pot. To the metal pot, add the maple syrup, vanilla, cinnamon, turmeric, nutmeg, and pepper. Stir and slowly add in the walnuts and cashews, and cook for about 4 minutes.

2 Press *Cancel*. Add the water, stir, and close the lid. Set the valve to *Sealing*, press *Pressure Cook (High)* and *Keep Warm (Off)*, and set the timer to 8 minutes using the +/− button. Meanwhile, preheat the oven to 300 degrees.

3 When the cooking completes, press *Cancel* and use *Quick Release* to remove the pressure.

4 Line a rimmed baking sheet with parchment paper and spray with cooking spray. Add the cranberries, sesame seeds, and salt to the pot, and combine with the nuts.

5 Spread the nut mixture onto the baking sheet. Place in the oven and bake for 8 minutes, stir, and then bake the remaining 6 minutes. Remove from the oven and let cool for 10 minutes. Serve.

NOTE: To make this recipe keto compliant, use 2 to 3 drops of monk fruit or stevia extract in place of the pure maple syrup.

TIP: Buy raw nuts from the bulk bins and store in the freezer for optimum freshness.

VARY IT! Use almonds and pecans for the nuts and swap in dried mango pieces for the cranberries.

| Pressure | High |
| 26 min | Natural Release |

Key Lime Cheesecake

Instant Pot function: Pressure Cook (High), Keep Warm (Off), Natural Release

Special tools: 7-inch springform pan

PREP TIME: 15 MIN	COOK TIME: 26 MIN	YIELD: 8 SERVINGS

INGREDIENTS

Two 8-ounce packages cream cheese

2 large eggs

¾ cup gingersnap cookies, crushed into fine crumbs

2 tablespoons unsalted butter, melted

¾ cup sugar

¼ cup Greek yogurt

2 limes, zested and juiced

1 teaspoon cornstarch

Fresh fruit, for garnish

Chopped nuts, for garnish

Lime curd, for garnish

DIRECTIONS

1 Set the cream cheese and eggs on the counter for 20 to 30 minutes to reach room temperature.

2 Meanwhile, in a medium bowl, mix together the cookie crumbs and melted butter.

3 Spray a 7-inch springform pan with cooking spray. Press the crumb mixture onto the bottom of the pan.

4 Beat the cream cheese and sugar on medium speed with a stand mixer or handheld mixer for 2 to 3 minutes until light and fluffy. Add in the yogurt, lime zest, and lime juice, and continue to mix 1 minute, scraping down the sides with a spatula to incorporate evenly. Add in the eggs and mix for another minute.

5 Pour the cheesecake batter into the pan. Tap the pan 4 times on the counter to release air bubbles. Cover the top with foil.

6 Add 1 cup of water to the Instant Pot. Insert the metal trivet over the water, and place the cheesecake pan on top. Secure the lid, press *Pressure Cook (High)* and *Keep Warm (Off)*, and set the timer to 26 minutes using the +/− button.

7 When finished, do a *Natural Release* of the pressure for 10 minutes. Press *Cancel* and remove the lid. Let the cheesecake rest for 10 to 15 minutes before removing from the Instant Pot. When it's cooled (about 30 minutes), set inside the fridge and loosely cover with a paper towel. Let set for at least 4 hours or overnight.

8 Serve cold with fresh fruit, chopped nuts, and/or lime curd drizzled on top.

Low-Carb Cheesecake

Pressure	High
30 min	Quick Release

Instant Pot function: Pressure Cook (High), Keep Warm (Off), Quick Release

Special tools: 7-inch springform pan

Fits diets: Gluten-Free, Vegetarian

PREP TIME: 15 MIN | **COOK TIME: 30 MIN** | **YIELD: 6 SERVINGS**

INGREDIENTS

Two 8-ounce containers Neufchâtel cream cheese

2 large eggs

⅔ cup plain 2 percent Greek yogurt

3 drops monk fruit extract

2 teaspoons vanilla extract

1 tablespoon fresh lemon juice

1 teaspoon lemon zest

¼ teaspoon salt

1 cup water

Fresh fruit, for garnish

Chopped nuts, for garnish

Chocolate syrup, for garnish

DIRECTIONS

1 Set the cream cheese and eggs on the counter for 20 to 30 minutes to reach room temperature.

2 After the cream cheese has reached room temperature, beat it on medium speed with a stand mixer or a handheld mixer until light and fluffy, about 2 or 3 minutes. Add in the yogurt and continue to mix for 1 minute, scraping down the sides with a spatula to incorporate evenly. Add in the eggs, vanilla, lemon juice, lemon zest, and salt. Mix for another minute.

3 Line a 7-inch springform pan with parchment paper and pour the cheesecake batter into the pan. Add the water to the Instant Pot. Insert the metal trivet over the water and place the cheesecake pan on top.

4 Secure the lid, press *Pressure Cook (High)* and *Keep Warm (Off)*, and set the timer to 30 minutes using the +/− button.

5 When finished, press *Cancel* and use *Quick Release* to release the pressure. Remove the lid. Let the cheesecake rest for 10 to 15 minutes before removing from the Instant Pot.

6 After the cheesecake has cooled (about 30 minutes), set inside the fridge and loosely cover with a paper towel. Let set at least 2 hours or overnight.

7 Serve cold with fresh fruit, chopped nuts, and/or chocolate syrup drizzled on top.

TIP: Use ⅓ cup powdered sugar instead of the monk fruit extract if you aren't trying to make this recipe keto compliant but you still want a lower-carb cheesecake.

Pressure | High

3 min | Natural Release

Quick Rice Pudding

Instant Pot function: Pressure Cook (High), Keep Warm (On), Natural Release

Fits diets: Gluten-Free, Mediterranean, Vegetarian

PREP TIME: 3 MIN	COOK TIME: 3 MIN	YIELD: 6 SERVINGS

INGREDIENTS

2 cups cooked white rice

3 cups whole milk

¼ cup sugar

¼ teaspoon cardamom

1 teaspoon vanilla extract

DIRECTIONS

1 Add the rice, milk, sugar, and cardamom to the inner pot. Secure the lid and set valve to *Sealing*. Select *Pressure Cook (High)* and *Keep Warm (On)* on the Instant Pot, and use the +/− button to set the timer to 3 minutes.

2 Do a *Natural Release* of the pressure for at least 20 minutes. Stir in the vanilla extract and allow the rice pudding to cool. As the rice pudding cools, it will thicken. Serve warm or cold.

NOTE: If you try to do a *Quick Release,* milk will splatter. Make sure you allow ample time for a *Natural Release* of pressure.

TIP: Top with fresh fruit for a simple breakfast option.

VARY IT! Replace the cardamom with cinnamon and nutmeg.

Dark Chocolate Zucchini Loaf Cakes

Instant Pot function: Pressure Cook (High), Keep Warm (Off), Quick Release

Special tools: Four 4-inch loaf pans

Fits diets: Mediterranean, Vegetarian

PREP TIME: 10 MIN	COOK TIME: 35 MIN	YIELD: 12 SERVINGS

INGREDIENTS

⅔ cup milk

1 teaspoon apple cider vinegar

1 cup all-purpose flour

⅔ cup whole-wheat flour

¾ cup dark cocoa powder

1½ teaspoons baking soda

½ teaspoon baking powder

¼ teaspoon salt

¾ cup cane sugar

⅓ cup plain Greek yogurt

2 tablespoons melted butter

2 teaspoons vanilla extract

2 large eggs

1 medium zucchini, skin removed and grated (about 1½ cups)

1½ cups water

¼ cup powdered sugar

Chopped nuts, for garnish

Raspberry sauce, for garnish

Whipped cream, for garnish

DIRECTIONS

1 In a small bowl or cup, whisk the milk and the apple cider vinegar together; set aside.

2 In a medium bowl, whisk the all-purpose flour, whole-wheat flour, cocoa powder, baking soda, baking powder, and salt; set aside.

3 In a large bowl, add and mix the sugar, yogurt, butter, vanilla, and eggs. Whisk in the milk and vinegar mixture, and gently fold in the zucchini.

4 Slowly add the dry mixture into the wet until all are uniformly combined.

5 Liberally spray four 4-inch loaf pans with cooking spray. Pour the batter into the pans and cover tightly with foil.

6 Place the water and metal trivet into the metal pot insert of the Instant Pot, and then place the pans on top of the trivet, two on the bottom and two in the opposite direction on top of the bottom two.

7 Press *Pressure Cook (High)* and *Keep Warm (Off)*, and set the timer for 35 minutes using the +/− button.

8 When cooking completes, do a *Natural Release* of the pressure for 10 minutes, and then use *Quick Release*.

9 Remove the pans from Instant Pot and discard the foil. Allow to cool for 5 minutes before removing the bread from the pans.

10 Place on a serving platter, sprinkle with powdered sugar, and serve with nuts, raspberry sauce, and/or whipped cream.

TIP: These cakes make excellent holiday gifts! Use aluminum pans, wrap with plastic wrap, and tie with a festive bow!

VARY IT! These cakes can easily be made into a cake shape. Use two 7-inch springform pans in place of the loaf pans. Layer with a whipped topping in between and top with fresh raspberries.

Cinnamon Walnut Monkey Bread

Instant Pot function: Sauté (High), Pressure Cook (High), Keep Warm (Off), Quick Release

Special tools: 7-inch springform pan

Fits diets: Vegetarian

PREP TIME: 15 MIN	COOK TIME: 39 MIN	YIELD: 8 SERVINGS

INGREDIENTS

½ cup brown sugar

2 tablespoons ground cinnamon

1⅓ cups all-purpose flour, divided

1 cup whole-wheat flour

2½ teaspoons baking powder

¼ cup finely chopped walnuts

⅓ cup butter, divided

⅓ cup plain 2 percent Greek yogurt

1 cup milk, divided

1 teaspoon vanilla extract

1 cup water

Powdered sugar, for garnish

DIRECTIONS

1 Spray a 7-inch springform pan with cooking spray and add the brown sugar and cinnamon to a large resealable bag. Set both aside.

2 In a medium bowl, add 1 cup of the all-purpose flour, the whole-wheat flour, the baking powder, and the walnuts. Using the backside of a fork or a pastry blender, add ¼ cup of butter to the flour. Add the Greek yogurt in the same way.

3 Combine ¾ cup of the milk with the vanilla extract; then slowly mix into the dough. The dough should be slightly sticky.

4 Place the remaining ⅓ cup of all-purpose flour on a large cutting board or pastry board, and add the dough to the center. Gently knead the dough with your hands for 5 minutes.

5 Punch down the dough and use a rolling pin to form dough into a 10-inch rectangle.

6 Cut the dough using a pizza cutter or knife into 1-inch pieces. Toss pieces into the resealable bag with the sugar and cinnamon mixture. Remove the dough pieces and evenly arrange in the springform pan. Do not discard the sugar and cinnamon that remains.

7 Press *Sauté (High)* on the Instant Pot, and set the timer to 4 minutes using the +/− button. Add the remaining butter, milk, and leftover sugar and cinnamon mixture to the pot. Stir until melted. Press *Cancel*.

8 Evenly pour the mixture over the top of the dough inside the pan. Cover the springform pan with foil, and set aside. Rinse the metal pot and dry the outside. Place back into the Instant Pot and add the water to the metal pot. Insert the metal trivet over the water and then place the springform pan on top.

9 Secure the lid and set the valve to *Sealing*. Press *Pressure Cook (High)* and *Keep Warm (Off)*, and set the timer to 35 minutes using the +/− button. When the cooking completes, press *Cancel* and use *Quick Release* to remove the pressure from the pot.

10 Carefully remove the pan from the pot and let cool for 5 minutes. Discard the foil.

11 Garnish with powdered sugar and serve.

Thai Rice Pudding with Mango Sauce

| Pressure | High |
| 17 min | Natural Release |

Instant Pot function: Pressure Cook (High), Natural Release
Special tools: Pot-in-pot metal bowl or casserole dish
Fits diets: Gluten-Free, Vegan, Vegetarian

PREP TIME: 10 MIN | **COOK TIME: 17 MIN** | **YIELD: 6 SERVINGS**

INGREDIENTS

1⅔ cups water, divided

1 cup Thai sticky rice or glutinous rice

1¾ cups full-fat coconut milk, stirred and divided

5 tablespoons sugar, divided

¾ teaspoon salt, divided

4 teaspoons cornstarch

2 teaspoons black sesame seeds, for garnish

1 cup chopped ripe mango

DIRECTIONS

1 Place 1 cup of water in the inner pot of the Instant Pot. Place the trivet into the pot.

2 Rinse the sticky rice under cold, running water until the water is clear, or soak the rice in water overnight and drain.

3 Place the rinsed sticky rice in a casserole dish and cover with the remaining ⅔ cup of water. Place the casserole dish onto the trivet and secure the lid. Set the valve to *Sealing*. Select *Pressure Cook (High)* and *Keep Warm (On)*, and use the +/− button to set the timer to 13 minutes.

4 After the cooking has completed, do a *Natural Release* of the pressure for 10 minutes before doing a *Quick Release*.

5 Meanwhile, in a small saucepan, heat 1 cup of the coconut milk over medium heat for 3 minutes. Whisk in 3 tablespoons of the sugar, ¼ teaspoon of the salt, and the cornstarch for 1 minute. Turn off the heat.

6 When the rice has finished cooking, transfer the rice to the saucepan, and mix with the coconut milk mixture. Transfer the sticky rice to a serving bowl and cover for 30 minutes or up to 2 hours at room temperature.

7 Add ½ cup coconut milk, the remaining 2 tablespoons of sugar, and the remaining ½ teaspoon of salt to a saucepan over medium heat, whisking until thickened.

8 Using a blender, blend the mango with the remaining ¼ cup coconut milk until smooth, about 2 minutes. Drizzle both of the sauces over the sticky rice and top with black sesame seeds.

Apple Pecan Maple Bread Pudding

Sauté/Pressure | High
25 min | Natural Release

Instant Pot function: Pressure Cook (High), Keep Warm (On), Natural Release
Special tools: 7-inch Instant Pot–friendly casserole dish
Fits diets: Vegetarian

PREP TIME: 5 MIN	COOK TIME: 25 MIN	YIELD: 8 SERVINGS

INGREDIENTS

1 Granny Smith or tart green apple, peeled and chopped

½ cup chopped pecans

2 large eggs, beaten

1½ cups whole milk

3 tablespoons brown sugar

⅓ cup real maple syrup

¼ teaspoon salt

¼ teaspoon cinnamon

⅛ teaspoon nutmeg

1 teaspoon vanilla extract

3 cups cubed day-old bread

1½ cups water

DIRECTIONS

1 In a medium mixing bowl, stir together the apple, pecans, eggs, milk, brown sugar, maple syrup, salt, cinnamon, nutmeg, and vanilla. Add in the cubed bread, and stir to mix.

2 Spray a casserole dish with cooking spray. Pour the bread pudding mixture into the casserole dish. Cover with foil.

3 Pour the water into the Instant Pot and place the trivet into the pot. Lower the casserole onto the trivet and secure the lid; set the valve to *Sealing*. Press *Pressure Cook (High)* and *Keep Warm (On)*, and use the +/− button to set the timer to 25 minutes.

4 When the cooking has completed, do a *Natural Release* of the pressure for 10 minutes before doing a *Quick Release* to release the remaining pressure. Serve immediately.

NOTE: Cut up stale bread and let sit overnight at room temperature for best results.

TIP: Serve with ice cream for a rich dessert or a dollop of vanilla yogurt for a sweet breakfast.

VARY IT! Add a tropical twist with chopped, dried mango and coconut flakes instead of apple and spice mixture.

Sautéed Peaches with Honey Ricotta

Sauté	High
8 min	N/A

Instant Pot function: Sauté (High)

Fits diets: Gluten-Free, Mediterranean, Vegan, Vegetarian

PREP TIME: 5 MIN	COOK TIME: 8 MIN	YIELD: 4 SERVINGS

INGREDIENTS

1 tablespoon butter

2 medium peaches, thinly sliced

1 teaspoon almond extract

½ teaspoon ground cinnamon

¼ teaspoon salt

1 cup ricotta cheese

1 tablespoon honey

¼ cup slivered almonds

DIRECTIONS

1 Press *Sauté (High)* on the Instant Pot and set the timer for 8 minutes using the +/– button. Add the butter to the metal pot and let it melt, using a spatula to move it evenly around the bottom of the pot.

2 Add the peaches and almond extract, tossing with the melted butter.

3 Stir in the cinnamon and salt.

4 When the peaches are soft (easily broken when a fork is inserted), press *Cancel*. Let cool 5 minutes.

5 Meanwhile, in a medium bowl, mix the ricotta cheese with the honey; set aside.

6 Portion the peaches into 4 serving dishes and top each with ¼ cup of the ricotta cheese and 1 tablespoon of the slivered almonds. Serve immediately.

NOTE: Check out the Ricotta Cheese recipe in Chapter 8 for a delicious, homemade variety.

VARY IT! Substitute vanilla extract for the almond and top with reduced balsamic vinegar.

Grandma's Simple Rhubarb Crisp

Instant Pot function: Pressure Cook (High), Keep Warm (On), Natural Release

Special tools: 7-inch casserole dish

Fits diets: Vegan, Vegetarian

PREP TIME: 10 MIN	COOK TIME: 8 MIN	YIELD: 6 SERVINGS

INGREDIENTS

4 cups diced rhubarb

½ cup sugar

1 large egg

1 cup plus 3 tablespoons flour, divided

¼ teaspoon cardamom

½ cup oats

½ cup brown sugar

½ teaspoon baking powder

¼ teaspoon salt

¼ cup unsalted butter, cut into slices

1½ cups water

DIRECTIONS

1. In a medium bowl, stir together the rhubarb, sugar, egg, 3 tablespoons of the flour, and the cardamom; set aside.

2. In another bowl, using your fingers, crumble together the remaining 1 cup of flour, oats, brown sugar, baking powder, salt, and butter until small, pea-size crumbs appear.

3. Spray a 7-inch casserole dish with cooking spray. Pour the rhubarb mixture into the casserole dish and top with the crumble mixture. Cover the casserole with foil.

4. Pour the water into the pot and lower the trivet. Lower the casserole dish onto the trivet and secure the lid, and set the valve to *Sealing*.

5. Select *Pressure Cook (High)* and *Keep Warm (On)* on the Instant Pot and use the +/− button to set the timer to 8 minutes.

6. After the cooking has completed, do a *Natural Release* of the pressure for 10 minutes.

7. Remove the foil and serve.

NOTE: If using frozen rhubarb, defrost and pat dry. Frozen rhubarb will add in more liquid to the dish.

TIP: Serve with yogurt for breakfast or ice cream for a delicious dessert.

VARY IT! Swap out rhubarb for tart apples or sour cherries, but decrease the sugar to 2 tablespoons in the filling.

Dark-Chocolate-Covered Strawberries

Sauté	High
20 min	N/A

Instant Pot function: Sauté (High), Keep Warm (On)

Fits diets: Gluten-Free, Keto, Mediterranean, Vegan, Vegetarian

PREP TIME: NONE	COOK TIME: 20 MIN	YIELD: 10 SERVINGS

INGREDIENTS

3 cups water

2 teaspoons coconut oil

12 ounces 60 percent or higher dark chocolate

20 large strawberries, washed and dried

½ teaspoon sea salt

Chopped nuts, for garnish

Crushed pretzel pieces, for garnish

DIRECTIONS

1 Add the water to the inner pot of the Instant Pot. Place a large glass bowl on top of the metal pot, acting as a double boiler.

2 Press *Sauté (High)* and set the timer for 20 minutes using the +/– button.

3 Add the coconut oil to the glass bowl and let it melt. Stir in the dark chocolate and continue to mix using a spatula until smooth.

4 When cooked, press *Cancel* and then *Keep Warm (On)* to keep the chocolate melted. Continue to occasionally mix if you're using as a self-service station.

5 Line a large baking sheet with parchment paper. Then take one strawberry at a time and dip it into the chocolate. Place the strawberries on a baking sheet, sprinkle with sea salt, and repeat for all the berries.

6 If topping with suggested garnishes, do so before the chocolate has cooled so they adhere to the chocolate.

7 Refrigerate until ready to serve.

VARY IT! Swap in your favorite fruit or chocolate!

Chapter 19

Baking and Sous Vide with the New Instant Pot

Go big or go home! That must be Instant Pot's slogan, because its newest pot has some *big* additions! Now you can fancy yourself a chef and use the skilled *sous vide* technique, which slowly infuses flavors deep into your food while it's submerged in water.

But wait, they didn't stop there! The newest model of the Instant Pot also has a special *Bake* feature. So, if it's hot outside but you're craving something sweet, you can satisfy that craving with a delicious cake without heating up your home!

Like traditional conventional oven baking, you can use your Instant Pot–friendly bakeware, set the recipe on the metal trivet, and let the pot do the rest! We recommend that you bake under pressure and finish with a little crisp in the customized *Bake* setting to keep time on your side, too.

In this chapter, we walk you through the differences between each setting. Now, sit back and enjoy your cup of coffee with a fresh-baked slice of Morning Glory Bundt Cake.

| Pressure/ Bake | Cake/ Custom |
| 40 min | Quick Release |

Morning Glory Bundt Cake

Instant Pot function: Pressure Cook (High), Keep Warm (Off), Quick Release, Bake (Custom)

Special tools: 7-inch Bundt cake pan

Fits diets: Mediterranean, Vegetarian

| PREP TIME: 5 MIN | COOK TIME: 40 MIN | YIELD: 10 SERVINGS |

INGREDIENTS

1 large egg

⅓ cup brown sugar

⅓ cup plain whole milk yogurt

½ cup plus 1 tablespoon milk, divided

1 teaspoon vanilla extract

¾ cup all-purpose flour

½ cup wheat bran

1 teaspoon baking soda

½ teaspoon baking powder

2 teaspoons ground cinnamon

¼ teaspoon salt

1 cup finely chopped shredded carrots

½ cup shredded coconut, sweetened, divided

¼ cup chopped nuts

¼ cup raisins

¼ cup seeds

1½ cups water

¼ cup powdered sugar

DIRECTIONS

1 In a medium bowl, whisk together the egg, brown sugar, yogurt, ½ cup of the milk, and the vanilla; set aside.

2 In a separate bowl, mix together the flour, wheat bran, baking soda, baking powder, cinnamon, and salt.

3 Slowly fold the dry ingredients into the wet. When combined, fold in the carrots, ¼ cup of the shredded coconut, the nuts, raisins, and seeds.

4 Spray an Instant Pot–friendly 7-inch springform pan with cooking spray. Pour in the batter and cover with aluminum foil. Place the metal trivet inside the pot and pour the water into the pot. Place the pan on top of the trivet, secure the lid, and set the valve to *Sealing*. Select the *Bake* function and use the knob to select the *Cake* setting; then press the knob in. Adjust the timer to 30 minutes, press the knob in, and then move on to adjusting the pressure. The pressure should remain on *High*, so press the knob in, make sure *Keep Warm* is turned *Off*, and then press *Start*.

5 When cooking completes, press *Cancel* and do a *Quick Release*. Carefully remove the pan from the pot and remove the foil. Discard the water and dry the metal pot; place the metal pot back inside the Instant Pot. Place the trivet inside.

6 Select the *Bake* function and use the knob to choose the *Custom* setting. Adjust the timer to 10 minutes. Press the knob in again. The pressure setting should appear. Turn the knob until *None* is selected. Then press the knob in again, and adjust temperature setting. It should read 347 degrees. Press the knob in and press *Start*.

7 When cooking has completed, press *Cancel*, remove the lid, and carefully remove the pan from the metal pot. In a small bowl, whisk together the remaining 1 tablespoon of milk and the powdered sugar. Drizzle over the Bundt cake and top with the remaining ¼ cup of coconut. Serve immediately.

TIP: Save time and buy shredded carrots!

Apple Crisp Under Pressure and Baked

Instant Pot function: Pressure Cook (High), Keep Warm (Off), Quick Release, Bake (Custom)

Special tools: 7-inch casserole dish

Fits diets: Mediterranean, Vegetarian

PREP TIME: 10 MIN	COOK TIME: 18 MIN	YIELD: 6 SERVINGS

INGREDIENTS

3 large Granny Smith apples, peeled and chopped

1 tablespoon unsalted butter, melted

2 tablespoons flour

2 tablespoons milk

1 teaspoon vanilla extract

3 tablespoons brown sugar

½ teaspoon cinnamon

¼ teaspoon salt

½ cup flour

½ cup oats

⅓ cup brown sugar

½ teaspoon baking powder

5 tablespoons unsalted butter, sliced

1 cup water

DIRECTIONS

1 In a medium bowl, add the apples, melted butter, flour, milk, vanilla extract, brown sugar, cinnamon, and salt. Stir to combine.

2 In a separate bowl, using your fingers or a pastry blender, mix together the flour, oats, brown sugar, baking powder, and sliced butter. Mix until you get tiny, pea-size butter crumbs.

3 Spray an Instant Pot–friendly casserole dish with cooking spray. Pour in the apple mixture and top with the flour mixture. Pour the water into the inner pot of the Instant Pot and place the trivet inside. Cover the pan with foil and lower onto the trivet. Secure the lid and set the valve to *Sealing*. Select *Pressure Cook (High)* and *Keep Warm (Off)* and use the knob to set the time to 8 minutes. Press *Start*.

4 When the cooking has completed, press *Cancel* and do a *Quick Release*. Remove the apple crisp and the foil. Dump the water and place the trivet in the inner pot again. Select *Bake* and use the knob to choose the *Custom* function. Adjust the time to 10 minutes. Press the knob in, and then adjust the pressure. Select *None*, and then press the knob in again. Adjust the temperature to 347 degrees. Place the apple crisp on the trivet. Secure the lid and keep the venting open. Press *Start*.

5 When the cooking has completed, press *Cancel* and remove the crisp from the pot. Serve immediately.

TIP: Serve with a scoop of ice cream for dessert or a dollop of yogurt for breakfast.

NOTE: When using the *Bake* function, the valve should always be opened, not sealed, so steam escapes while baking.

Sugar Cookie Pizookie

Pressure/ Bake	High/ Custom
25 min	Quick Release

Instant Pot function: Pressure Cook (High), Keep Warm (Off), Quick Release, Bake (Custom)

Special tools: 7-inch springform pan

Fits diets: Vegetarian

PREP TIME: 10 MIN	COOK TIME: 25 MIN	YIELD: 6 SERVINGS

INGREDIENTS

⅓ cup butter

¼ cup plus 1 tablespoon packed brown sugar

1 large egg

½ teaspoon vanilla extract

1 cup all-purpose flour

½ teaspoon baking powder

¼ teaspoon baking soda

¼ teaspoon salt

1 cup water

¼ cup powdered sugar

1 tablespoon milk

DIRECTIONS

1 In a medium bowl, use a hand mixer to mix together the butter, sugar, egg, and vanilla.

2 In a small bowl, mix the flour, baking powder, baking soda, and salt. Slowly add the dry ingredients into the wet, and mix until combined.

3 Spray an Instant Pot–friendly 7-inch springform pan with cooking spray. Pour in the cookie dough and cover with aluminum foil. Place the metal trivet inside the pot, pour in the water, and place the pan on top. Secure the lid and set the valve to *Sealing*.

4 Select *Pressure Cook (High)* and *Keep Warm (Off)*, and use the knob to adjust the time to 15 minutes. Then press *Start*.

5 When cooking completes, press *Cancel* and do a *Quick Release*. Carefully remove the pan from the pot and remove the foil. Discard the water and dry the metal pot. Place the pot back inside the Instant Pot. Place the trivet inside.

6 Select the *Bake* function and use the knob to choose the *Custom* setting. Adjust the time to 10 minutes. Press the knob in again. The pressure setting should appear. Turn the knob until *None* is selected. Then press the knob in again, and adjust the temperature setting. It should read 347 degrees. Press the knob in and press *Start*.

7 When the cooking has completed, press *Cancel*, remove the lid, and carefully remove the pan from the metal pot.

8 In a small bowl, whisk together the powdered sugar and milk, and drizzle over the cookie. Serve immediately.

Lemon Olive Oil Cake

Instant Pot function: Pressure Cook (High), Keep Warm (Off), Quick Release, Bake (Custom)

Special tools: 7-inch springform pan

Fits diets: Mediterranean, Vegetarian

PREP TIME: 5 MIN	COOK TIME: 40 MIN	YIELD: 8 SERVINGS

INGREDIENTS

½ cup extra-virgin olive oil

½ cup plus 1 tablespoon cane sugar

2 large eggs

⅔ cup plus 1 tablespoon milk, divided

1 teaspoon vanilla extract

3 tablespoons fresh lemon juice

1½ cups all-purpose flour

1½ teaspoons baking powder

¼ teaspoon salt

1½ cups water

¼ cup powdered sugar

2 tablespoons fresh lemon zest

DIRECTIONS

1 In a medium bowl, whisk together the olive oil, sugar, eggs, ⅔ cup of the milk, vanilla, and lemon juice.

2 In a separate bowl, mix together the flour, baking powder, and salt.

3 Slowly fold the dry ingredients into the wet ingredients.

4 Spray an Instant Pot–friendly 7-inch springform pan with cooking spray. Pour in the cake batter and cover with aluminum foil. Place the metal trivet inside the pot and pour the water into the metal pot. Place the pan on top of the trivet, secure the lid, and set the valve to *Sealing.*

5 Select the *Bake* function and use the knob to choose the *Cake* setting; then press the knob in. Adjust the time to read 30 minutes, press the knob in, and then move on to adjusting the pressure. The pressure should remain on *High*, so press the knob in, make sure *Keep Warm* is turned *Off*, and then press *Start.*

6 When the cooking completes, press *Cancel* and do a *Quick Release.* Carefully remove the pan from the pot and remove the foil. Discard the water; dry the metal pot and place it back inside the Instant Pot. Place the trivet inside.

7 Select the *Bake* function and use the knob to choose the *Custom* setting. Adjust the time to read 10 minutes. Press the knob in again. The pressure setting should appear. Turn the knob until *None* is selected. Then press the knob in again, and adjust the temperature setting. It should read 347 degrees. Press the knob in and press *Start*.

8 While cooking, prepare the glaze by mixing the remaining 1 tablespoon of milk, powdered sugar, and lemon zest in a small bowl.

9 When the cooking has completed, press *Cancel*, remove the lid, and carefully remove the pan from the metal pot. Let the cake cool 5 to 10 minutes; then drizzle with powdered sugar glaze and serve immediately.

NOTE: If you prefer a sweeter cake, increase the cane sugar to ¾ cup.

Fudgy Baked Brownies

Bake | Cake/Custom
35 min | Quick Release

Instant Pot function: Pressure Cook (High), Keep Warm (Off), Quick Release, Bake (Custom)

Special tools: 7-inch springform pan

Fits diets: Vegetarian

PREP TIME: 10 MIN	COOK TIME: 35 MIN	YIELD: 12 SERVINGS

INGREDIENTS

¼ cup coconut oil

⅓ cup plus 1 tablespoon cane sugar

1 large egg

2 tablespoons milk

1 teaspoon vanilla extract

1 cup all-purpose flour

1 teaspoon baking powder

⅓ cup plus 1 tablespoon dark cocoa powder

¼ teaspoon salt

⅓ cup mini chocolate chips

1½ cups water

DIRECTIONS

1 In a medium bowl, mix together the coconut oil, sugar, egg, milk, and vanilla.

2 In a small bowl, mix the flour, baking powder, cocoa powder, and salt. Slowly add the dry ingredients into the wet, and mix until combined. Fold in the chocolate chips.

3 Spray an Instant Pot–friendly 7-inch springform pan with cooking spray. Pour in the brownie batter and cover with aluminum foil. Place the metal trivet inside the pot and pour the water into the metal pot. Place the pan on top of the trivet, secure the lid, and set the valve to *Sealing*.

4 Select the *Bake* function, and use the knob to choose the *Cake* setting. Press the knob in. Next, adjust the time to read 25 minutes, press the knob in, and then move on to adjusting the pressure. The pressure should remain on *High*, so press the knob in, make sure *Keep Warm* is turned *Off*, and then press *Start*.

5 When cooking completes, press *Cancel* and do a *Quick Release*. Carefully remove the pan from the pot and remove the foil. Discard the water and dry the metal pot. Place the pot back inside the Instant Pot. Place the trivet inside.

6 Select the *Bake* function and use the knob to choose the *Custom* setting. Adjust the time to read 10 minutes. Press the knob in again. The pressure setting should appear. Turn the knob until *None* is selected. Then press the knob in again, and adjust the temperature setting. It should read 347 degrees. Press the knob in and press *Start.*

7 When the cooking has completed, press *Cancel,* remove the lid, and carefully remove the pan from the metal pot. Serve immediately.

NOTE: If you're looking for a gluten-free brownie, use almond flour instead of all-purpose flour and use almond extract instead of vanilla extract.

Sous Vide Shrimp Salad Sandwiches

Sous Vide	130°F
1 hr	N/A

Instant Pot function: Sous Vide

Special tools: Resealable plastic bag or *sous vide* bag

PREP TIME: 10 MIN	COOK TIME: 1 HR	YIELD: 4 SERVINGS

INGREDIENTS

4 quarts water

1 pound shrimp, peeled and deveined

2 cloves garlic, minced

2 tablespoons butter, melted

2 tablespoons extra-virgin olive oil

1 tablespoon chopped fresh dill

1 teaspoon salt

¼ cup finely chopped red onion

½ cup finely chopped celery

1 small carrot, grated

⅓ cup mayonnaise

1 teaspoon white wine vinegar

¼ teaspoon black pepper

2 tablespoons chopped fresh dill

4 brioche rolls, cut in half lengthwise and toasted

DIRECTIONS

1 Add the water to the inner pot of the Instant Pot. Select the *Sous Vide* function. Then use the knob to select the *Seafood* function. Press the knob in and adjust the temperature to 130 degrees. Twist the knob again to adjust the time to 1 hour. This will allow the water to begin heating as you prepare the recipe.

2 In a resealable plastic bag or *sous vide* bag, place the shrimp, garlic, butter, olive oil, dill, and salt. Seal the bag.

3 Immerse the bag in water to remove the air bubbles from the bag and follow the water immersion method described in Chapter 2. Make sure the water is below the max fill line, and remove any excess if needed.

4 Secure the lid and keep the venting open. Press *Start.*

5 When the cooking has completed, use tongs to remove the bag from the water. Remove the shrimp from the bag and place the shrimp on a cutting board. Allow the shrimp to rest for 5 minutes.

6 Chop the shrimp into small, bite-size pieces. Place the shrimp in a mixing bowl. Add the onion, celery, carrot, mayonnaise, white wine vinegar, pepper, and dill. Stir to combine.

7 Chill the shrimp salad for 2 hours prior to serving to allow the flavors to combine. Serve on toasted brioche rolls.

NOTE: If using frozen shrimp, defrost under cold running water prior to using.

VARY IT! Go with a Moroccan flair by adding in ½ teaspoon curry powder.

4

The Part of Tens

Chapter **20**

Ten Tips for Making the Most of Your Instant Pot

A wise person once said, "Practice makes perfect." And that saying couldn't be more true for learning how to successfully (and consistently) use your Instant Pot. In this chapter, we provide ten tips you can practice in order to get the most out of your Instant Pot.

Cleaning Your Instant Pot

Sounds simple, right? It is, but honestly not being sure how to clean the Instant Pot is one of the top reasons people haven't used their Instant Pots yet! Here's how to clean your pot:

1. **Take the pot out of the box.**

   Every journey begins with a single step.

2. **Wash the inner pot, trivet, lid, and sealing ring with dish detergent (or run them through the dishwasher — they're dishwasher safe!).**

3. **Make sure the outer edges and bottom of the metal pot are dry before inserting it into the Instant Pot to begin cooking.**

Voilà! You're ready to make your first Instant Pot recipe!

Some people don't use their Instant Pots consistently because of the odor that lingers after making something, like a roast. Don't worry, we've felt that way before, too. But the smell won't last forever! And if you follow the deep-cleaning tips in Chapter 21, the smell will disappear in less than 10 minutes.

Our suggestion is to follow the meal plan guide (see Chapter 7) and prep all your savory items at once. Then deep clean your Instant Pot and make your sweet dishes. Easy-peasy!

Keeping Your Instant Pot Out

If you're one of those people who insist on having a bare countertop, this tip may not suit you. But hear us out! The old adage "out of sight, out of mind" is especially relevant when you're not used to using a new tool or piece of equipment. Sure, you can store your toaster in a cupboard because you've been making toast since you were a kid. But you've probably been cooking for years without an Instant Pot, so you may forget you even have it if it's buried in the back of the cupboard behind those three blenders you were given when you got married. We want you to *see* the Instant Pot and be reminded to use it! If you do, it'll soon become your favorite kitchen gadget, and then you'll wonder how you ever lived without it.

Starting Simple

As tempting as it can be to skip ahead in chapters and jump-start your Instant Pot journey with a whole meal, we recommend taking it slow. If you've never used your Instant Pot before, try a few of the basic recipes in Chapter 8 first. Get familiar with the functions of the pot before barreling ahead with something more complicated. You crawled before you walked, and you walked before you ran. If you try something super-complicated right off the bat, you may feel frustrated and give up. And you don't want to be crawling the rest of your life!

Exploring the Functions of Your Instant Pot

With the Instant Pot, you can now throw away all those bulky gadgets like your rice cooker and slow cooker. Talk about freeing up kitchen space — that is, until you decide to buy two or three Instant Pots, like we've done! Why? Because these compact pots are multifunctional and ease our stress in the kitchen.

From rice and beans to your slow-cooking needs, the Instant Pot can do it better and faster. We get it: It's tempting to only use the pot for pressure cooking, but by doing so you're really missing out on all the multifunctional fun you could be having, from cocktails to yogurt to one-pot wonders!

On any given night, we may cook rice first, then make a dish like Beefy Green Curry (Chapter 15), and then clean it up and cook yogurt overnight for the next morning. *Multitask* is the Instant Pot's middle name!

Feeling Confident with Your Instant Pot

REMEMBER

We get it — high-pressure cooking may not be familiar to you. But when you get the hang of it, you'll be pleasantly surprised at just how enjoyable it is. So, consider these tips:

>> Always ensure your venting is in the correct position.

>> Watch your hands and face when releasing the pressure from your pot.

>> Don't force the lid open if all the pressure is not out.

>> Be sure the lid is securely locked in place while cooking.

>> Have a towel handy to cover the top when releasing the pressure.

>> Don't overfill the pot — observe the fill lines!

>> Liquid is necessary, so be sure there's always a minimum of 1 cup of liquid in the pot.

>> Place the pot away from cupboards while cooking to avoid moisture seeping into the wood.

Finally, approach your Instant Pot with confidence! When you're using it regularly, these reminders will stay fresh in your mind.

Trying One New Recipe per Week

Shake things up a bit! As registered dietitian nutritionists, we often hear what holds people back from continuing a healthy lifestyle is the feeling of boredom that comes with the standard roasted vegetables and flavorless meat they think they need to eat. But that's not the case at all!

Choose one new recipe to make in your Instant Pot a week. Starting with one recipe per week will help keep it manageable and remind you how amazing the Instant Pot really is when it comes to creating a healthy lifestyle for you (and your family!).

Starting with something simple like the Salsa Verde Shredded Chicken (see Chapter 10) will help demonstrate the ease and simplicity that the Instant Pot can provide, in addition to the delicious and flavorful source of protein. Plus, you can use that chicken and try out one of our ten tips to carry over pulled meats (see Chapter 22) for meals throughout the week!

Comparing Recipes

Who wants to be starving for dinner and end up having to get takeout instead? Not us, and we don't want that for you either. So, shop before you chop! In other words, take time to look around at different recipes before trying a new one. If you have an idea of a recipe you'd like to try and you can't find it in our book, go online and compare recipes or look at a variety of cookbooks before trying a recipe. Yes, there are some trusted bloggers, and if you find one you love that's a bonus.

REMEMBER

Bottom line: Success with the pot is what will keep you coming back day after day, so be selective when menu planning and recipe testing.

Shopping the Sales

We firmly believe consistency and affordability go hand in hand. That's why we include *Vary It!* options in many of the recipes so you feel comfortable and encouraged to venture out of the rigid recipe guidelines and come up with your own variations.

We do this all the time, and frankly, it's because we shop the sales. Shopping the weekly ad at your local market helps keep your budget in check.

Say, for instance you've flagged Chapter 11 as quick and convenient recipes you'd like to try out, and you notice lean beef is on sale. Stocking up on beef allows you the flexibility to use your Instant Pot and create your own variation of the Korean Beef Bulgogi Bowl.

TIP

Having this game plan mentally in your head as you shop the sales cultivates a mind-set of consistency, allowing you to succeed at successfully using your Instant Pot more regularly.

Investing in Accessories

We're both pretty minimalistic in our kitchens. We're pretty savvy when it comes to using what came with our initial Instant Pot purchases. But then we fell in love with the variety of recipes you can create in the Instant Pot and we knew we had to invest in a few accessory staples.

In Chapter 4, we outline the many Instant Pot accessories you can purchase. For instance, the 7-inch springform pan has quickly become our pot's best friend! We use it for everything from savory dishes like Nonna's Lasagna (Chapter 15) to the delicious Cinnamon Walnut Monkey Bread (Chapter 18) that will joyfully wake a house with its sweet aroma on a Sunday morning.

Because every cook is unique in what sparks his or her culinary interest, we won't say, "Buy X instead of Y." Instead, we encourage you to find those recipes that light your passion in the kitchen and consider purchasing the accessories you need to make them come to life. Part of what keeps people in their kitchens consistently is having a fire inside them, so harness that energy and use it to blow some steam (or allow your Instant Pot to blow the steam for you!).

Buying Extra Basics

If you've got some extra kitchen space, you may want to consider investing in a second sealing ring and/or metal pot insert. It's sort of like your Tupperware drawer — you don't necessarily wash the same container multiple times a day to store things in, but you consistently use them, right?

Same thing goes for your Instant Pot. You're more apt to use your Instant Pot if you don't have to wait for the dishwasher cycle to run from the recipes you made the night before. If you have a second, you can whip up a batch of Hard-Boiled Eggs (Chapter 8) before work in the morning for a nourishing, protein-packed way to start your day.

Plus, this tip goes hand in hand with cleaning your pot! Having a second sealing ring allows you to use one for sweet recipes and the other for savory recipes, eliminating any potential for the residual smell that can be absorbed by the material.

Chapter **21**

Ten (or So) Tips to Care for Your Instant Pot

on't you hate it when you feel like you're continually buying the same new appliance year after year at those Black Friday sales? We do, too! That's why we can promise you this: If you care for your Instant Pot correctly, it'll stay with you long into the future.

In this chapter, we cover how to clean your Instant Pot to keep it smelling like new. We also share a few tips and tricks we've picked up along the way.

Cleaning Your Instant Pot

Have you noticed the stainless-steel exterior that your pot is so elegantly housed in? This exterior is easily washable with a kitchen towel and dish soap, but be sure to keep the base out of water.

TIP

If you take the time to wash off the pot's exterior and any residue every time you use it, you won't have to scrub too hard. Plus, you'll have a shiny appliance that is appealing to the eye (which means you won't have to hide it in a cabinet where it never gets used).

In addition to this basic, every-time-you-use-it cleaning, you should perform a deep clean after every 10 to 15 uses. To perform a safe, chemical-free deep clean, follow these steps for a 6-quart Instant Pot:

1. **In the metal pot of the Instant Pot, add 1 cup of distilled vinegar, 1 cup of water, and the juice of one citrus fruit (like a lemon or orange). Mix well.**

2. **Place the citrus fruit on top of the liquid.**

3. **Secure the lid, set the valve to *Sealing,* and set to *Steam (High)* for 1 minute.**

4. **Allow the pot to *Naturally Release* the pressure so the cleaning solution can penetrate the steam release valve as well.**

5. **After the pressure has been released, discard the liquid from the pot, rinse the metal pot and lid under hot water, and dry them off.**

Voilà! Your Instant Pot has been given a deep cleaning and smells citrusy clean.

REMOVING BLUISH MARKS FROM THE INNER METAL POT

Have you noticed a slight bluish hue to the bottom of your Instant Pot? Don't worry — it's not some strange bacteria growing in there! Just like your other stainless-steel kitchen pots, the Instant Pot's inner metal pot can develop this blue hue from minerals and salt that come into contact with it from the food and water you cook with.

To remove this blueish hue, you can try either one of the following tips:

- Clean it with a nonabrasive stainless-steel cleanser.
- Cover the bottom with white vinegar and let it sit for 5 minutes; then discard the vinegar and rinse the inner metal pot.

Remember: Having a slight discoloration to your pot only means you're succeeding at using it! You aren't doing anything wrong, so keep cooking!

Keeping Strange Odors at Bay

TIP

We may have learned the hard way (which is actually quite lucky for you) what to do to ensure your delicious cheesecake doesn't take on that fish taco smell. If you follow these tips, you won't experience the odd-tasting cheesecake we did.

>> **Wash your inner metal pot, lid, and each of their components after each use.** Detach the sealing ring from the lid, remove the cover from the steam release valve on the bottom part of the lid, take off the condensation collector, and wash all these parts with hot, soapy water. Of course, you also need to wash the lid and the metal pot as well! But often we find the components of the lid aren't manually washed themselves, which may result in a smell building up over time.

>> **Run the inner metal pot through the dishwasher.** If you aren't a fan of handwashing, you can definitely put the lid, sealing ring, condensation collector, and inner metal pot inside the dishwasher. The high temperature inside the dishwasher will help rid the pot of any residual smell. Just make sure you place the lid and sealing rings on the top rack.

>> **Soak the sealing ring in boiling water.** With some of the more pungent smells, like fish, the sealing ring is typically what absorbs the flavor due to the material that it's made of. To help get the smell out faster so you can quickly switch from beef roast to chocolate cake, let the sealing ring soak in soapy, boiling water for 5 minutes.

>> **Store your sealing rings in the freezer.** If your sealing ring starts to take on an odor or seems to be stretching out, pop it in the freezer! We've found that freezing helps eliminate the stink and also helps shrink the sealing ring a bit.

>> **Clean the anti-block shield.** These parts of the Instant Pot can be easily removed. Plus, you should wash them after each use. To remove the anti-block shield, push the side of it and lift up toward the rim using your finger. You may need to use a little extra pressure, but it should help make the anti-block shield pop off. Give it a good scrub and a soak, and see if that helps. To reposition the anti-block shield, simply push it back down on the bottom portion of the lid.

Storing Your Instant Pot

You can keep your Instant Pot on your counter (and we highly encourage you to do so to make sure you get the most use out of it!), but we understand that space may be tight and storing your Instant Pot on the counter may not be feasible. If that's the case, no worries! You can easily store your pot (and the accessories) safely and securely to help keep it looking as good as new.

You can simply put it away wherever you have room for it, with the lid secured on top. Simply tuck the cord, condensation collector, metal trivet, and measuring cup inside the inner metal pot. We even store our manuals inside our pots, just in case we have questions.

If you want to keep the exterior looking like new, avoid placing it in an area that collects condensation from the stovetop (such as a cabinet above the stove).

If you're taking your Instant Pot on the road, you may want to invest in a carrying case that has a soft protector you can place your pot into. The carrying case will help prevent scratches that naturally happen when you carry and store your pot.

Chapter **22**

Ten Ways to Carry Over Pulled Meats

The best part about using the Instant Pot to cook your favorite meats is the endless possibilities those leftovers can provide. We're big fans of saving time (and sanity) in the kitchen, and leftovers do just that. But we're not about to tell you to eat the same meal five days out of the week. (Of course, if that's your jam, no judgment!)

Having a variety of quick and convenient ways you can repurpose that pulled pork or roasted chicken is crucial to not only keeping your love for the Instant Pot alive, but also satisfying your taste buds and encouraging creativity in the kitchen. Use this chapter as a guide to think outside the box when it comes to carrying over your favorite pulled meats.

Bowls

Chapter 11 is all about beautiful bowls. But you can skip a step and whip up a bowl on a whim by using the pulled meat from your latest Instant Pot meal prep day and highlight it in your bowl. Made pork instead of the chicken called for in the Mediterranean Bowl with Feta and Herb Yogurt Dressing (see Chapter 11)?

Don't fret! Use pork instead, and rest easy knowing you'll still be getting plenty of solid nutrition like protein, vitamin B12, and many other nutrients.

Casseroles

Casseroles are not just reserved for ground meats. Pulled meats, like chicken, pork, and beef, make excellent additions to your favorite comfort classic casserole recipes. The meats are precooked, so you should be able to adjust the cooking time a bit to throw dinner together more quickly.

REMEMBER

Every recipe will vary so a general rule of thumb is to allow yourself the time to be able to keep an eye on the recipe while it's cooking on your first run through, so you don't end up with an overcooked casserole!

Enchiladas

Enchiladas are a family favorite in our homes. Simply shred your leftover meat into even pieces. Using your Instant Pot and 7-inch springform pan, make a quick enchilada lasagna in just under 14 minutes! Just as you would with a traditional lasagna, layer your tortillas, cheese, sauce, and leftover meat. You can even kick it up a notch by adding in precooked vegetables you may have on hand.

TIP

Make it gluten-free by using corn tortillas.

Omelets

Power up your breakfast and make a protein-packed omelet. Omelets are a go-to food recommended on most keto and paleo diets. Plus, they're easily customizable for the entire family. A nice way to kick off a weekend would be to use up any leftover meats you had from the week and create your own in-home, build-your-own-omelet bar! Not only will you save a *ton* of money (because you won't be dining out), but you'll also help clean out your fridge to get ready for Sunday meal prep. Some of our favorite combos include pairing garden-fresh vegetables like tomatoes, bell peppers, and fresh cilantro with the leftover Carnitas (Chapter 10).

Salads

It's pretty obvious you can throw whatever pulled meat you have on a delicious crisp salad any season of the year (and we recommend that as a variation in many of our recipes). But this tip uses those pulled meats in a way that you may not have thought of before: yogurt-based salads!

Yes, you can amp up the nutrition of those traditional mayonnaise-based salads by using a blend of plain yogurt and mayonnaise (or if you're a yogurt fan, just use it entirely in the recipe and hold the mayo). We recommend using fresh herbs to enhance the flavor of your salads, although the meats are seasoned when cooked. Serve them atop a bed of butter-leaf lettuce and whole-grain crackers for a simple yet satisfying meal.

Sandwiches

Did your house suddenly become a landing spot? Don't stress, you can feed your friends and family with a quick sandwich platter using that leftover pulled meat.

Take out whatever bun or bread you have (even hot dog buns cut in half will work well for this) and assemble a variety of hot and cold sandwiches with whatever meat you have on hand. Plus, you can easily take your hot dog bun pulled pork sandwich to a new level by adding a drizzle of one of the homemade dressings from the bowls in Chapter 11. Your guests may even think you had them catered in with that gourmet touch!

Soups

Boost the protein of those vegetarian classic soups like Minestrone Soup (Chapter 14) and other vegetable-based soups by tossing in leftover pulled meats! If you're making them in the Instant Pot, simply wait until the cooking completes for your soup, and stir in the pulled meat pieces at the end. Carry-over cooking from the pressure of the pot will naturally reheat the meat (without toughening it) to the proper temperature that's safe to consume!

REMEMBER

If you plan to use a leftover pulled meat in a soup that uses a bone-based cut of meat, it may not have the depth of flavor intended (bones naturally add flavor to the broth). So, you may need to add a little beef, chicken, or pork-based bouillon to amplify the flavor.

Tacos

Tacos aren't just for Tuesdays! We highly encourage you to keep tortillas on hand so you can enjoy those leftover pulled meats in taco form any day of the week. Craving barbecue? Take that tortilla, stuff it with your pulled meat, and top with cabbage slaw and barbecue sauce and you've got yourself a portable taco sandwich that most Texans would be proud of. A double bonus: Tacos can be made in just about anything that folds! Following a low-carb diet? Swap lettuce leaves for the tortilla.

Tamales

Whether you're preparing tamales for the holiday season or just because it's a Thursday, leftover pulled meats are a *huge* time-saving hack! Instead of spending the time and labor involved in making the meat from scratch on the day of your tamale assembly, batch cook the meat ahead of time and it'll be ready to go when you're ready to assemble. Also, just think of the fewer number of dishes you'll have if you use leftover meat this way! A win-win!

Toast

Avocado toast is super trendy (and delicious) but it's often lacking an important nutrient group that could really help leave you more satiated and satisfied hours after enjoying it: protein! Those leftover pulled meats all pair wonderfully shredded, heated, and topped on your avocado toast morning, noon, and night. We recommend taking this simple recipe up a notch by adding pickled vegetables and red pepper flakes on top.

Chapter 23

Ten Meals to Modify for Baby

Babies all over the world have been enjoying curried lentils, steamed rice, and stews long before blenders existed. Even a baby who is just beginning his feeding journey can share a meal with his family, and the food doesn't necessarily need to be pureed.

In this chapter, we explore ways to serve up our top-ten family-favorite meals with babies who are just beginning to eat, as well as with babies who are slightly more skilled (such as 10-month-old infants). For easy reading, we designate these two categories as *Beginner Eater* and *Novice Eater.*

As dietitians, we encourage families to advance infants to solids quickly, so even if you choose to blend at the beginning, remember that your baby needs to advance to finger foods sooner rather than later. Use this as a guide when your little one is ready to embrace more solid foods.

TIP

Here are some helpful tips to consider when serving up foods for your baby:

>> **Make sure the texture is very soft.** To test the texture, gently press the food between your fingers; if it mashes with ease, that's a safe texture. Another way to test the texture is to put the food in your mouth and gently press the food to the roof of your mouth with your tongue; if the food mashes with ease, it's the right texture.

WARNING

>> **Know infant CPR and understand the differences between an infant gagging and an infant choking.** The more you know, the better you'll be able to face any situation that comes up. Take a class, watch videos online, and speak to your pediatrician before you start feeding your infant solid and pureed foods.

>> **Adjust your seasonings.** Instead of adding an extra dash of Sriracha or salt to your food, consider who is eating. Babies have more taste buds on their tongues than you do, so go easy on the seasoning. Don't skip the fresh herbs and spices completely, though — babies are entitled to have tasty foods, too! If an infant in India can enjoy curry, your baby can, too!

>> **Be sure your baby is sitting up in a secure chair at the table.** Not only is this important for safety reasons, but it ensures that they can see you enjoying the meal, too.

>> **Ditch the sugar and sugar substitutes.** Infants don't need their oatmeal sweetened, we swear! They can enjoy it plain, and maybe you can, too!

>> **Stick with foods that don't have a lot of preservatives, food dyes, or additives.** Sharing a meal with an infant doesn't need to include your chips (which are a choking hazard anyway). Speak to a dietitian or pediatrician about which foods are safe and appropriate for infants and toddlers before their first bite.

WARNING

>> **Skip the honey.** Honey contains *Clostridium botulinum,* which can kill an infant. Yes, serious talking point here! Even in baked items, the spores can thrive.

>> **Keep the casseroles coming!** Why casseroles? Because many kids have an issue with mixed foods. There's no guarantee who will be picky or more selective. Realize that all children go through a picky phase, and some have extreme picky-eating habits. By regularly introducing foods with different shapes, textures, and mixtures, your chances of avoiding extreme picky eating improve.

⚠ AVOIDING CHOKING HAZARDS

WARNING

Now that your baby is ready to join you at the table be sure to take note of foods that pose a significant choking risk, and let your family members know, too!

- Grapes
- Popcorn
- Hot dogs
- Hard fruits or vegetables (such as apples and carrots)
- Marshmallows
- Whole nuts
- Candy

When you're ready to advance your toddler or young child with these foods, be sure to consult your pediatrician on the best way to safely serve them.

Sloppy Joes (Chapter 12)

Beef is packed with iron, zinc, and selenium, which are key nutrients for infants. You can omit the salt in the recipe and salt your own personal dish instead. We suggest pairing this with a salad, and serving your baby a dissected salad with avocado and grated carrots.

How to serve:

» **Beginner Eater:** Serve the sauce meat finely minced on a baby-safe spoon. You can either hand it to your baby or let her pick it up. Let her have one bite at a time for beginners. Dish out a teaspoon at a time, following your baby's cues if she wants more or is finished and only playing. Skip the bread for now. Serve with a very ripe avocado wedge and finely grated carrots in olive oil to complete this meal.

» **Novice Eater:** Novice eaters can have an open-faced sandwich or finger sandwiches to keep it fun. Serve with chopped avocado and grated carrots to complete the meal.

Nancy's Stuffed Bell Peppers (Chapter 12)

This was one of Wendy Jo's daughter's very first mixed meals at 7 months old, and she devoured the peppers and still does today.

How to serve:

>> **Beginner Eater:** Give your baby ½ to 1 teaspoon meat and rice mixture with tomato sauce. You can either preload it on a spoon or let your baby use his palm to scoop it up and feed himself. Dish out a teaspoon at a time, following your baby's cues if he wants more or is finished and only playing. Remove the bell pepper pulp from the skin and serve on a spoon or in thin strips on a tray, one strip at a time.

>> **Novice Eater:** Give your baby ¼ cup of filling with sauce. Serve with a spoon so he can practice with the spoon, or he may still choose to use both hands. Serve tiny, bite-size pieces of cooked bell pepper to help him work his pincer grasp.

Madras Lentils (Chapter 15)

Prepare the less-spicy version for family! Serve with rice and raw cucumber slices. Lentils are an excellent source of fiber and vegetable-based protein. If your infant is constipated you may decide to put this recipe on your weekly rotation!

How to serve:

>> **Beginner Eater:** Give your baby 3 teaspoons lentils and 3 teaspoons rice. You can either preload it on a spoon or let your baby use her palm to scoop it up and feed herself. Dish out a teaspoon at a time, following your baby's cues if she wants more or is finished and only playing. Grate about 1 tablespoon of fresh cucumber for infants to begin getting the taste for raw cucumber.

>> **Novice Eater:** Give your baby ¼ cup of filling with sauce. Serve with a spoon so she can practice with the spoon, or she may still choose to use both hands. Serve tiny, bite-size pieces of cooked bell pepper to help her work her pincer grasp. Instead of grating the cucumber, at this stage, you can move to serving your baby a spear (the size should be two adult fingers in width and one finger in length). Allow the infant to gnaw on the spear or serve in julienned strips (one to three pieces at a time). Freezing a cucumber can also help the cucumber break down and become mushy. It's also a great teething tool!

Farmers Market Frittata (Chapter 9)

Tough vegetables are still hard to master for an infant, so be sure all vegetables inside of the frittata are soft and can be easily mashed.

How to serve:

>> **Beginner Eater:** Serve one spear of frittata (the size should be two adult fingers in width and one finger in length) so the infant can grasp the egg, or chop finely and add plain yogurt to help create a softer texture.

>> **Novice Eater:** Give your baby two or three frittata spears at a time, or ¼-inch cubes for bite-size pieces, to enhance pincer grasp skills. Or you can give your baby an infant fork.

Carne Guisada (Chapter 10)

Serve with *pico de gallo* (chopped salsa) and soft corn tortilla.

How to serve:

>> **Beginner Eater:** Give your baby ½ teaspoon of shredded meat loaded on a spoon and drizzled with olive oil. Serve a soft corn tortilla in strips. You can also introduce tiny pieces of tomato, minced onion, and minced cilantro, but we suggest skipping jalapeño this early!

>> **Novice Eater:** Make your baby a mini soft taco. Fill a soft corn tortilla with 1 tablespoon of shredded meat and a teaspoon of *pico de gallo* (finely chopped); then roll and serve.

Chicken Sausage and Ancient Grain Casserole (Chapter 12)

Skip the chipotle version, and stick with the milder versions. Be sure to mince the sausage to make it safe for your infant to swallow. A variety of grains offer varied nutrient profiles, different textures, and fiber.

How to serve:

» **Beginner Eater:** Mince the sausage and make sure the vegetables have a tender texture. You can opt to preload a spoon or embrace the grainy mess and allow your infant to dig in with her palms. Less is more, so opt for starting off with ½ teaspoon infant spoon servings or 1 to 2 tablespoons for the infant to scoop.

» **Novice Eater:** Quarter the sausage or chop and allow your baby to use her pincer grasp to pick up the sausage. Serve ¼ cup rice mixture with an infant-friendly spoon for her to use.

Cinnamon Spice Steel-Cut Oats (Chapter 9)

Before you run out and buy baby oatmeal, realize that it's more a gimmick than a necessity. Much like baby yogurt and other clever marketing titles for babies, there is no need to buy these types of food specifically for an infant. Regular oatmeal can be thinned down to make the texture less gummy, which is ideal for an infant just starting out on the eating journey. Be sure to cook oats fully and consider adding plain yogurt, kefir, or even a tiny amount of nut butter to introduce allergens.

How to serve:

» **Beginner Eater:** Give your baby 3 tablespoons of oatmeal in a baby-friendly bowl or plate and let him dig in with his hands, or load three spoons with ½ teaspoon of oatmeal on each and refill as needed.

» **Novice Eater:** Give your baby ¼ cup oatmeal and allow your baby to use an infant-friendly spoon to eat, refilling as needed.

Plain Yogurt (Chapter 8) and Coconut Milk Kefir (Chapter 8)

Fermented foods, such as yogurt and kefir, are great for mixing into foods to help create a more moist texture. For children under 1 year old, we don't recommend serving kefir as a beverage because it could be too filling and replace breast milk or formula. Serve up yogurt in place of mayo in recipes, or drizzle coconut kefir on cooked vegetables.

REMEMBER

Both milk and coconut are high-allergen foods. It's important to introduce these high-allergen foods early on in the feeding journey to help prevent food allergies later on. We hope these tips help get you started!

How to serve:

>> **Beginner Eater:** Mix ½ teaspoon nut butter (peanut or almond butter) with 1 tablespoon of plain yogurt and serve to your baby on a preloaded spoon. Coconut kefir can be drizzled on any meat or vegetable to moisten the food; start with 1 teaspoon at a time.

>> **Novice Eater:** Give your baby ¼ cup of yogurt in a bowl with quartered blueberries or finely chopped strawberries mixed in or on the side. Use coconut kefir as a dip for banana spears or canned mandarin oranges.

Simple Spanish Paella (Chapter 15)

Shrimp is great as an early-introduction food due to risks of a shellfish allergen.

How to serve:

>> **Beginner Eater:** Mince cooked shrimp and give your baby 1 tablespoon or three individual loaded spoons with creamy sauce mixed in. Mash softened broccoli to ensure a safe texture. If your baby doesn't have teeth yet, you can serve a large broccoli stalk and allow him to gnaw on the stalk — a raw stalk is too hard for infant gums to break. Make sure the stalk is an inch or more thick and monitor your baby closely so he doesn't break any pieces off. Raw introduction is equally important for future flavor acceptance by your growing child. You can also finely grate broccoli if it makes you feel more comfortable.

>> **Novice Eater:** Chop ¼ cup shrimp into tiny, bite-size pieces along with broccoli, continuing to ensure very soft textures, with sauce on top. Continue to expose your baby to raw broccoli at this time as well, but take note that your baby's teeth can easily break off an unsafe piece of raw broccoli. Grate broccoli and serve with olive oil and vinegar over the top.

Texas Beef Chili with Beans (Chapter 14)

This is a Texas favorite in our homes, and we hope your family loves this iron- and fiber-packed meal, as well. You can opt to use less chili powder while pressure cooking, and add more at the table for those with seasoned palates. Serve with grated cheese and a dollop of yogurt.

How to serve:

>> **Beginner Eater:** Give your baby 1 teaspoon of the meat and bean mixture mashed with a fork into smaller pieces. Be sure each bean is mashed at the beginning. Drizzle with plain yogurt and 2 teaspoons finely grated cheddar cheese.

>> **Novice Eater:** Give your baby ¼ cup of chili with beans. Be sure to cut the beans in half and finely chop large pieces of ground meat. Serve the chili in a child-friendly bowl with a dollop of plain yogurt and grated cheese on top. Allow your growing infant to explore using a spoon (or her hands if she chooses). This is one of those dishes you may choose to serve outside or with a full-body bib!

Chapter 24

Top Ten Keto-Friendly Meals

I f you're on a keto diet, you've got your eyes on carbs, keeping them to a minimum. We provide lots of keto-friendly recipes in this book, but some you'll need to modify in order increase the fat. You can do that by adding healthier unsaturated fats (like avocado, nuts, and seeds) or by topping the recipe with a finishing oil (like olive oil, avocado oil, coconut oil, or macadamia nut oil). You may want to add a higher-fat beverage, like coconut water mixed with a medium-chain triglycerides (MCT) oil, to your meal.

TIP

If you've heard about the keto diet, but you're not sure where to start, check out *Keto Diet For Dummies,* by Rami Abrams and Vicky Abrams (Wiley), for tons of useful information.

Here are ten recipes you'll want to try if you're on (or interested in) the keto diet.

Coconut Milk Kefir

Our Coconut Milk Kefir recipe (see Chapter 8) has a small amount of sugar to help ferment the coconut milk into kefir, but it's a great option for those who are following a modified keto diet. Use this as your liquid in a coconut-based cereal made of unsweetened coconut flakes, chopped nuts, and a small handful of fresh berries. The berries will provide a small amount of carbohydrate, but they'll help to balance out the meal and give it a more satisfying texture.

Poached Eggs

If you're a fan of eggs, you'll still be allowed to enjoy them on the keto diet! Eggs are a nutrient-rich choice that pairs perfectly with some of the lower-carbohydrate vegetables, like chopped broccoli, spinach, and mushrooms! You can also toss in some cheddar cheese and chopped meat for a higher-protein meal. Our Poached Eggs recipe (see Chapter 9) is a great place to start.

Beef Bone Broth

Avoid paying the high price for a glorified bone broth at your local market, and make your own in your Instant Pot. Our Beef Bone Broth recipe (see Chapter 8) is an excellent way to bring rich flavor to the low-carbohydrate soups that tend to be prominent on the keto diet. Plus, bone broth is a great source for many vitamins and minerals because of the bone used to flavor the broth.

Seasoned Pulled Pork

Our Seasoned Pulled Pork recipe (see Chapter 10) is very rich, mainly from the fattier pork shoulder used in the recipe. The recipe suggests pairing this with a simple coleslaw, which traditionally is high in fat from mayonnaise. But if you're on the keto diet, we recommend pairing this recipe with low-carbohydrate veggies to add more fiber to your diet and prevent some of the unfortunate side effects of a high-fat diet, like constipation.

Carne Guisada

Though Carne Guisada (see Chapter 10) is traditionally served with tortillas, to remain keto compliant you can serve it alongside some butter-leaf lettuce or spoon it into a halved avocado. Avocados are a nutrient-rich food that helps to provide satiety alongside the better-for-you fats that aren't found in meats.

Korean Beef Bulgogi Bowl

Our Korean Beef Bulgogi Bowl recipe (see Chapter 11) does call for sugar, but to remain keto compliant, you can substitute the brown sugar with stevia or monk fruit. This delicious recipe can certainly fit into your low-carb meal plan when paired with a simple cauliflower rice. Cauliflower rice is a freezer-friendly staple, so you won't have to spend hours in the kitchen ricing your own.

Turkey and Mushroom Meatloaf

Nothing is worse than showing up to an event without something to eat! That's why our prep-ahead Turkey and Mushroom Meatloaf (see Chapter 12) can be a keto follower's best friend for a weekend away. Going camping? Cook ahead and modify by using an almond flour in place of the breadcrumbs. Reheat to 165 degrees (yes, you can do this over an open flame in the woods), and you'll have a nourishing meal (not out of a package) in a matter of minutes.

Garlic Green Beans and Tomatoes

Green beans are non-starchy vegetables (along with artichokes, bok choy, cabbage, celery, mushrooms, and spinach — think of vegetables that grow aboveground). Though tomatoes are a bit higher in carbohydrates, when eaten in moderation, they can absolutely fit into a keto diet! Pair our Garlic Green Beans and Tomatoes recipe (see Chapter 13) with any meat, and we promise, you'll be satiated and satisfied!

Cheese Fondue with Jalapeños

Our Cheese Fondue with Jalapeños (see Chapter 16) is a party-friendly appetizer that you and your friends on the keto bandwagon can enjoy! Serve this recipe alongside celery sticks, cauliflower, radishes, or even rolled meats. Remember, though: This is a pretty high-sodium dish, so be mindful of your portions and drink lots of water.

Spiced Walnuts and Cashews

Need to satisfy a sweet tooth but recognize that keto means saying no to your favorite desserts? Then our Spiced Walnuts and Cashews recipe (see Chapter 18) is a great go-to. Walnuts are rich in omega-3 fatty acids, a heart-healthy fat that has shown to have many promising effects within the body. When preparing this recipe, you can swap the maple with commonly approved sugar substitutes on the keto diet, like stevia, monk fruit, erythritol, or xylitol.

WARNING

A word of caution, though: If you're new to sugar substitutes, be mindful of portions and see how your body responds. Some people report tummy troubles upon eating sugar substitutes.

5

Appendixes

Convert measurements to metric.

Find important safe cooking temperatures for your foods.

Appendix A

Metric Conversion Guide

Note: The recipes in this book weren't developed or tested using metric measurements. There may be some variation in quality when converting to metric units.

Common Abbreviations

Abbreviation(s)	What It Stands For
cm	Centimeter
C., c.	Cup
G, g	Gram
kg	Kilogram
L, l	Liter
lb.	Pound
mL, ml	Milliliter
oz.	Ounce
pt.	Pint
t., tsp.	Teaspoon
T., Tb., Tbsp.	Tablespoon

Volume

U.S. Units	Canadian Metric	Australian Metric
¼ teaspoon	1 milliliter	1 milliliter
½ teaspoon	2 milliliters	2 milliliters
1 teaspoon	5 milliliters	5 milliliters

(continued)

(continued)

U.S. Units	Canadian Metric	Australian Metric
1 tablespoon	15 milliliters	20 milliliters
¼ cup	50 milliliters	60 milliliters
⅓ cup	75 milliliters	80 milliliters
½ cup	125 milliliters	125 milliliters
⅔ cup	150 milliliters	170 milliliters
¾ cup	175 milliliters	190 milliliters
1 cup	250 milliliters	250 milliliters
1 quart	1 liter	1 liter
1½ quarts	1.5 liters	1.5 liters
2 quarts	2 liters	2 liters
2½ quarts	2.5 liters	2.5 liters
3 quarts	3 liters	3 liters
4 quarts (1 gallon)	4 liters	4 liters

Weight

U.S. Units	Canadian Metric	Australian Metric
1 ounce	30 grams	30 grams
2 ounces	55 grams	60 grams
3 ounces	85 grams	90 grams
4 ounces (¼ pound)	115 grams	125 grams
8 ounces (½ pound)	225 grams	225 grams
16 ounces (1 pound)	455 grams	500 grams (½ kilogram)

Length

Inches	Centimeters
0.5	1.5
1	2.5
2	5.0

Inches	Centimeters
3	7.5
4	10.0
5	12.5
6	15.0
7	17.5
8	20.5
9	23.0
10	25.5
11	28.0
12	30.5

Temperature (Degrees)

Fahrenheit	Celsius
32	0
212	100
250	120
275	140
300	150
325	160
350	180
375	190
400	200
425	220
450	230
475	240
500	260

Appendix B

Safe Cooking Temperatures

For food safety, it's always wise to have a thermometer on hand to test the inner temperature of the foods you're preparing. Here's a guide to safe food temperatures for a variety of foods.

You can apply these cooking temperatures to the recipes you make outside the Instant Pot as well.

Cooking Temperatures

Food	Temperature (°F)
Eggs	145
Red meat (whole)	145
Red meat (ground)	160
Pork	145
Poultry	165
Seafood	145
Casseroles or leftovers	165

Index

U

Ultra model, 17

V

vanilla extract, 43
Vegan category, 3
vegetable broth
   Chicken Sausage and Ancient Grain Casserole, 115
   Corn and Potato Chowder, 143
   Cream Cheese and Chive Mashed Potatoes, 124
   Creamy Butternut Squash Orzo Risotto, 156
   Frijoles Negros Plantain Bowl, 98–99
   Madras Lentils, 160
   Minestrone Soup, 138
   Parmesan Pancetta Polenta Bowl, 106
   Sara's Lightened-Up Macaroni Cheese, 122
   Sourdough Stuffing, 135
   Southern-Inspired Sautéed Kale Bowl with Spicy Peanut Dressing, 104–105
   White Bean and Garden Vegetable Soup, 140
Vegetable Broth recipe, 70
vegetable stock
   Beefy Green Curry, 158
   Broccoli Potato Cheese Soup, 142
   Creamy Tomato and Basil Soup, 139
   Lentil Soup, 141
   Mexican-Inspired Roasted Sweet Potatoes, 125
   Persian Stew, 147
   Sausage, Potato, and Kale Soup, 144
   Sautéed Balsamic Mushrooms, 132
   Southwestern Queso, 174
vegetables, 28, 34, 49. *See also specific types*
Vegetarian category, 3
vegetarian meal plan, 55–56
Viva model, 17
Vodka, 184
volume conversions, 243–244

W

walnuts, 85, 86, 100–101, 127, 135, 190, 196–197
Warm White Russian recipe, 184
Warning icon, 4
water chestnuts, 116–117
water immersion method, for Sous Vide, 20
weight conversions, 244
wheat bran, 204–205
whipped cream, 182, 184, 194–195
whisk, 37
White Bean and Garden Vegetable Soup recipe, 140
white beans, 140
white fish, 168
white wine, 119, 132, 133, 169

Y

yellow peas, 147
yogurt
   about, 62
   Chicken Tikka Masala, 162
   Chocolate Chip Muffins, 86
   Cilantro Lime Fish Tacos, 168
   Corn and Potato Chowder, 143
   Feta and Herb Yogurt Dressing, 101
   Lemon, Blueberry, and Chia Breakfast Cake, 83
   Madras Lentils, 160
   Morning Glory Bundt Cake, 204–205
   Plain Yogurt, 62
   Ranch Dressing, 103
   Red Lentil Curry, 157
Yogurt feature, 22

Z

zest, 33
zester, 37
zucchini, 119, 138, 152–153, 158, 194–195

About the Authors

Wendy Jo Peterson, MS RDN: Wendy Jo is an award-winning author, speaker, culinary nutritionist, proud military wife, and mom. Whether at work or at the table, Wendy Jo believes in savoring life. Check out her most popular books: *Born To Eat* and the *Mediterranean Diet Cookbook For Dummies*. When she's not in her kitchen, you can find Wendy Jo strolling the beach with her Labradors and daughter or exploring the great outdoors in #OlafTheCampervan. You can catch her on social media at @just_wendyjo or check out her website, www.justwendyjo.com.

Elizabeth Shaw, MS RDN CPT: Liz is a national nutrition expert and best-selling author of the *Fertility Foods Cookbook* who works as a spokesperson and nutrition professor in San Diego. Her passion for breaking down science-based facts into digestible sound bites has led her to what she loves doing most: helping others understand the important role nutrition can play in their lifelong health. You can find Liz sharing her recipes on her website, www.shawsimpleswaps.com, or over on social media at @shawsimpleswaps with her #ShawKitchen crew (her husband and daughter!).

Dedication

To our daughters and husbands, Miss A, H, Brandon, and Wayne, thank you for giving us plenty of reasons to need an Instant Pot! To our family and friends, the best taste testers around. And to every person who needs an extra minute to breathe, stress free, and get a wholesome meal on the table. We hope you enjoy this book as much as we loved creating it for you!

Authors' Acknowledgments

We would like to acknowledge our agent, Matt Wagner, for bringing this incredible project to us. We're forever grateful for Tracy Boggier, Senior Acquisitions Editor at Wiley, and the Instant Brands family, who believed in us and the power of two registered dietitian nutritionists to create an entire collection of recipes using the Instant Pot. We appreciate the ideas, guidance, and support we've received throughout this project. It's been invaluable!

Publisher's Acknowledgments

Senior Acquisitions Editor: Tracy Boggier

Proofreader: Debbye Butler

Production Editor: Siddique Shaik

Cover Photos: Courtesy of Wendy Jo Peterson and Elizabeth Shaw